UNITED STATES
FOREIGN POLICY
AT THE
CROSSROADS

GLOBAL PERSPECTIVES IN HISTORY AND POLITICS, *edited by George Schwab*, is a subseries to CONTRIBUTIONS IN POLITICAL SCIENCE.

Recent titles include:

Nationalism: Essays
Edited by Michael Palumbo and William O. Shanahan

Global Mini-Nationalisms: Autonomy or Independence
Louis L. Snyder

Socialism of a Different Kind: Reshaping the Left in France
Bernard E. Brown

UNITED STATES FOREIGN POLICY AT THE CROSSROADS

Edited by
GEORGE SCHWAB

Contributions in Political Science, Number 96
Global Perspectives in History and Politics

GREENWOOD PRESS
Westport, Connecticut • London, England

Library of Congress Cataloging in Publication Data
Main entry under title:

United States foreign policy at the crossroads.

  (Contributions in political science, ISSN 0147-1066 ;
no. 96. Global perspectives in history and politics)
  Proceedings of the Fourth CUNY Conference on History
and Politics, held Dec. 11-12, 1980 at the City
University of New York.
  Bibliography: p.
  Includes index.
  1. United States—Foreign relations—1945- —Con-
gresses. I. Schwab, George. II. Conference on
History and Politics (4th : 1980) III. Series: Con-
tributions in political science ; no. 96. IV. Series:
Contributions in political science. Global perspectives
in history and politics.
E840.U7 1982   327.73   82-15588
ISBN 0-313-23270-9 (lib. bdg.)

Library of Congress Catalog Card Number: 82-15588
ISBN: 0-313-23270-9
ISSN: 0147-1066

First published in 1982

Greenwood Press
A division of Congressional Information Service, Inc.
88 Post Road West
Westport, Connecticut 06881

Printed in the United States of America

10 9 8 7 6 5 4 3 2 1

In Memory of
Hans Joachim Morgenthau
Inspiring Thinker, Honored Colleague,
Devoted Friend

Contents

In Memoriam, Hans Joachim Morgenthau

ARTHUR M. SCHLESINGER, JR.

It is fitting that this volume should be inscribed to the
memory of Hans Morgenthau in part because the papers were
originally presented at the Graduate School of the City University of New York, where Hans Morgenthau was a cher-
ished teacher and remains an abiding influence. A less parochial and a more compelling reason for the dedication is that
students of world affairs everywhere stand in Hans
Morgenthau's debt. His intellectual leadership over 40 productive years helped effect a revolution in the way scholars
think about international relations.

Born in Coburg, Germany, in 1904, Morgenthau studied
jurisprudence in Berlin, Frankfurt, and Munich, was admitted
to the German bar in 1927, entered law practice, and for a
time presided over the Labor Law Court in Frankfurt. But
foreign affairs enticed him; soon he was at the Institute of
International Studies in Geneva; and when Hitler came to

power, he became a member of the political science faculty of the University of Geneva. In 1937 he joined the great migration of Jewish intellectuals to the United States. Here he taught at Brooklyn College, at the University of Kansas City, and, beginning in 1943, the year he became an American citizen, at the University of Chicago. In 1950 a grant from the Lilly Endowment enabled him to establish at Chicago his influential Center for the Study of American Foreign Policy.

When Morgenthau arrived in the United States, international relations was an academic field in some disarray. On the historical side, it consisted of careful but essentially descriptive accounts of particular transactions. In political science the predominant approach was legalistic in mode and idealistic in purpose, for it was organized around the longing for a better world. Notable individuals—Nicholas J. Spykman, Walter Lippmann, Edward Mead Earle, Frederick J. Schuman—insisted on the primacy of power in the international structure, but their somber ideas had not permeated the mainstream of academic analysis.

Coming from a continent consumed by nationalist rage and trembling on the abyss of war, Morgenthau brought a distinct pessimism about human nature and a profound skepticism about the power of law and of ideals to order international affairs. He brought also the vigorous conviction that there existed objective and universally-valid truths about political matters and that these truths were accessible to human reason. He affirmed in particular that the struggle for power was the essence of international politics and that national interest was the only authentic basis for a state's foreign policy.

These were the themes of Morgenthau's lectures at Chicago and of *Politics Among Nations* (1948), the book that set forth his general theory of international relations. It is hard now, 40 years later, to recall the shock that these propositions produced. But wide oceans had long shielded the republic from the logic of *Realpolitik*. Americans were accustomed to viewing their actions abroad as the expressions of disinterested national virtue. Many, especially in academic life, were still moved by Wilson's noble vision of a world rejecting the bad old balance of power in order to construct a "community of power" that would ensure lasting peace. To men of goodwill Morgenthau's acrid realism appeared to be heresy, outrageous as well as dangerous. He was denounced as amoral and cynical—a new Machiavelli.

In fact, although Morgenthau abhorred sentimentalism, moral self-righteousness, and ideological crusading in foreign policy, his own sensibility was deeply moral. The wishful optimism of the idealist school seemed to him to ignore the evidence of history, the nature of man, and the tragedy of human striving. "To act successfully," he wrote in *Scientific Man and Power Politics* in 1946, ". . . is political wisdom. To know with despair that the political act is inevitably evil, and to act nevertheless, is moral courage. To choose among several expedient actions the least evil one is moral judgment. In the combination of political wisdom, moral courage and moral judgment, man reconciles his political nature with his moral destiny." Prudence—the weighing of the consequences of alternative courses—was, he wrote in *Politics Among Nations,* "the supreme virtue in politics."

Realism drew much of its force from its reliance on the evidence of history. Morgenthau himself, perhaps initially in the hope of legitimizing his heresies, began to inquire into the foreign-policy ideas of the Founding Fathers. To his great satisfaction he found that Washington, Hamilton, Franklin, and Jefferson (in his actions) were thoroughgoing realists, staunch devotees of the national interest, and careful calculators of the international balance of power. His Chicago center encouraged the reexamination of American diplomacy as an aspect of intellectual history—as, for example, in the valuable studies of Franklin and Hamilton undertaken under Morgenthau's direction by the Austrian historian Gerald Stourzh. Realism, far from being a heresy imported from abroad, emerged as a reaffirmation of the sturdiest American tradition in international affairs.

Morgenthau was by no means the only warrior engaged in the battle for realism. In Great Britain E. H. Carr had opened the assault on the utopian approach to foreign affairs the year the Second World War broke out. The war itself offered a generation of Americans bitter instruction in the facts of international life. The cold war placed the United States in the center of the power struggles of a dangerous planet. Reinhold Niebuhr, George F. Kennan, Lippmann, Arnold Wolfers, and others helped demolish the bastions of idealism. But *Politics Among Nations* was the most systematic and comprehensive formulation of the realist position. It was the most influential textbook of its time, and it gave international relations a new framework as an academic discipline.

Verified by the tide of events, the realist approach grew rapidly less controversial, and each revised edition of *Politics Among Nations* grew correspondingly less polemical. In 1953 Robert E. Osgood's *Ideals and Self-Interest in America's Foreign Relations,* another production of the Chicago center, provided a valuable historical survey of the debate; a few years later Osgood's categories seemed irrelevant to the discussios of foreign affairs. By 1960 the argument had ended, with Morgenthau, Carr, Niebuhr, and their allies undisputed victors.

The utopians were routed, and the battle shifted ground. Acting on the best balance-of-power model, new critics arose, determined to prevent the domination of the field by a single approach. Much concern was focused on the key concept of national interest. Was national interest after all so easily identifiable? Morgenthau might think that

German leaders had twice in one generation violated
Germany's national interest; but would the kaiser and Hitler
have agreed? Indeed, when have statesmen ever deliberately
acted against the national interest of their countries? May not
one man's violation be another man's defense of national
interest? Defenders of the concept managed to rescue a "hard
core of the national interest" derived from geography; but
evidently the concept itself, so "hard" against the backdrop
of utopian idealism, turned out to be rather "soft" on its
own.

Certainly realism did not provide unequivocal policy
guidance to statesmen—a fact dramatically revealed in the
American debate over the Vietnam War. In the 1960s the
leading realists—Lippmann, Kennan, Niebuhr, Morgenthau
himself—passionately denounced American participation in
the war as wholly unwarranted in terms of the national interest; and they were surely right. Yet the advocates of American participation—President Johnson, Secretary of State
Rusk, and the rest—argued with equal vehemence that the
national interest demanded the Americanization of the war.
History may return the final verdict; but who could *prove* at
the time where the national interest truly lay?

Some critics turned the realists' favorite weapon—
history—against realism. Was not realism simply an unjusti-
fied extrapolation from the pattern of interstate relations
that had prevailed in Europe in the eighteenth and nineteenth
centuries? Its operative ideas—the balance of power, limited
national objectives, secret diplomacy, foreign policy conducted by professional elites and protected from the vagrant
emotions of domestic politics—all might be no more than the
functions of a specific historical epoch, when states agreed on
the rules of the game and citizens made no claim to democratic control. Was realism not therefore inadequate to understanding a new age characterized by the democratization of
foreign policy, by ideological crusades, by absolute weapons,

and by the intrusion into the international equilibrium of new states that did not agree on the rules of the game?

Members of the "bureaucratic politics" school further objected that realism imputed excessive rationality to foreign-policy choices by portraying the state as a unified national entity that devises calculated solutions to international problems. The "rational actor model," it was said, overlooked the impact of bureaucratic and political rivalries on foreign-policy decisions; it overlooked too the role of irrational factors—of accident, misperception, ignorance, stupidity, madness. Moreover, the concept of power as the single *raison d'être* was both amorphous and ambiguous; the concept covered a baffling diversity of variables; nor in any event could the infernal complexity of international relations be reduced to a single goal.

Such criticisms, however, amounted to useful qualifications and refinements of the realist position rather than to root-and-branch rejection of the realist ideas of interest and power or of the realist methods of political analysis. Other challenges were more ambitious and more fundamental.

Among historians there arose a "revisionist" school dedicated to the thesis that the mainspring of foreign policy was economic rather than political or strategic; that states, at least capitalist states, sought power less to ensure public security than to increase private gain; that capitalism had to expand in order to survive; and that, in particular, the foreign policy of the United States was dictated by the unrelenting quest for world economic hegemony. Morgenthau regarded this interpretation of foreign policy with contempt. Imperialism, he pointed out, had existed long before capitalism; in the capitalist age it existed among anticapitalist as well as capitalist states. Against the revisionist doctrine that capitalists used government as their tool to secure profits, Morgenthau invoked history to show that in most cases governments used capitalists as their tools to enhance power.

The economic theories of imperialism, he wrote scornfully in *Politics Among Nations,* were "completely at variance with the facts of experience." As the revisionist vogue subsided, Morgenthau's conviction of the primacy of politics over economics began to prevail among a new generation of diplomatic historians.

The challenge emanating from Morgenthau's own field, political science, concentrated more on method than on substance. Once the idealist versus the realist debate was settled, a different contention arose—between defenders of the "classical" approach, who relied on history, philosophy, and law and doubted that rigorous empirical verification was practical in discourse in which insight came from judgment and wisdom; and truculent champions of the new "behavioral" faith, who were ardent in their assertions that highly abstract models of the international system and/or computer-based quantitative inquiries could transform the study of international relations from an art into a science.

If Morgenthau regarded the revisionist school of diplomatic historians with contempt, he regarded the behavioral school of political scientists with incredulity. The rejection of practical wisdom from Machiavelli to Cambon and Nicolson, the substitution of models for history, the subordination of insight to methodology—all seemed to him a new and repellent form of utopianism. Power, he said, was not susceptible to quantification; and models were an affront to reality, for history, as he wrote in *International Affairs* in 1967, was "the realm of the accidental, the contingent, the unpredictable." The behavioral approach told us nothing we need to know about the real world. "The new theories," he concluded, "... are in truth not so much theories as dogmas. They do not so much try to reflect reality as it actually is as to superimpose upon a recalcitrant reality a theoretical scheme that satisfies the desire for thorough rationalization. Their practicality is specious since it substitutes what is

desirable for what is possible. The new theories are in truth
utopias, differing from the utopias of old only in that they
replace the simple and obvious deductions from ethical
postulates with a highly complex and sophisticated method-
ological and terminological apparatus, creating the illusion of
empirical demonstration."

The pretense of neutral, scientific investigation seemed
to him to serve an unacknowledged function. It provided, he
wrote, "a respectable protective shield behind which members of the academic community may engage in non-
controversial theoretical pursuits," thereby enabling foreign-
affairs specialists to escape the responsibility of pronouncing
on the urgent issues of war and peace. This was a responsibility that Hans Morgenthau never evaded. He did not flinch
from testing scholarly analysis against hard questions of
immediate choice. His defense of the national interest
mocked the illusion of American omnipotence as well as of
Soviet benevolence; and his courage and eloquence were
never more manifest than in his devastating critique of the
American role in Vietnam.

As the revisionist enthusiasm has receded, so too has the
behavioral crusade; in each case Morgenthau's realism has
won vindication. No one can doubt that his penetrating in-
sights into power politics and *raisons d'état* will endure long
after the economic speculations and computerized investi-
gations of recent times are forgotten. His basic work endures
as a monumental effort to impose intellectual discipline on
the chaos of international politics and to infuse rational order
into the analysis of the travail of nations.

It only remains to be said that this master diagnostician
of *Realpolitik* was a gentle and a kindly man, civilized,
sardonically humorous, and unexpectedly affectionate, a
splendid teacher and a generous friend.

Preface

GEORGE SCHWAB

On December 11 and 12, 1980, the fourth CUNY Conference on History and Politics was held at the Graduate Center of the City University of New York to examine the "Foreign Policy Goals of the United States: Do We Need to Change Them?" Because Hans Joachim Morgenthau was to have been a participant, this volume, which contains the collected papers of the conference, is dedicated to him, my late friend and colleague.

I doubt whether the quality of the volume would have been the same without the participation of the audience and the chairmen of the panels. In this context I express my special gratitude to Jacob L. Mosak of the United Nations Secretariat and to Ivo D. Duchacek, Benjamin Rivlin, and Arthur M. Schlesinger, jr., of the Graduate Center.

For organizing this gathering, sponsored by the CUNY Conference on History and Politics, the CUNY Academy for the Humanities and Sciences, and the Center for European Studies at the Graduate Center, gratitude is due to the president of the Graduate Center, Harold M. Proshansky, to the former provost of the Graduate Center, Hans J. Hillerbrand, and to the dean of research and university programs, Solomon Goldstein. I am greatly indebted to Mrs. Dorothy Weber, the executive assistant to the former provost, who once again helped most graciously with the numerous details that are involved in arranging a gathering of this kind.

I would once more like to thank my assistant, Miss Edwina McMahon. Without her skilled editorial assistance this volume could not have appeared in its present form.

George Schwab, Director
CUNY Conference on History
and Politics

Introduction

G. L. ULMEN

Implicit in the question posed at the Fourth CUNY Conference on History and Politics in the fall of 1980, "Foreign Policy Goals of the United States: Do We Need to Change Them," was the answer; there had already developed widespread agreement that United States foreign policy had reached a critical juncture. The ending of the Vietnam War in 1975 made the debate imperative, but in the years thereafter the country turned inward and was preoccupied with domestic concerns, most notably the Watergate affair. The events of November 4, 1979, when the American embassy in Teheran was seized and the hostages taken, and December 27, 1979, when the Soviet Union invaded Afghanistan, brought the political dimension of the problem into sharper focus. The one signaled the loss of a critical American presence and the other the gain of a critical Soviet presence in the Persian Gulf—the foremost power vacuum in the world today.

Moreover, the invasion of Afghanistan underscored the greatly advanced Soviet military capability and the readiness tc
use it outside the Soviet power bloc, whereas the aborted
American rescue operation underscored the decline in American military capability—the apparent consequence of the
hesitancy to use it following the Vietnam debacle.

The debate was joined in 1980; the battle lines were
drawn. On the one side are those who strongly criticize or
reject outright the major doctrines of American foreign policy since the 1960s—principally detente, human rights, and
the so-called north-south agenda. On the other side are those
who are attempting to justify these doctrines in whole or in
part while concurring in the judgment that there has been a
tilt in the balance of power toward the Soviet Union and that
the United States must take measures to offset it. This debate
then is not between hawks and doves but between analysts
who perceive the national interest differently.

More so than in previous debates, when superior American power perhaps allowed the luxury of idealizing the goals
of American foreign policy, this debate is centered on differing conceptions of the national interest. If, as Arthur
Schlesinger jr. states, Morgenthau and the political realists
had won out over the political utopians by 1960, their victory was not unrelated to the relative change in the balance
of power between the United States and the Soviet Union
that had already become evident. The forced withdrawal of
Soviet nuclear missiles from Cuba in 1962 was, in retrospect,
the beginning of the end of American predominance.[1] To
prevent a repetition of such a showdown, the Soviet Union
undertook a massive military buildup that continues, despite
SALT. The American response was quite the opposite. To
prevent a repetition of such a showdown, detente was advanced. In his 1963 speech at American University, President
Kennedy acknowledged mutual responsibility for the cold
war and expressed the judgment that the national interest,

not ideology, is the fundamental determinant of foreign policy and that the overriding national interest of both the Soviet Union and the United States is the avoidance of nuclear war. Detente suited the mood of the leaders of the United States, who sought to end the dangerous cycle of the arms race with the Soviet Union; it suited the method of the leaders of the Soviet Union, who sought to buy time to pursue their goals of achieving parity and superiority vis-à-vis the United States. The Soviet view of detente has never included ideological coexistence, which would threaten the coherence of the Soviet state. Precisely because Marxist-Leninist ideology serves to justify Soviet rule, ideology is an essential component of the Soviet national interest and therefore of its foreign policy.[2] American leaders who have assumed responsibility for interpreting the national interest can no more ignore this fact than they can ignore the present tilt in the balance of power toward the Soviet Union. Nor can they ignore the necessity of preventing nuclear war and sustaining peaceful coexistence with the Soviet Union. The hour of political realism in the United States has come, is indeed here, and we must contend realistically with the difficult problems of politics and prudence, power and peace. Given this reality, understanding peace as the avoidance of war is the essence of political wisdom; understanding power as the means of avoiding war is the essence of political prudence.

Morgenthau's conception of political realism is evident in the present circumstances of international politics and is thus relevant to the present debate both theoretically and substantively. The first edition of *Politics Among Nations* stressed "the obsolescence of the sovereign national state"; the following editions emphasized "the attempt to create novel supranational institutions."[3] To be sure, the infusion of militant ideologies into politics,[4] the limitations of sovereignty, the uncertainty of geographical boundaries brought about by overarching power blocs, and the proliferation of many new political entities in the world arena, among other factors, have led to a transformation of the nature of the state and its relations.[5] This fact served not to undermine but to strengthen the thesis of political realism—the struggle for power is central to international politics: The national interest is the only basis for a state's foreign policy.

Morgenthau realized that the United States was being forced by circumstances to perceive itself as a state among other states at precisely the moment when the traditional nature of the state had changed. Moreover, it was called upon to be the guardian of the balance of power at precisely the moment when the traditional nature of power had changed. The balance of power *per se* had not become "outdated," as many contended; it had been transformed. The new balance of power required a new perspective. The theorists of political realism have drawn on history, philosophy, and law, but the practitioners of political realism must confront the present on its own terms. A historical truth is true only once; political truth is a child of its times.[6]

The foremost practitioner of political realism in our time is undoubtedly Henry Kissinger, whose memoirs, published on the eve of the current debate, provide a focus for contesting views.[7] Because much of the debate is concerned with why United States foreign policy has reached a critical juncture and because detente is central to virtually every issue involved, no analyst of foreign policy can avoid reference to the thinking and the actions of Kissinger, who dominated American foreign policy from 1969 to 1977 and who is widely acknowledged as the "architect of detente."[8] Kissinger's assumption of office coincided with the end of the period during which the United States was overwhelmingly more powerful than any other state and could solve its problems alone or entirely with its own resources.[9] Characterizing America's power-political position, Kissinger observed:

For the first time in American history we can neither dominate the world nor escape from it. Henceforth this country will be engaged in world affairs by reality and not by choice. America must learn to conduct its foreign policy as other nations have had to conduct it—with patience, subtlety, imagination and perseverance. [10]

The power-political position of the United States that Kissinger inherited and the foreign policy that he pursued are at issue in the present context only to the extent that they impinge on the major concerns of this volume. The focus of Kissinger's foreign policy, as he himself acknowledges, was ending the war in Vietnam. The detente that he pursued with the Soviet Union had as much to do with the problems of the United States in Vietnam and the political fallout in the United States as it did with the growing might and political will of the Soviet Union.[11] Kissinger understood that Vietnam was not a cause but a symptom of America's new power-political position, as was unease on the home front.[12] Indeed, he saw his options circumscribed by this situation.[13] Whether he had an alternative that he should have taken is moot in the current debate because the situation has changed, and the question is what to do now.[14] Current opinions are open to debate, but Kissinger rightly cautions that it is not the fact of detente that should be debated but its content.[15]

In his own words, the most important thing that Kissinger tried to do was "to attempt to base American foreign policy on some fundamental principles of national interest and to avoid those oscillations between euphoria and panic which have been so characteristic." He states: "If I didn't succeed, somebody else will have to do it,"[16] and it appears that the major conceptual battle must still be won. It is in this light that we must approach the current debate in general and the papers of the CUNY conference in particular.

The collected papers of this conference fall generally into four categories. The first focuses on United States foreign policy in the context of the overarching conflict between the two superpowers (Walter LaFeber, Vojtech Mastny, George Schwab); the second, on the impact of natural resources and international trade on shaping foreign policy (Dankwart A. Rustow, William Diebold Jr.); the third, on United States foreign policy toward the third world and the United Nations (N. A. Pelcovits, Seymour Maxwell Finger); the fourth, on United States foreign policy in the context of the nuclear age and other global problems of human survival (John H. Herz, Kenneth and Beverly Thompson). Among the questions raised and discussed are the relations between consensus and the conduct of foreign policy, how the United States should respond to the ideological dimension of Soviet foreign policy, whether a consensus of free-world concerns might bind the United States and its allies and friends in a common struggle, the political and the military consequences of the "consensus of strategic concerns" in the Persian Gulf that has placed the United States in the same position as that of its friends in Europe and Japan, the threat of oil price rises to the economic future of the United States and other industrial nations, the relation between the international economic order and the conduct of United States foreign policy, how the United States should respond to the economic interests of the third world in the light of overriding political considerations, whether the internal or the external behavior of foreign governments should be decisive in determining United States foreign relations, whether the national interest of the United States should now be merged with the interests of all in global survival, whether national initiatives or international programs are more effective in coping with global problems?

Despite the global expertise of the contributors to this conference, none evidences any specific concern with Europe, the focal point of the cold war and the policy of containment. This omission undoubtedly can be ascribed to the presumed victories of detente—particularly the Ostpolitik

pursued by the Federal Republic of Germany and the legit-
imation of once disputed borders in the Helsinki agreements
of 1975. Moreover, none of the contributors evidences any
specific concern with Southeast Asia, the focal point of
American political and military concern in the years when
detente was vigorously pursued. This omission undoubtedly
can be ascribed to the conclusion of the Vietnam War and the
desire to put it out of mind.

Whatever the reasons, these omissions and indeed the
CUNY conference raise a number of critical questions. In an
age when international politics is truly global, can the United
States continue to conduct its foreign policy in an isolated
and episodic manner? Should United States foreign policy be
conducted in relation to such amorphous economic and political constellations as the "south" and the "third world"? Is
there not a need for a global approach to foreign policy
capable of contending with political, economic, ideological,
social, military, and other forces that together make up the
struggle for power and peace today? United States foreign
policy is at the crossroads of West and East, of power and
decline, of decision and doubt, of leadership and withdrawal,
of political realism and political irresponsibility, and perhaps,
ultimately, of peace and war.

NOTES

1. See Arthur M. Schlesinger jr., "Detente: An American Perspective" in *Detente in Historical Perspective*, eds. George Schwab and
Henry Friedlander, 2nd. printing (New York, 1981), pp. 125 ff.
2. In this respect, the article by George F. Kennan, a.k.a. Mr. X,
remains valid: "The Sources of Soviet Conduct," *Foreign Affairs*, vol.
XXV, July 1947, pp. 566-582.
3. Hans J. Morgenthau, *Politics Among Nations: The Struggle for
Power and Peace* (New York, 1948, 1954, 1960, 1966, 1978).
4. See George Schwab, "Enemy oder Foe: Der Konflikt der
modernen Politik," *EPIRRHOSIS: Festgabe fuer Carl Schmitt*, eds.
Hans Barion, Ernst-Wolfgang Boeckenfoerde, Ernst Forsthoff, Werner
Weber (Berlin, 1968), pp. 671 ff.

5. The causes of the end of the traditional European state are delineated in Carl Schmitt, *Der Begriff des Politischen: Text von 1932 mit einem Vorwort und drei Corollarien* (Berlin, 1963). See Carl Schmitt, *The Concept of the Political,* Translation, Introduction, and Notes by George Schwab, with Comments on Schmitt's Essay by Leo Strauss (New Brunswick, N.J., 1976).

6. See Carl Schmitt, "Die geschichtliche Struktur des heutigen Welt-Gegensatzes von Ost und West" in *Freundschaftliche Begegnungen. Festschrift fuer Ernst Juenger zum 60. Geburtstag* (Frankfurt am Main, 1955), pp. 147 f.; Hans J. Morgenthau, *Politics Among Nations,* Preface to the third edition, 1960. The influence of the German political and legal theorist, Carl Schmitt, is implicit in Morgenthau's conception of political realism developed in his many writings and particularly in *Politics Among Nations.* The explicit link is forged in his critique of Schmitt's friend-enemy criterion elaborated in Schmitt's essay, "Der Begriff des Politischen," first published in 1927 in *Archiv fuer Sozialwissenschaft und Sozialpolitik,* vol. 58, no. I, pp. 1-33, and further elaborated in a book in 1932; Morgenthau, *La notion du "politique" et la théórie des differends internationaux* (Paris, 1933), pp. 35-37 and pp. 44-64.

7. Henry Kissinger, *White House Years* (Boston and Toronto, 1979). Kissinger has long acknowledged the influence of Morgenthau on his thinking, and it is particularly evident in *White House Years.* In his review of this first volume of Kissinger's memoirs, Stanley Hoffmann draws attention to the influence of Schmitt's friend-enemy criterion on Kissinger's notion of constant and inevitable struggle; see "The Case of Dr. Kissinger," *New York Review of Books,* December 6, 1979, pp. 22 f.

8. Ibid., pp. 55 ff. The consistency and development of Kissinger's position in *White House Years* are evident from his early writings. See *Nuclear Weapons and Foreign Policy* (New York, 1957) and *The Necessity for Choice: Prospects of American Foreign Policy* (New York, 1961).

9. Kissinger, *For the Record: Selected Statements, 1977-1980* (Boston and Toronto, 1981), p. 73.

10. Ibid., p. 75.

11. Ibid., p. 163.

12. Kissinger, *White House Years,* pp. 62 ff, 117, and 118 ff. See Carl Schmitt, *Der Begriff des Politischen* (Berlin, 1963), pp. 18 f., and *Theorie des Partisanen: Zwischenbemerkung zum Begriff des Politischen* (Berlin, 1975), pp. 18 ff.

13. Kissinger, *For the Record,* pp. 123 f., 136, 138, 198 f., and 237.

14. Kissinger's record should be judged from the perspective of how he saw himself (*White House Years,* pp. 55 ff.) and his self-criticism (*For the Record,* pp. 198, 237, 243 f).

15. Kissinger, *For the Record,* pp. 143 f., 145, 243 f., 262, 272, 289 f.

16. Ibid., p. 163.

UNITED STATES
FOREIGN POLICY
AT THE
CROSSROADS

I.

Consensus and Cooperation: A View of United States Foreign Policy, 1945–1980

WALTER LaFEBER

If Americans hope to answer Tocqueville's classic criticism that their democracy is singularly ill equipped to formulate and carry out a long-term, consistent foreign policy, they must first solve the problem of creating a consensus to support that policy. That consensus does not have to shape mass opinion (not in a society in which public-opinion polls consistently show 70 to 80 percent of the citizens ignorant of the issues about which they are supposed to have opinions). But the consensus does have to include the attentive or informed public that follows foreign-policy problems and, in many instances, has access to the media. A consensus must also manifest a second characteristic: It should be strong enough to place primary emphasis on foreign policy in domestic debates, for in debating internal problems, a democracy tends naturally to fragment. This essay suggests the characteristics of the consensus that marked U.S. policy in the early cold war (an era becoming known as Cold War I), why that consensus disintegrated in the 1950s and 1960s, and how officials tried to resurrect it in the 1970s and early 1980s (Cold War II).

Support for American foreign policy in the immediate post-World War II years was fashioned from disarray and quickly evolved into a consensus that fragmented again into disarray. Early in Cold War II there are enough indications to suggest how a consensus might develop to support policy. For a historian, many of the indications seem familiar: the almost exclusive focusing of attention on the Soviet Union (or, as Ronald Reagan said in June 1980, "Let's not delude ourselves. The Soviet Union underlies all the unrest that is going on"[1]) and the articulation of great concern over indigenous revolutionary outbreaks in the Middle East and the Caribbean; a growing moral concern among Americans but a growing willingness to work with repressive military regimes; an avowed commitment to remove the government from the private sector but a strong commitment to a larger national-security state that will necessarily create a growing governmental presence; and the attempt to renew and release the forces of American individualism but attempts to force-feed a sprouting anticommunist consensus in which dissenters—especially among minorities—could be forced further toward the margins of society.

These indications resemble the characteristics of the first cold war. More specifically, they indicate that policymakers might try to resolve twenty-first-century problems by using the weapons of the 1980s while operating on the basis of the assumptions of the 1950s.

The cold war policies of the 1950s rested on four assumptions: U.S. dominance in the Western alliance system, overwhelming American power in the global economy, a politically potent domestic consensus that a President could summon to provide almost automatic support for overseas ventures, and unquestioned U.S. superiority in strategic forces and in conventional capabilities in areas not adjacent to the Soviet Union. These assumptions about American power in Cold War I shared characteristics that should be underlined. They were valid assumptions in the 1940s and 1950s but became increasingly less so in the 1960s and 1970s. They shaped a unique era of American and world history that had no precedent and will have little in common with any future era. And the assumptions became invalid in roughly the order listed: The foundations of the Western alliance cracked, the dominance of the U.S. economy began to erode, then the consensus fragmented (and major fragments appeared on Capitol Hill where single-interest-group lobbyists soon outnumbered even the cold warriors), and, finally, U.S. strategic superiority disappeared.

It may well be that these characteristics of the first cold war did not attenuate in this particular order. The chronology indicates a cause-and-effect relationship that not only suggests how and when Americans moved from the first to the second cold war but why future U.S. policymakers may have difficulty if they try to make policy by reading cold war history backward, that is, if they believe that the quest for a margin of U.S. military superiority will lead to a new consensus, a global resurrection of U.S. economic power, or a reunified Western alliance. The cause-and-effect relationship did not seem to work that way in the recent past. The sequence of events is fundamental also in understanding that past, for it generally provides a thread to tie together 35 years of American foreign policy (or, alternatively, a bridge across which we can move to examine the gaps that separate the first and the second cold wars). More specifically, it provides a tool with which to analyze recent revisionist analyses of the Vietnam War, analyses that distort the historical record of that war and do so in part, it seems, to make more acceptable similar diplomatic and military policies for the 1980s.[2]

The Western Alliance

In these new revisionist accounts of the Indochina conflict, one part of the history is often omitted, the failure of Washington's closest allies to support its position in Southeast Asia. The war revealed fundamental disagreements within the Western alliance, but these differences did not suddenly become manifest in the mid-1960s. The growing conflict among national interests in the West had deep historical roots.

The divisions were at first neutralized by the overwhelming reaction to the U.S. hegemony that shaped the Marshall Plan, the 1949 NATO alliance, and the rearmament of the Federal Republic of Germany. Washington could virtually dictate terms to the British and did so in the 1946 loan arrangements. State Department officials dealt with the French by buying them off with Marshall Plan aid and then exerting political pressure that forced French leaders, despite their bitter objections, to accept West German rearmament. Providing nearly 80 percent of the French military budget in Indochina enabled the United States to decide whether the French were to be saved. After Dwight Eisenhower flashed the thumbs-down signal during the Dienbienphu crisis, he accelerated the schedule for pushing out the French. Americans then moved into Indochina to do the job in a proper, noncolonial fashion. Truman and Eisenhower handled other allies with some sensitivity. Western European concerns about Truman's policies in Korea seem to have been an important counterbalance to General Douglas MacArthur's unlimited goals. Eisenhower did not try to rescue the French at Dienbienphu because, at least in part, Winston Churchill's government in London refused to go along.[3]

Above all others, the Federal Republic of Germany enjoyed a special position in U.S. diplomacy. A realistic assessment of the economic and military situation seemed to require the rapid rehabilitation of the German economy and army. The unusual American empathy dates to the 1870s and 1880s and especially to the interwar years; it did not suddenly develop during Cold War I. The empathy was broken when Americans declared war on the Germans after discovering that Berlin's and Washington's priorities were quite different after all. In the 1950s and into the 1960s, however, a relationship of empathy was the cornerstone of the alliance. It was strikingly underscored by the close Dulles-Adenauer friendship, by John Kennedy's dramatic visit to Berlin, and when the West Germans reversed themselves, on U.S. insistence, and withdrew from a lucrative pipeline deal with the Russians in 1962-1963.

Even in the early postwar period, however, alliance relationships were changing, and U.S. dominance was ebbing. The pivotal event occurred in 1956 when the United States turned on the British, the French, and the Israelis and forced them to halt their drive into Egypt. Eisenhower was not subtle; he threatened to wage war on the pound and cut off oil shipments at the beginning of winter unless the two NATO allies accepted his terms. For a host of reasons, the Suez episode and the simultaneous Soviet invasion of Hungary appear to be a turning point in the cold war.[4] The divisions within the alliance became obvious, and Konrad Adenauer, despite his close friendship with Dulles, privately asserted to beleaguered French leaders that their revenge on the United States would be the creation of an independent Europe. Within the next two years, the formation of the European Economic Community (EEC) and France's accelerated development of the atomic bomb began to transform Adenauer's words into reality. The tremendous success of the U.S. multinationals that moved inside the EEC's tariff walls to gain control over key sectors of Western Europe's economy masked a long-term transformation. Led by the French, the EEC was becoming an economic power. By the late 1960s the European Economic Community had cut sharply into Washington's control over the alliance. The most direct expression of that control then became U.S. dominance in NATO. But even that once sharp instrument was blunted by France's withdrawal from the military structure of NATO between 1963 and 1966 and West Germany's Ostpolitik, or new opening toward the communist bloc, after 1970.

Ironically, United States control over its Western allies began to diminish as early as the 1950s, as the extent of its power was being most dramatically demonstrated at Suez. John Kennedy inherited a disintegrating alliance system. Raymond Aron accurately wrote that the system continued to fragment in the 1960s because "the Grand Design of the New Frontiersmen was incompatible with the Grand Design" of Charles de Gaulle.[5] The 1963 Franco-German treaty and the continued exclusion of Great Britain from the EEC (because, to French eyes, the British were an American Trojan horse) exemplified how the national interests of Western Europe and the United States were drifting apart.

John Kennedy's and Lyndon Johnson's Vietnam policies made the gap almost unbridgeable. The United States had mutual defense treaties with 42 nations and the Southeast Asia Treaty Organization (SEATO), which included Great Britain and France, but only three nations—Australia, New Zealand, and South Korea—finally sent combat troops to help Americans and Vietnamese. The South Koreans dispatched a second division only after being bribed to the extent of one billion dollars.[6] Thirty-seven nations helped with aid (symbolic aid in many instances), but in general, Vietnam had a devastating effect on the alliance system. The involvement raised basic questions about U.S. judgment and priorities, and it led Washington to exert pressures that angered its allies. U.S. officials in turn became angered, most famously at Dean Rusk's farewell party, when the secretary of state sought out a British journalist and unloaded eight years of frustrations: "All we required was one regiment. The Black Watch would have done. Just one regiment, but you wouldn't. Well, don't expect us to save you again. They can invade Sussex, and we wouldn't do a damned thing about it."[7]

Vietnam split the alliance in another direction as well. After the Cuban missile crisis, Kennedy apparently believed that the Soviets had learned a lesson but that the Chinese communists had replaced the Russians as the major threat, especially in South Asia. The President sent this word to de Gaulle,[8] but neither the French leader nor other European leaders shared Kennedy's view. Equally important, Washington's most important Asian ally, Japan, adopted the Europeans' outlook. When U.S. officials warned about Chinese expansionism in the mid-1960s, Japan responded by quietly opening informal channels that created a half-billion dollar trade with mainland China. Tokyo had little interest in U.S. containment policy. "It seems," said a Japanese Defense Agency official, "that the Pentagon wants us to play the infield while you play the outfield against the Chinese."[9] The Japanese did not consider it in their interest to do so.

In the aftermath of the missile crisis and the first major U.S. military commitments to Vietnam, the allies doubly damned Washington's policy. Not only was it unduly anti-Chinese, but it was moving too rapidly and without sufficient consultation toward a new bilateral relationship with the Soviet Union. The test ban treaty of 1963 and Johnson's attempts amid a worsening Vietnam crisis in 1967-1968 to work out a detente policy with Moscow raised French fears of a Yalta-type deal between the two superpowers. The West Germans and the French, however, made the best of the situation: Since at least the mid-1960s, they have enjoyed rapidly growing trade with the newly-respectable Eastern communist bloc. Ironically, that trade has also sharply divided the allies; when Jimmy Carter asked them to cut it back after the Soviet invasion of Afghanistan, the West Europeans did not comply with the request. The disintegration of the alliance and especially of U.S. control within the alliance had been in progress for more than a decade when Richard Nixon came to power in 1969. His surprise opening to China stunned the Japanese, and his sudden economic moves in 1971 shocked both the Japanese and the Europeans. Differences over the 1973 war led to policy arguments about the Middle East, and by late 1973 French officials privately accused Henry Kissinger of encouraging the OPEC oil embargo in order to weaken energy-dependent West Europe. Kissinger's pledge that 1973-1974 was to be "the year of Europe" in U.S. diplomacy was swept away by the new political and economic tides that engulfed the alliance. Given the record to this point, however, the "year-of-Europe" pledge promised to be no more than a quick fix for a problem that required basic surgery. By 1974 Kissinger termed certain West European governments "contemptible" and soon after said privately that given present trends, Europe could be Marxist by the mid-1980s.[10] The hope for a "year of Europe" had changed into a fear of Europe.

The Carter administration was not as gloomy at first, but it could do little to reverse the two-decade-old decay in the alliance. A stagflation that caught up with the West German economy weakened both NATO military planning and, particularly when Carter pushed Chancellor Helmut Schmidt and other Western leaders to do more to pump-prime the West German and other Western economies, U.S. relations with key countries in the alliance. The failure to coordinate economic sanctions in the aftermath of the Afghanistan invasion created more bitterness. Americans have realized that particularly since Chancellor Willy Brandt's successful Ostpolitik of 1970-1971, Western Europe has become more independent, more concerned about good relations with the communist bloc, and especially more dependent on Soviet oil and gas—a dependency that in some instances may increase fourfold in the 1980s. A former State Department official, Charles Maechling, Jr., wrote in November 1980 that "Unlike France, [which] is self-centered in its foreign policy but captive to no one, . . . West Germany is now so locked into relationships with the East that its value in any crisis short of outright Soviet aggression in Europe is open to question."[11] Such a judgment about the nation that historically served as the United States' strongest ally during the cold war is severe, and its significance lies in part in understanding that these differences in national interests are not evanescent but have been sharpening for a quarter of a century.

The Economy

The alliance's disruption over the Suez crisis initially signaled that the conditions of the first cold war were changing. The problems that soon began to plague the American economy signaled that U.S. policymakers were losing a most important tool for maintaining U.S. hegemony in the alliance. Between 1944 and 1948 this tool was the most potent weapon in the U.S. diplomatic arsenal particularly after the nearly bankrupt British accepted Washington's monetary and trade policies in 1946. Through the Bretton Woods arrangements that established the World Bank and the International Monetary Fund, the General Agreements on Tariffs and Trade, the Marshall Plan, and the enormous military expenditures of the Korean War, the United States created a liberal, multilateral trading area west of the Iron Curtain that was as remarkable for its duration as for the spectacular growth it generated. The Soviets never accepted these economic ground rules. Indeed, in retrospect those few weeks in February 1946, when Stalin refused to join the Bretton

Woods organizations, the United States angrily responded to
that refusal, and George Kennan wrote the "long telegram"
that offered systematic reasons for containing Soviet power,
marked a major turning point away from the wartime alliance
and toward the cold war's ideological-political conflict.

The extent of U.S. economic power in the early years of
that conflict can be measured not only by the rapid reconstruction of Western Europe and Japan but by Truman's ability to quadruple U.S. defense expenditures within six months
after the Korean War began. Eisenhower cut back military
budgets by more than one-quarter. The former general believed with some fervor that the passion with which some
Americans sought higher military expenditures, higher tariffs,
and possibly unbalanced budgets demonstrated "the short-
sightedness bordering upon tragic stupidity of many who fan-
cy themselves to be the greatest believers in and supporters of
capitalism . . . but who blindly support measures and conditions that cannot fail in the long run to destroy any free
economic system," or so Eisenhower wrote in his diary in
mid-1953.[12] The President condemned those who sought
high tariffs and other mercantilist devices much as he condemned the power of the military-industrial-university complex eight years later. In the interim, however, he found it
necessary to increase defense expenditures once again and,
more significantly, to use such government-directed, neo-
mercantilist devices as the Export-Import Bank, the Development Loan Fund (in which monies were tied to U.S. exports), and the Inter-American Development Bank. The policy assumption throughout the decade was that mammoth
American economic power was a major weapon to be used in
the cold war. A government, in this instance controlled by
Republicans, only had to intervene to direct that power precisely or to use its political authority to clear away obstacles
that confined that power, as, for example, in Iran, when
Eisenhower released five major U.S. oil companies from the

threat of antitrust action so that they could replace British power in that country and help the young shah consolidate his newly-regained power in 1954.

The validity of this assumption about U.S. economic power began to change after 1957-1958. The EEC threatened U.S. economic hegemony at the same time Americans were hit from another direction by a new and a spectacularly efficient Japanese productive system. Future historians will probably conclude that the turn of U.S. economic power away from the triumphs of Cold War I to the stagflation and frustrations of Cold War II began not with Vietnam but in the late 1950s. The Vietnam conflict worsened conditions and made them more visible because in prosecuting both the war in Vietnam and the war on poverty, U.S. officials were demonstrating their determination to find a new frontier abroad and build a great society at home. Not even the American economy of the first cold war could do both at once.

The strain appeared in 1958-1959 when U.S. manufactured exports could no longer easily pierce the EEC or compete in other global markets. For a time in 1959, the value of American merchandise imports actually exceeded the value of merchandise exports—the first time such an unfavorable trade trend had developed since the 1890s. American manufactured goods, it seemed, were losing the competitive edge that they had enjoyed internationally since the late nineteenth century.[13] The imbalance worsened during the 1960s. Manufactured imports accounted for less than 50 percent of all imports in 1961 but for more than 65 percent by 1971.[14] Not only did the percentage share of such goods in world trade decline, but Americans found themselves supplying increasing amounts of agricultural goods and raw materials abroad while taking, in return, finished manufactured products, much as they had done in the nineteenth century.[15] The growing trade imbalance and the accelerated U.S.

investment overseas created a fundamental problem in the
nation's balance of payments and ultimately caused a run on
U.S. gold reserves. Because those reserves supported the dollar as the key international currency, a run on the dollar,
orchestrated in the mid-1960s by the United States' ally in
Paris, also occurred.

Theodore Sorensen expressed the belief that "few
subjects occupied more of Kennedy's time in the White
House or were the subject of more secret high-level meetings"
than the balance-of-payments situation. "Almost to a man,"
Sorensen recounted, "Kennedy's associates . . . thought he
was excessively concerned about the problem."[16] The President apparently understood, however, that some restoration
of the U.S. hegemony in the world marketplace was required
if his plans for an expanded arms budget were to be realized
and if his pledge to "support any friend, oppose any foe" was
to be honored. This requirement became a fine irony in postwar U.S. foreign policy: At the point when its economic base
began to weaken, a newly-ambitious American foreign policy
placed impossible demands on that base.[17] One result was
that in Vietnam the irony turned into tragedy. A second
result was a skewing of the U.S. economy until inflation took
hold. Gross domestic investment dropped after 1960 to
about half the rate in West Germany and Japan, and employment—and the stock market—during the 1960s depended
increasingly on military expenditures.[18] A third result was an
inflation that created a dollar so overvalued that the strain
finally destroyed the quarter-century-old Bretton Woods system in 1971 and in 1973 persuaded OPEC nations to raise oil
prices so that they could pay the inflated prices of Western
goods.

By 1973 U.S. policymakers confronted deep fissures in
their economic policies that ran north-south as well as East-
West. A distinguishing characteristic of the new cold war that
appeared in the 1960s was the increased U.S. dependence on

newly emerging, independent nations for markets and the most basic raw materials. Developing nations now take more U.S. exports than the EEC and Japan combined.[19] Henry Kissinger first confronted the political meaning of this new economic dependence in 1974-1975. Understandably, given the deep roots and the complexity of the problem, neither he nor Carter-administration officials devised policies that arrested the relative decline of U.S. economic power and dealt with the resulting political problems. In Latin America and Africa, however, U.S. policymakers were more realistic and successful after 1976 than before that date. They realized that given the devolution of political and economic power from the major industrial nations to the so-called third world, which has occurred since the formation of OPEC in 1960, gunboat and dollar diplomacy are less useful than coming to an accommodation with the advocates of the new nationalism.

The Reagan administration believes that the long-term economic decline can be arrested by instituting more free-market measures. It has indicated that problems in such areas as Latin America and Africa can be handled by what might be termed neorealism; as an expression of one of its more extreme forms, a Reagan adviser during the presidential campaign, General Daniel Graham, proposed that order and good diplomatic relations could be maintained by a NATOlike treaty that linked the military governments of South America with the South African government.[20] If this brief survey of post-1959 American economic history is correct, the new administration's international policies will less resemble the free-market principles of Adam Smith than the mercantilism of the Earl of Shaftesbury. Reagan's apparent determination to contain both the Soviet Union and revolutionary nationalism, combined with the two trends evident in the post-1958 United States—a relatively declining economy and the development of governmental institutions and policies to wield that economic strength most effectively in the international arena—will force the new administration to use more governmental power to direct relatively smaller economic resources against Soviet power and third-world revolutions. Given the economic trends of Cold War II, a reinvigorated national-security state cannot be built nor can its power be expanded abroad on free-market principles.

The Declining Consensus

Nor can such a state be built and its power exercised overseas over a long period without an effective political consensus. Harry Truman and Dean Acheson showed that they understood this basic fact in 1947 when they effectively ended months of public debate about how to respond to Soviet policies by devising the Truman Doctrine. Since the end of World War II, the administration had been whipsawed by Henry Wallace on the left (who wanted to recognize explicitly Soviet dominance in Eastern Europe and then work out tighter U.S.-Soviet economic links) and by Republicans on the right (who, especially after their smashing election victories in 1946, wanted to fight communism but not make expensive overseas commitments). Suddenly confronted in February 1947 with the collapse of England's power in Turkey and Greece because of the broken British economy, Acheson and the President devised a remarkable formula that allowed for the creation of a *pax Americana* to replace the old *pax Britannica* and to rest the creation on a solid consensus at home.[21]

Defining the threat as both ideological and military and exploiting the historic American fear of Russia, the Truman administration successfully established an anticommunist consensus that lasted throughout the first cold war into the second cold war of the early 1970s. The consensus supported, among other ventures, Truman's policies in Korea until he appeared too moderate or ineffective in ending the war; Eisenhower's policies in the crises of the offshore islands of Quemoy and Matsu, Suez, and Lebanon; and Kennedy's Bay-of-Pigs fiasco to the extent of giving him his highest level of support in the public-opinion polls after that disaster. The consensus rolled on into the Vietnam years, muting debate in Washington and New York corridors of power until, in frustration, debate erupted into teach-ins in universities and demonstrations on city streets. In retrospect, the extent of public support for the Vietnam War was remarkable. Top officials, such as the State Department officers who, in 1966, summarily dismissed dissenters as "a small though vocal minority of the population,"[22] and Richard Nixon, who asserted that his 1970-1971 policies were supported by a "quiet majority," were quite right in their perceptions of the political climate. Bipartisan foreign policy was threatened by a very small group of Democrats, not by Republicans who, unlike the Republicans of 1918 and 1940, attacked a Democratic President for doing too little militarily.[23]

And if, as Congress threatened, the legislators turned dovish and repealed the 1964 Gulf of Tonkin resolution, Johnson (and Nixon) believed, in the Texan's words that, "I could still carry out our commitments" in Vietnam.[24] After all, as Undersecretary of State Nicholas Katzenbach told a Senate committee in 1967, the act of declaring war is the expression of an outmoded phraseology"; the Founders simply gave Congress "an opportunity to express its views" on the question of war.[25] The legislative branch offered no effective response to this weird constitutional interpretation for another three years. Such close observers as George Ball, Bernard Cohen, and Herbert Schandler, among others, agree that throughout the 1960s, the Johnson administration successfully ignored dissent over Vietnam policy and instead shaped public opinion.[26]

This point should be emphasized especially during the current debate over the so-called Vietnam syndrome. It is impossible to prove, as some now argue, that the American defeat in Southeast Asia was the result of a lack of will at home or the inability of two Presidents to mold public opinion in favor of their policies. The United States lost politically in Vietnam because Japan and the most important Western European allies refused to become involved in what they believed was a bad cause, economically because the American economy proved incapable of paying for such a war and militarily because the United States could not devise a way of saving Vietnam without destroying it.

The collapse of the political consensus had considerably more complex origins than those suggested by the military failure in Vietnam. In one important sense, the collapse began as long ago as the 1890s when, as one persuasive analysis argues, a new kind of political party system began to evolve to deal with massive immigration, a communication and transportation revolution, and global responsibilities that Americans willingly assumed.[27] Despite the successes of the New Deal coalition, this party development had not reached fruition in 1948 when intensified ticket splitting, third parties, and such explosive issues as civil rights and antiwar movements began to tear apart the party system. "Ideological politics," in the words of the analysis, "has rapidly displaced patronage politics."

In foreign policy, these centrifugal forces were temporarily masked or circumvented by the success of the Truman-Acheson formula of 1947 and by a successful appeal to bipartisanship. Foreign policy, always directed by elites, became more so. It continued to be insulated against the political forces of the 1940s and the 1950s as long as it was successful on its own terms, that is, in containing communism, and continued to provide ever-larger economic rewards through access to cheap raw materials and fresh markets for trade and

investment. In the 1960s U.S. foreign policy showed a
distressing inability to blunt communist power in such areas
as Southeast Asia, Cuba, and Czechoslovakia, but, of perhaps
greater importance, it failed to demonstrate to enough
Americans that it was profitable. Indeed, given decreasing
productivity, inflation, the loss of foreign and even of domestic markets, and a roller-coaster unemployment rate, overseas
commitments were questioned even as loss leaders.

By the 1970s, therefore, the great contradiction in U.S.
diplomatic history had reasserted itself. It is impossible to
decentralize power at home, as has occurred in social and
political areas since the 1960s (if not the 1890s or 1820s),
and simultaneously centralize power to carry out overseas
policies. Tocqueville recognized this contradiction 150 years
ago, and at least four Presidents (Johnson through Carter)
have helped demonstrate it. Vietnam sharpened, not created,
the contradiction. It was implied in 1962 when *The Wall
Street Journal* warned of impending political problems and
lamented that no one apparently knew how to meet them:
"National politics today is pretty much a vacuum or at least a
desert. It is arid of ideas."[28] Becoming aware of the problems he confronted, President Kennedy told Arthur
Schlesinger that while conservative thinking was "so naive,"
liberals "ought to . . . provide new ideas, and they don't
come up with any."[29] One Kennedy response was to centralize even further certain diplomatic decision-making activities.
That eloquent defender of State Department prerogative,
Dean Acheson, condemned the new power of the National
Security Council: Kennedy's "distrust [of the State Depart-
ment] and desire for a more personally controlled instrument, combined in Washington, as they had in Moscow, to
create an inner and private politburo to control and supervise
a foreign office whose new head the President hardly
knew."[30]

The evolution of the NSC continued throughout the

1960s and the 1970s, but it did nothing to resolve the great contradiction. NSC's increased power without constitutional responsibility worsened the problem by raising suspicions in Congress and among the public and confounded policy-making. Post-1960s politics sharpened the contradiction: Voting participation declined, and political-party ties gave way to special-interest lobbying groups; new ideologies combined with weakened parties to make those who did cast ballots more volatile in their political behavior; regionalism, ethnicity, states rights—or what one observer called the Balkanization of America—grew.[31] These changes particularly affected Congress, and its power surged after 1972 when President Nixon increasingly based his foreign policies—especially detente—on trade treaties and other economic measures. When he approached Congress, Nixon (and his successors) discovered, much as had Charles I, that the legislature could exact a high price for loosening its power over the purse.

Congress's power, however, was also being dispersed. Seniority and deference to executive authority gave way to more democratic procedures and rapidly growing staffs that listened less to White House officials and committee chairmen than to the proliferating lobbyists. By 1974-1975, Henry Kissinger recognized the extent of this political earthquake; he devoted large amounts of time to soothing congressional egos and, through nationwide speaking engagements, informing public opinion. This effort constituted one of the most fascinating periods in Kissinger's tenure. Jimmy Carter also perceived the new conditions, but except for the success of the Panama Canal treaties, he failed to tame for policy purposes the political system that had raised him to power.

Carter's State Department press secretary, Hodding Carter, caught a central aspect of the change with nicely mixed metaphors: Once Americans "strode the world like a colossus so that it was all a gravy train," but now there is a "clawing for survival." Anyone having "a direct stake in foreign policy," Hodding Carter continued, has "a client institution [Washington] fighting for it."[32] The deeper meaning was perceived by Hans Morgenthau, who wrote in 1974 that the fear of the authors of the *Federalist Papers* was coming true, "for it is the great political paradox of our time that a government too weak to control the concentrations of private power that have usurped much of the substance of its power has grown so powerful as to reduce the citizens to impotence." The result, Morgenthau concluded, is "political apathy, political violence, and the search for new communities outside the official political structure."[33]

A Note on the Military Dimension

The dilemmas resulting from the great contradiction in U.S. foreign policy would be less critical if the United States possessed, as it did in Cold War I, the raw power to protect its avowed overseas interests. But as the alliance weakened and economic tools became blunt, so U.S. military power declined relative to that of the other superpower. As early as the 1950s, Washington policymakers carefully excluded Eastern Europe as an area for U.S. military involvement. The so-called Sonnenfeldt Doctrine of 1975, which recognized the need for organic evolution and not sudden change if Eastern Europe was to become more autonomous and liberal, dates at least to the Eisenhower-Dulles view that the "liberation" of the communist bloc had to be peaceful and gradual.

Outside Eastern Europe, however, U.S. power, resting on an absolute superiority in atomic and then nuclear weapons, was so great that in a number of instances American Presidents could consider or threaten the use of such weapons with the confidence that the United States was immune to retaliation. Examples included Truman's actions in the 1948 Berlin crisis, his refusal to exclude atomic weapons from the fighting in Korea after Chinese armies overran U.S. positions in late 1950, Eisenhower's threat to employ atomic bombs against North Korea and China in 1953 and against China in 1954 and 1958, and the consideration given to their employment in Indochina.[34]

The ultimate test nearly occurred in the 1962 missile crisis. Walt Whitman Rostow wrote that the crisis was "a kind of Gettysburg of the Cold War," and so it was, although not quite in the way Mr. Rostow meant.[35] Soviet leaders, in the words of one Russian official at the United Nations, determined that such a thing would never happen to them again; they undertook a massive military spending program, achieving strategic parity with the United States by the mid-1970s. Although by the end of the 1960s Americans had 700,000 soldiers stationed in 30 countries, placed military advisory teams in 38 nations, signed mutual defense treaties with 42 governments, and furnished military and/or economic aid to nearly 100 countries,[36] the war in Vietnam could not be won, changes in the newly-emerging nations could not be controlled as U.S. officials wished, and military elements often exacerbated rather than improved alliance relationships.

The United States reaction to these frustrations, Soviet arms expenditures, the invasion of Afghanistan, and revolutionary outbreaks in the Middle East and Central America has been to increase the Pentagon's budget until it will account for over one trillion dollars during the next five years. Public-opinion polls, especially a CBS-*New York Times* poll published in January 1980, showed a remarkable lack of public support for forceful measures in response to the Iranian and Afghanistan crises.[37] A high State Department official's interpretation of the Afghanistan situation, however, sounded familiar: It was a "clear demonstration," Matthew

Nimetz said in July 1980, " . . . that the Soviets now possess both the ability and the willingness to project their power abroad, beyond the territory of the Warsaw Pact, and to do so in an area of Western sensitivity and vulnerability."[38] That is a close paraphrase of Truman's and Acheson's interpretations of the invasion of South Korea in 1950. In the threats that they posed to U.S. interests, the two situations are not comparable, but they certainly are comparable in the sense that both interpretations have provided a rationale for greatly expanded arms budgets.

Summary

The definition and the main conclusions are similar. Only the world is different. How it is different can be encapsulated:

—There has not been one cold war but two quite different cold wars. The new cold war did not begin with the failure of SALT II or the invasion of Afghanistan. In important respects it dates to the late 1950s.

—Cold War II has been shaped by a growing divergence among national interests of the members of the Western alliance. Former Secretary of Defense Harold Brown captured this divergence with his comment in late 1980 that "Sometimes, some of the allies imply 'Yes, there should be a division of task—we'll sell stuff to the Russians and you defend us.' That's not what I mean," Mr. Brown observed, "by a division of task."[39] The problem predates Brown's tenure, however. It can be traced to at least the Suez crisis of 1956, the EEC's birth, Japan's recovery in the late 1950s, and Vietnam. Gaullism and Brandt's detente policies were more the results than the causes of the divergence.

—The second cold war has been marked by the inability of the United States economy to carry the burdens placed on it by Kennedy, Johnson, and their successors, but, again, the fundamental economic problems became apparent in the late 1950s.

—The new cold war has been characterized by a breakdown of the 1947 consensus and the consequent decline of presidential power in conducting foreign policy. The roots of this problem can be traced to the early 1960s, indeed to 1948 and even to the nineteenth century.

—Finally, the fundamental problems that trouble U.S. policy in Cold War II, if these historical developments can serve as a guide, will not be resolved in the American political system by viewing them strictly within the context of a bipolar U.S.-U.S.S.R. relationship or by trying to resolve them by creating a much larger national-security state[40] and simultaneously applying free-market principles. That approach contains contradictions that will only worsen the problems that have arisen during the two-decade development of Cold War II.

NOTES

1. *New York Times,* October 20, 1980, p. 23.

2. This point is discussed at length in Walter LaFeber, "The Last War, the Next War, and the New Revisionists," *Democracy,* I (January 1981), especially pp. 93-101.

3. The best recent overview of Eisenhower's policies in these areas is Robert Divine, *Eisenhower and the Cold War* (New York, 1981), chapters I and III.

4. A provocative analysis that makes this point is the special report on the decline of American power in *Business Week,* March 12, 1979.

5. Raymond Aron, *The Imperial Republic: The United States and the World, 1945-1973,* translated by Frank Jellinek (Englewood Cliffs, New Jersey, 1974), p. 85.

6. *Washington Post,* September 13, 1970, p. 1.

7. Louis Heren, *No Hail, No Farewell* (New York, 1970), p. 230.

8. William R. Tyler, Oral History Interview, March 7, 1964, John F. Kennedy Presidential Library, Cambridge, Massachusetts.

9. George R. Packard III, "Living with the Real Japan," *Foreign Affairs,* XLV (October 1967), pp. 195-196; *New York Times,* August 14, 1966, p. 22.

10. *Ibid.,* February 16, 1976, p. 1; *Washington Post,* March 17, 1974, p. A12.

11. Charles Maechling, Jr., "Schmidt: Walking a Tightrope, . . . " *Ibid.,* November 20, 1980, p. A19.

12. Diary entry of July 2, 1953, D. D. Eisenhower Presidential Library; I am indebted to Professor James Gilbert, University of Maryland, for a copy of this document.

13. Harold G. Vatter, *The U.S. Economy in the 1950s* (New York, 1963), pp. 19-20.

14. Lewis Beman, "How to Tell Where the U.S. Is Competitive," *Fortune* LXXXVI (July 1972), pp. 54-55.

15. Seymour Melman, *The Permanent War Economy* (New York, 1974), pp. 112-114.

16. Theodore C. Sorensen, *Kennedy* (New York, 1965), pp. 405, 408.

17. *New York Times,* October 10, 1980, p. D2.

18. James L. Clayton, ed., *The Economic Impact of the Cold War* (New York, 1970), p. 51.

19. Department of State, Bureau of Public Affairs, "North-South Relations," *Gist,* June 1980.

20. *New York Times,* September 22, 1980, p. A12.

21. This argument is elaborated in the author's "The Truman Doctrine," in Alexander DeConde, ed., *Encyclopedia of American Foreign Policy* (New York, 1978).

22. Bernard Cohen, *The Public Impact on Foreign Policy* (New York, 1973), p. 124.

23. James Reston's column in the *New York Times,* November 19, 1965, p. 23.

24. *Public Papers of the Presidents . . . Lyndon Baines Johnson, 1966* (Washington, 1968), p. 222.

25. A good discussion of these statements is in Arthur M. Schlesinger, jr. *The Imperial Presidency* (Boston, 1973), pp. 181-182.

26. George Ball's quote in *New York Times Magazine,* April 1, 1973, p. 43; Cohen, *Public's Impact, passim;* Herbert Y. Schandler, *The Unmaking of a President: Lyndon Johnson and Vietnam* (Princeton, 1977), p. 179, footnote.

27. Joel Silbey and Lee Benson, "1854-1984," unpublished paper, pp. 81-84, 86-88.

28. Louis Heren, op. cit., pp. 118-119.

29. Arthur M. Schlesinger, jr. *1000 Days* (Boston, 1965), p. 739.

30. Dean Acheson, "The Eclipse of the State Department," *Foreign Affairs,* IL (July 1972), 602.

31. Kevin Phillips, "Balkanization of America," *Harper's,* CCLVI (May 1978), p. 38.

32. *Washington Post,* June 26, 1980, p. A19.

33. Hans Morgenthau, "Decline of Democratic Government," *New Republic,* CLXXI (November 9, 1974), pp. 14-16.

34. Robert Divine, *op. cit.,* chapter II; Memorandum "Discussion at the 131st Meeting of the NSC, . . . February 11, 1953," Ann Whitman Files, Eisenhower Papers, Eisenhower Library.

35. W. W. Rostow, *Diffusion of Power* (New York, 1972), p. 250.

36. Ronald Steel, *Pax Americana* (New York, 1967), p. 10; *New York Times Magazine,* September 17, 1967, pp. 30-31.

37. *Public Opinion,* III (February/March 1980), p. 13.

38. Matthew Nimetz, "Health of the Atlantic Alliance," U.S. Department of State, *Current Policy,* no. 199.

39. *New York Times,* December 7, 1980, p. 44.

40. Robert Lindsey, "What the Record Says about Reagan," *New York Times Magazine,* June 29, 1980, pp. 18, 32.

II.

The Soviet Challenge
to United States
Foreign Policy

VOJTECH MASTNY

Little doubt exists that the Soviet Union poses a challenge to the United States; opinions differ about the nature of the challenge. President Carter lost much prestige when he confessed that the Soviet invasion of Afghanistan "has made a more dramatic change in my opinion of what the Soviets' ultimate goals are than anything they've done in the previous time that I've been in office."[1] But although few have been so honest or innocent to admit openly their misperceptions of Moscow's true intentions, misperception has plagued American foreign policy. This is not to say that the policy has been recurrently wrong. It is to say that it has often been difficult to gauge whether successes in foreign policy resulted from good judgment or merely good luck.

The first part of the judgment pertains to the character of Soviet expansionism. During the 65 years of its existence, the Soviet state has grown into the world's mightiest, and probably last, imperial power. Its imperialism can be defined simply as the relentless quest for direct or indirect control of additional territories. Whatever the deficiencies of that definition, it conveys the essential fact that the pursuit of what Moscow regards as its national interest has repeatedly threatened the independence and the integrity of other nations. The United States has usually, although not always, perceived this kind of international behavior as a threat to its national interest.

The intensity of Soviet assertiveness has been by no means uniform, although Moscow's readiness for genuine as opposed to merely tactical accommodation has always been suspect—another reason why Soviet-American relations have normally been tense. With few exceptions, the only difference has been between periods of high and low tension. But this can be a vital difference when both countries possess the means to wreak mutual destruction. Coming to grips with what provokes high as opposed to low tension is therefore the key to managing the troublesome relationship.

According to one school of thought, the Soviet Union needs to feel more secure in order to be accommodating. But there is no less logic in the opposite view that only insecurity induces the readiness for accommodation on the part of an inherently aggressive regime. The interpretation hinges not only on a judgment about the nature of the regime. It also depends on what security, both internal and external, means to Soviet leaders at any given time. Internal security includes the security of their empire, although this is even more likely than external security to be subject to change.

Because American policy inevitably shapes Soviet perceptions of security, it is within American power and certainly in the American interest to influence those perceptions. Traditionally policymakers have been much more preoccupied with influencing the external aspects of Soviet security, which are easier to grasp, than the elusive internal determinants. This may seem a sound preoccupation because it addresses what is more feasible. Nevertheless, it can impair the effectiveness of policies by neglecting what is more critical.

The transformation of the Soviet state into an empire with global involvements has been a salient development of our time. Yet Soviet power and imperialism have not always been intertwined. In 1917 the former was born of the rejection of the latter. The Bolsheviks associated imperialism with the decay of capitalism and acted accordingly. Their attempt to expand their power and influence was initially made to spread their revolutionary gospel abroad rather than promote territorial dominion. The difference could have become merely semantic had they succeeded in exporting revolution to Poland and possibly farther west through the force of arms in 1920. But they failed and never tried again to accomplish the same purpose by using the same means.

The subsequent Soviet commitment to the building of "socialism in one country" at the time of Europe's recovery during the 1920s suggested the recognition that expansionism does not pay. Nor did the advent of the Great Depression alter that recognition, for the crisis of capitalism coincided with the Soviet Union's own crisis caused by its forced industrialization and collectivization of agriculture. Inhibited from waging an assertive foreign policy, Moscow tried to do its best to accelerate capitalism's eargerly-awaited collapse by sponsoring the Comintern's often annoying but largely ineffective subversive activities abroad. Only the unexpected victory of fascism in Germany led Stalin to curb these activities in an effort to encourage the Western powers to take a firm stand against German aggressiveness and thus avert a rising threat to Soviet security.

Having effectively abandoned the pursuit of international revolution, Stalin gradually developed a concept of imperialism as a policy linked to Soviet security—his distinctive and most durable contribution to Soviet political culture. While trying to set an example for the Western powers by supporting the Spanish republic in its struggle against the nationalists and their fascist allies, he established a massive presence in Spain in 1936-1938. This involvement did not serve to promote communist revolution, for his agents treated the indigenous revolutionaries as harshly if not more so than their nationalist enemies. Nor is it certain that Stalin had originally aimed at creating a client state in that distant country. But that was what he in fact proceeded to do when the conditions seemed right, although he was forced to retreat and abandon the lost cause by 1939.

By then Hitler, abetted by the Western policies of appeasement, posed a direct threat to the Soviet Union by accelerating his eastward expansion after Munich. For his part Stalin had by this time consolidated his regime by bringing the Great Purge to an end. Thus even though he faced a greater external danger, he was in a better position to defuse it by coming to terms with his chief ideological adversary. This approach was not an inevitable step for him after years of preaching unconditional resistance to fascism. But the strengthening of Stalin's domestic base made the turnabout possible. Besides, Hitler provided not only the challenge but the inspiration. The success of both his aggressive foreign policy and his efficient domestic repression conveyed to Stalin the message that imperialism might pay after all, particularly if carried out by methods similar to his own.

Thus Soviet imperialism was born of the strange liaison between nazism and Stalinism. The Stalin-Hitler pact of August 1939 brought the Soviet Union substantive territorial gains for the first time. Its expansion in 1939-1940 occurred at a time of relative external weakness and internal strength that Stalin had ruthlessly achieved. In securing his regime against the rising Nazi power, he had the choice of either seeking cooperation with his neighbors—as he had done ten years before when he negotiated nonaggression treaties with them—or of resorting to coercion. Because he had strengthened internal security, he could afford to pursue the latter course and subjugate not only eastern Poland but the Baltic states and Bessarabia as well. He proved that defensive concerns need not preclude aggression nor make it any less reprehensible.

Stalin overestimated his strength when he attacked Finland in 1939; his inability to win easily compounded the embarrassment of this blatantly imperialistic war. When Soviet forces finally subdued the Finns, Stalin did not extinguish their indpendence as, it appears, he had originally intended. The outcome demonstrated another hallmark of Soviet imperialism that distinguished it from Hitler's variety —an ability to scale down original aims when faced with determined resistance. Keenly sensitive to cost, Stalin—unlike Hitler—despite all his abominations, was not an unmanageable conqueror provided there was enough will to wage such resistance.

Flexible rather than fixed, Stalin's aims were not strictly limited. In 1939 he exacted from Hitler an upward revision of their initial agreement on spheres of interest. He proceeded to test German willingness to acquiesce in the assertion of Soviet primacy in territories that had not been mentioned in the agreement nor were part of the historic Russian area of influence—Bukovina, the Baltic Straits, even Sweden. Rebuffed in November 1940, Stalin had to settle for those that happened to have belonged to Russia under the tsar. This reconquest did not make his imperialism any less reprehensible; only more akin to the tsarist one. The notion that the weak were less entitled to security than the strong was their common denominator.

But the Soviet concept of imperialism as a safeguard of security soon proved not only immoral but ineffective, even counterproductive. The magnitude of the original German concessions led Stalin to underestimate Hitler's aggressive intentions. The arrogant but ineffective Soviet insistence on further concessions whetted the aggressive appetite of the Nazi leader and clinched his decision to attack the Soviet Union. Nor did the recently acquired territories, inhabited by sullen or hostile populations, help Moscow blunt the force of the German attack when it was finally launched. Inasmuch as Stalin's quest for security through imperial expansion failed so pathetically, why was the idea not consigned to the proverbial rubbish heap of history?

The simple answer is that Stalin neither wanted nor had to admit that he had erred. At the critical time, Great Britain and the United States extended to the Soviet Union their unconditional assistance. The bulk of the Russian people rallied behind Stalin even though their margin of support was razor thin. If expansion was not topical while the Soviet Union was fighting for its survival, it became only too topical once the fortunes of the war turned in its favor. By attacking and failing to conquer the Soviet Union, Hitler ensured the continuity and the growth of Soviet imperialism.

While insisting on regaining the territorial gains that he had made during his association with Hitler, Stalin let the course of the war determine the aims that were worth striving for. Until 1944 the Red Army's advance beyond what he considered Soviet territory was neither inevitable nor an unmixed blessing from his point of view. Germany's collapse, not the Allies' invasion, could have ended the war before he faced the necessity of pursuing the enemy abroad. The exposure of Soviet troops to more advanced and hostile foreign lands was replete with risks certain to complicate Stalin's domestic and foreign policies. In planning to project his power abroad, he therefore relied more on diplomacy than on the direct use of military force. However, once compelled by the course of events to carry the war beyond the home territory,

Stalin had to come to grips with the consequences of conquest.

Although Stalin must have considered the amenities flowing from additional territorial acquisitions, he wisely ruled out any extensive ones. As a result of the war, he eventually incorporated largely depopulated East Prussia and the Kurile Islands as well as the Carpathian Ukraine, about which its Czech owners shed few tears. The wartime upsurge of nationalism among the Soviet Union's diverse ethnic groups gave Stalin sound reasons to abstain from conquering further potentially-restive nationalities. Instead, he directed the thrust of Soviet imperialism toward the subordination of nominally independent states.

When the defeat of the Axis was within reach, Stalin insisted on an eastern European "glacis" as a supposedly legitimate safeguard of Soviet security. The acceptance of this notion placed Soviet security from a hypothetical attack above other countries' security from the far from hypothetical Soviet interference. Stalin did not necessarily decide in advance what form eastern Europe's dependence should take. He acted as if he preferred to obtain deference to his wishes by directing Communist parties responsive to Moscow to exercise in their countries the critical margin of influence rather than actual power. However, because Stalin was aware of the meager communist following and anti-Russian sentiment in most of the prospective glacis, he wanted any order that he would eventually impose to be underwritten by his powerful Western partners. For this main reason, Soviet imperialism evolved from a merely regional into a global issue.

Despite their commitment to the principle of self-determination, the British and the Americans did not initially challenge Stalin's alleged right to effect his security as he saw fit. This was not because they were prepared to underwrite it at the expense of the east Europeans but because they were unwilling to consider a serious conflict of interest. In this best of all cases, amid the profusion of goodwill that would follow the war's end, Stalin would not interfere to ensure the installation of pro-Soviet governments, whereupon grateful east Europeans would freely elect them in accordance with his wishes. But his reluctance to clarify the limits of his security requirements and the means toward their attainment presaged trouble, whereas the Western failure to insist on the clarification compounded it. As George Kennan grasped in early 1945, "We have refused to name any limit for Russian expansion and Russian responsibilities, thereby confusing the Russians and causing them constantly to wonder whether they are asking too little or whether it was some kind of trap."[2]

In his well-known discourse with Djilas, Stalin observed that "this war is not as in the past; whoever occupies a territory also imposes his own system as far as his army can reach."[3] But although this was a telling prediction of what eventually happened, it obscured the reasons why it happened. The Soviet Union had choices and exercised them; it decided when, where, and how it could try to apply its power. In so doing, it consulted its interests but also considered the actual and the probable reactions of others. None was more crucial than that of the United States. As the world's most powerful nation, its actions and inactions inevitably influenced the calculations that shaped the course of Soviet imperialism.

Stalin overestimated the American willingness to sanction the kind of control he deemed indispensable in eastern Europe to satisfy his inflated notions of security. He also underestimated the difficulty of attaining that control without resorting to policies certain to alarm the West about his intentions. For its part, the United States underestimated Stalin's desire for Western endorsement of his east European aspirations and overestimated his reluctance to apply the repulsive policies that alone could ensure their fulfillment. At the Yalta conference in February 1945, the two sides reached a sham agreement, having papered over their differences for the sake of the alliance. Not a partition of Europe, as the popular myth suggests, but mutual deception and self-deception were the legacies of Yalta.

When the sham was exposed, Soviet-American relations soon began to deteriorate not in a straightforward manner but in the untidy way of action and reaction. In the last weeks of the war, Stalin made matters worse by overreacting. Reversing his previous policy of restrained advance, he ordered his armies to seize for political purposes as much of the remaining enemy territory as they could. When the West failed to respond in kind, he was able to overrun much of central Europe, including Berlin, and more of the Far East thanks to his last-minute declaration of war on Japan.

But it was not so much this outright deployment of military power on legitimate battlefields as its growing indirect use for intimidation that made Soviet imperialism a threat to international order. After the end of the war, Moscow rattled sabers in trying to wrest territorial concessions from Turkey and Iran—behavior that even Soviet critics, including Khrushchev, retrospectively judged as gratuitously provocative.[4] Even if Stalin did not pursue any master plan of conquest, it was bad enough that he acted so recklessly in testing how far he could go in extending the geographical limits of his tyranny.

Opportunities without excessive risks continued to present themselves as long as the United States, uncertain about Soviet intentions, vacillated between resistance and conciliation. Indeed, at least from Moscow's point of view, the future of the whole Western world remained uncertain during those chaotic early postwar years. But so did Stalin's prospects of consolidating his new empire while having to face the formidable task of his own country's reconstruction —enough uncertainties to restrain his adventurism. For all these reasons, the cold war continued to evolve in fits and starts rather than relentlessly, making occasional accommodation possible.

The pattern changed in 1947 when the United States' adoption of containment precipitated, even if it did not cause, a confrontation. The new policy responded to an almost certainly erroneous perception of an imminent Soviet military threat to Greece and Turkey, thus making the ensuing military assistance given to the two countries ill-suited to meet the actual thrust of Soviet imperialism. Nor was the Truman Doctrine, with its assumption of Moscow's global design for aggression, based on an accurate assessment of the essentially opportunistic character of that imperialism. Rebuffed in his efforts to exploit his military might in order to expand farther in the Near East, Stalin hedged his bets on political and economic collapse in western Europe, which he proceeded to encourage to the best of his limited ability by providing assistance to his local communist followers.

The Soviet Union therefore did not show much alarm when the United States extended military aid to Greece and Turkey, where no vital Soviet interests could be sustained. Instead, Stalin acted as if he believed that neither the modest American engagement in the two Mediterranean countries nor the rhetoric of the Truman Doctrine but the subsequent Marshall Plan, with its profound economic and political implications for the recovery of Europe, was the true watershed necessitating a reassessment of his own posture. In a deeper sense, however, American aid, no matter how timely, merely mobilized rather than created western Europe's strength. Stalin's policies had been predicated on his underestimation of that strength; this error of judgment led to his reassessment.

In November 1947 Walter Lippmann posited that "the

Russians have lost the Cold War and they know it."[5] But Stalin evidently did not think so, for he began to prepare himself for a confrontation. He knew that he had a choice, which can be inferred from his hesitation before deciding to oppose the Marshall Plan and proceed with the effective separation of his part of Europe following the creation of the Cominform in September 1947. His answer to the anticipated resurgence of western Europe was the final subjugation of eastern Europe, which, however, did not enhance but instead impaired Soviet security in the long run. Ironically, if the American policy of containment was right but for the wrong reasons, Stalin's response to it was wrong but for the right reasons: He had indeed lost in the competition between systems and ideas but refused to admit it.

Stalin might have chosen the path of accommodation, as he proved capable of doing at other times, had he been compelled to do so by a deteriorating internal situation. But the internal situation was improving, thus nourishing his hope that he could prevail in an international confrontation. Nineteen forty-seven marked the peak of his prestige as the leader of international communism. The reconstruction of the Soviet Union, facilitated by the tribute it exacted from its new dependencies, was progressing rapidly. And their consolidation was making strides in the wake of the crushing of the last remnants of domestic opposition.

But Stalin pressed his advantage too hard and too fast. In 1948 he backed the communist seizure of power in Czechoslovakia, until then his most submissive noncommunist client. He attempted to topple Tito—a loyal disciple who merely wanted to be treated as a partner rather than a puppet. The attempt coincided with the Soviet imposition of the Berlin blockade, which had been calculated to exploit local strategic advantage in humiliating the United States. But the Czechoslovak coup prompted West Europeans to rally more closely behind American leadership, and the Yugoslav and the Berlin ventures proved no less counterproductive. Tito's defiance threatened to undo the consolidation that Stalin had achieved elsewhere in eastern Europe, and the successful Western resistance in Berlin humiliated him, not the Americans. Unlike the events of 1947, the convergence of internal and external setbacks in 1949 produced a temporary Soviet retreat, particularly the lifting of the blockade.

But Stalin's willingness to risk a military clash in Berlin had done damage by raising the level of confrontation. The creation of NATO during the crisis reflected the American estimate that the Soviet Union had become a military menace, not only a political and an ideological adversary. Even if the Soviet Union did not contemplate starting a war at that time—and there is no evidence that it did—the American estimate was fair. Having exploded its first atomic bomb in 1949, Moscow proved ready to take risks in exploiting its military assets for political gain provided the conditions were right. And Stalin evidently thought they were right when he permitted the aggression in Korea in 1950. He might not have taken the risk had internal difficulties not been checked. But they diminished after he cut his losses in Berlin and managed to contain the Tito heresy by tightening his grip over his remaining possessions.

If before 1950 the Soviet Union had given no conclusive sign of anticipating war with the United States, the Korean miscalculation changed the signal. Not only did the United States send troops to Korea, but it decided to rearm West Germany to help meet an expected Soviet attack in Europe as well. And indeed, according to latest evidence from communist archives, Stalin in January 1951 secretly summoned his East European lieutenants to tell them to prepare for such an attack.[6] Even if he did not mean what he said—and no operational directives are known to have followed—he must have considered a *Western* assault on his empire probable enough to order such a high state of alert.

Stalin could afford to generate high international tension because his domestic front held firm. By sheer terror he intimidated opposition before it could coalesce while exacting from his subjects sacrifices that enabled eastern Europe to achieve the highest rate of economic growth in its history. Whatever the price, the Soviet empire was more stable than ever at the time its relations with the United States reached the nadir. As long as stability lasted, Stalin felt little compulsion to conciliate his external adversaries, thus making improbable any abatement of the cold war. Conversely, as soon as his death cast doubt on the future of the system of coercion that he had established, the prospects brightened for Moscow's more conciliatory attitude abroad.

So pervasive had been the state of tension in Soviet-American relations under Stalin that it blurred his few but significant shifts between assertion and accommodation. After his death, the pattern became more pronounced, as periods of "thaw" alternated in discernible ways with periods of "frost." Changes became more frequent and, with the growing complexity of the international environment, more susceptible to forces beyond the leaders' control.

The first era of accommodation began in 1955 and relapsed into confrontation after the onset of the second Berlin crisis in 1958. Another tentative thaw ensued the next year, followed by renewed tension reinforced by the erection of the Berlin wall and culminating in the 1962 Cuban missile crisis. Afterwards the third and longest period of detente began. It gained momentum after 1969 and made seeming but deceptive progress by 1975.[7] Since then, the pattern has been one of almost continuous deterioration, leading, by the early 1980s, to the greatest uncertainty about the future of East-West relations since the advent of the cold war.

In 1953 Stalin's departure from the scene coincided with the arrival in Washington of a new Republican adminis-

tration whose campaign promises, made at the time Stalin
was at the helm, included repudiation of containment as both
immoral and ineffective. The United States vowed to embark
on the more principled and activist policy of "rolling back"
the Soviet empire and liberating its subject peoples in the
process. Even though the prospect of implementation was
questionable, there could be no doubt that the American
policy hardened at the time when Stalin's death created the
conditions for the opposite change on the Soviet side. It
cannot be proved that the new mood in Washington made the
Moscow leaders more accommodating. But it certainly did
not prevent them from beginning to move in that direction.

Unlike the change in policy signified by the Truman
Doctrine in 1947, the change in American policy in 1953
coincided with an evolving internal crisis in the Soviet bloc.
Aside from their internecine struggle for power, Stalin's successors had to face almost immediately unprecedented challenges to their inherited order, including open revolts in
Pilsen, East Berlin, and even in one of the Gulag labor camps
in the Soviet Union. Although these uprisings were suppressed easily by applying Stalin's methods, the handwriting
was on the wall. For all these reasons, Moscow had an interest in winding down the cold war, as it demonstrated especially by concluding a compromise armistice in Korea.

The interest did not rule out contradictory impulses as
long as the unresolved leadership struggle hampered the development of consistent policies. Thus, in contrast to Stalin's
disparagement of the atomic bomb, Moscow signaled its desire to avoid war when Premier Malenkov stated publicly that
nuclear war would be an unmitigated disaster for capitalism
and socialism alike. Yet other Soviet spokesmen subsequently
affirmed commitment to the concept of preventive war,
which was presumably justified by the threat implicit in the
American doctrine of liberation,[8] although in different ways,
both postures showed a sense of vulnerability that further

increased once Khrushchev, having prevailed in the struggle for power, attempted internal de-Stalinization.

It was less the certainty of Khrushchev's new leadership status than the uncertainty raised by his impending reform program that bred in 1955 Moscow's desire for disengagement. Such Soviet concessions as the neutralization of Austria, reconciliation with Yugoslavia, and the establishment of diplomatic relations with West Germany warmed the international atmosphere. This transformed, not ended, the Soviet-American rivalry, for Khrushchev evidently figured that he could better prevail by selective accommodation and assertion, including especially aggressive penetration into the third world. As practiced by him, "peaceful coexistence" did not preclude and sometimes accentuated the Soviet use of military instruments for political ends—starting with the 1955 Egyptian arms deal. Nevertheless, the geographical extension of conflict amounted to its dilution, as Khrushchev's cold war of movement replaced Stalin's cold war of positions.

The 1956 upheaval in Eastern Europe, which produced the Polish and the Hungarian crises, ended the thaw. The outcome could have been different if the internal challenge that Moscow faced had been matched by a consistent and determined American policy. However, at a time when the Soviet Union proved ready to acquiesce in a substantive diminution of its imperial power in its critical sphere of influence, particularly by tolerating the advent of a nationalist communist government in Poland, the United States was unprepared to take advantage of the development. Yet the course of events in Eastern Europe vindicated the premises on which the professed policy of rollback and liberation was based. Inasmuch as the Russians agonized before sending troops into Hungary, the opportunity to test whether they would accept its neutralization under conditions similar to those that they found acceptable for Austria the year before was missed.

It is uncertain whether even a timely international

recognition of Hungary's neutrality would have averted the Soviet intervention and possibly restored the momentum of disengagement. What is certain is that Khrushchev found resort to force less risky and more justifiable because of Western inaction compounded by the contemporaneous Anglo-French expedition against Suez that ended in defeat. As a result, at the time the West's main colonial powers were learning painfully that imperialism does not pay, Moscow learned the opposite lesson.

Subsequent developments added reasons for Khrushchev's satisfaction. Not only did he restore order in Eastern Europe, but he broke up a conspiracy directed against him in 1957. He was able to take credit for his country's impressive technological progress, which was demonstrated the next year by the launching of the first Sputnik. In October 1958 the Soviet leader confided to the Yugoslav ambassador that he "did not count on a worsening of East-West relations and certainly did not believe there was danger of a serious conflict breaking out."[9] Only one month after he offered his benign assessment, he provoked gratuitously the second Berlin crisis and thus initiated another round of confrontation with the United States.

As Stalin had done in the same city, Khrushchev overreached himself. Western resistance denied him the diplomatic victory he sought. Whether because of this sobering experience or because of new internal problems that included incipient conflict with China—most likely because of the combination of both factors—Khrushchev soon allowed a second period of detente to evolve in 1959-1960. But this relaxation of tensions never amounted to much, nor did it last very long. It succumbed to his irresistible temptation to exploit the Soviet capture of the U-2 spy plane in order to embarrass the United States.

The Soviet Union maintained pressure in Berlin despite its growing sense that it was counterproductive, an assessment reinforced by the defection of so many East Germans to the West that the viability of the Soviet-imposed regime was put in question. Overwhelmed by the forces he had set in motion, Khrushchev had little choice but to prop up the shaky regime by erecting the Berlin wall. Unable to force the Americans to retreat, as he had originally intended, he at least hoped to consolidate East Germany. Subsequent developments proved him right. But in the short run, the building of the wall created the worst war scare since Korea, thus casting doubt on his previous assumption that a serious East-West conflict was unlikely.

If Khrushchev, despite his setbacks, chose to manage the crisis rather than conciliate his adversaries, his decision was facilitated by the impression of weakness conveyed by the American policy, particularly at the time of the Bay of Pigs fiasco. The new Kennedy administration did little to discourage the Soviet leader from seeking a way out of his internal difficulties by undertaking a foreign adventure—the introduction of offensive missiles in Cuba in 1962. Only when the threat became imminent did the United States take a firm stand by impressing on Moscow its readiness to go to war unless the missiles were withdrawn. Brinkmanship worked, although barely so—an example of crisis management in which good luck mattered as much if not more than good policy.

The threatened disaster proved that under Khrushchev the Soviet challenge had not diminished; it had merely grown more diversified and therefore more difficult to meet. Having overestimated and then underestimated it, the United States failed to adapt to the change, enabling Khrushchev to score points initially by using greater flexibility. Later on, when his internal problems worsened because of his own faults rather than the merits of the American policies, the Unites States failed to deter him from taking risks greater than Stalin had dared to take. Khrushchev proved that a less autocratic

Soviet leader need not necessarily be more peaceful, especially if he felt compelled to demonstrate his prowess to his rivals in the Kremlin. Only after the Cuban rebuff intensified his internal problems—the faltering economy, dissension in Eastern Europe, the open break with China—did Khrushchev develop a readiness for accommodation, thus ushering in a third period of detente. After discouraging experiences in the Congo, he scaled down Soviet involvement in the third world. Starting with the 1963 Nuclear Test Ban Treaty, he expanded areas of cooperation with the United States. Under these circumstances, the new American policy of "bridge building" was well-conceived to encourage the internal momentum that kept alive Moscow's interest in detente. But Khrushchev, apparently contemplating rapprochement with West Germany, seemed poised to proceed faster than some of his colleagues thought prudent. When they overthrew him in 1964, they cast doubt on the continuity of his policies.

Khrushchev's successors did not repudiate detente, but after a brief period of uncertainty, they began to prepare for a more assertive policy. They started a massive military build-up that prompted the deposed leader to observe ruefully "that the economizing trend we started seems to have been reversed" and express privately his misgivings about the "new trend of military overspending."[10] Resuming efforts to isolate West Germany and split the Western alliance, the Soviet Union launched a campaign for a European security conference from which the United States would be excluded. In a renewed bid for influence in the third world, the new leaders proceeded more deliberately than Khrushchev. They extended aid for specific purposes rather than for the sake of prestige. One project involved equipping the Arabs to enable them to wage the 1967 war against Israel, in the wake of which Soviet influence in the Middle East reached its peak.

If, despite this new assertiveness, there occurred no relapse into the cold war, the probable reason was the worsening internal strains that beset both power blocs simultaneously—their "competitive decadence," as Pierre Hassner put it.[11] The Soviet leaders were constrained by the array of domestic and imperial problems that they had inherited from Khrushchev and failed to solve. But the West was no less inhibited because of its unfolding political, economic, and moral crises. The United States tried to act from a position of strength, as its growing involvement in Vietnam was meant to demonstrate, but the underpinnings of its power were giving way. In 1968 the crisis climaxed for the West in the riots in Paris; for the East it culminated in the upheaval in Czechoslovakia.

The decisive Soviet turn toward accommodation occurred the following year. It can be dated from the March 1969 Budapest declaration of the Warsaw Pact countries, which dropped for the first time any precondition for convening the European security conference. The Russians not only professed their interest in better relations, but they acted accordingly. Before the end of the year, they responded favorably to initiatives made by the new West German government of Willy Brandt, and the normalization of relations with Bonn, which had eluded Khrushchev, eventually unfolded. East-West trade surged, and Soviet-American rapprochement proceeded apace.

Had the Soviet Union become more accommodating because it felt more secure after having suppressed by force the heresy in Czechoslovakia? Shortly after the intervention, in the fall of 1968, Brezhnev proclaimed his doctrine, reiterating the integrity of the "Socialist Commonwealth" and Moscow's ostensible right to uphold it by any means, including military force. But at the time of the proclamation, integrity was more a postulate than a reality. Nor had the coveted "normalization" in Czechoslovakia occurred when the Soviet Union embarked on the new course charted by the Budapest declaration. What had occurred a few weeks before was the precipitous deterioration of the conflict with China resulting from the Ussuri River clashes that threatened for the first time to escalate into a war. The Soviet interest in detente stemmed from the need to obtain greater security, not its attainment.

Given the unsettled condition of the Soviet empire, the decision to expand its relations with the West entailed a calculated risk. In allowing for greater interaction, the Soviet leaders had to take into account a variety of trends—some favorable but others unfavorable to them. It was a tribute to their growing sophistication that they chose to expand relations rather than simplify them by withdrawing into isolation as Stalin had done. The assumption was that enough chance existed for the Soviet Union to come out ahead of the West in the "competitive decadence" and that the chance was growing. The course of events soon seemed to vindicate the calculation.

Although Eastern Europe erupted again in 1970, when workers' riots flared in Poland, order was restored without Soviet intervention. In proceeding with the consolidation of its empire, Moscow could draw comfort from President Nixon's public certification that the United States would not "seek to exploit Eastern Europe to obtain strategic advantage against the Soviet Union," for the American "pursuit of negotiation and detente is meant to reduce existing tensions, not to stir up new ones."[12] By the early 1970s Moscow's European domain could be rightly described as the world's "forgotten region"—the optimal condition for its rulers.[13] The Eastern Europeans had achieved a measure of economic prosperity that contributed to the stability of the region.

In the worldwide competition with the United States, the Soviet Union lost its enormous investment in Egypt following the expulsion of its advisers in 1971. But the loss was not immediately translated into an American gain. On the contrary, the 1973 Middle East war, which the Soviet investment had made possible, triggered the oil embargo and aggravated the world's energy crisis in a manner that hurt the West much more than the East. The crisis coincided with the time when the United States was sinking ever deeper into the Vietnam quagmire, a decline compounded by the Watergate scandal. The worst thing that happened to Moscow was the Sino-American rapprochement. But even that potential Soviet calamity was used by the embattled Nixon administration to promote detente with the Soviet Union and conclude in 1972 the Moscow agreement on the principles of mutual relations, which responded to the Soviet desire to be treated as America's equal. By then the massive Soviet armament program had paid off by convincing the United States that approximate strategic parity between the two superpowers had been achieved.

During the Moscow negotiations, the Soviet leaders demanded recognition of their right to "equal security." Although their insecurity was based much more on internal rather than external factors and therefore transcended the scope of official Soviet-American relations, the Nixon-Brezhnev declaration affirmed the dubious right as at least a mutually-desirable postulate if not a full-fledged reality.[14] The elastic formulas of the document conveyed the erroneous impression that the advent of military parity satisfied Moscow's craving for security and thus would lead to the appreciable reduction of its challenge to the United States. But Soviet spokesmen never left any doubt that their version of detente did not preclude but in fact necessitated intensified political and ideological struggle. In 1973 their ambivalent conduct during the new Middle East war led to near confrontation. But the crisis passed, and detente resumed. It led two years later to the Helsinki agreement on European security that marked the successful achievement of a longstanding Soviet goal.

Rarely before Helsinki had the Soviet Union had better reasons to feel secure, both externally and internally, than at this moment of its diplomatic triumph made possible by the growth of its military might and enhanced by the quiescence of its empire. Yet, faithful to the imperialistic pattern, this desirable state of affairs fostered not restraint but greater assertiveness abroad. During the second half of the 1970s, Moscow chose to employ its surrogate Cuban troops in order to project its power into parts of Africa where no vital Soviet interest was at stake, thus inaugurating a new phase in the evolution of Soviet imperialism. Soviet arms began to flow into the arsenals of some of the third world's most detestable and irresponsible regimes, such as those of Qaddafi's Libya and Amin's Uganda. By training and in other ways supporting Arab extremists, Moscow abetted, even if it did not necessarily mastermind, the upsurge of international terrorism that erupted at that time. As a result, tension with the United States mounted despite the professed Soviet desire to pursue detente.

Although President Ford vowed to discard the word *detente* in 1976,[15] there was little change in the American behavior that might have made the Soviets doubt the value of their understanding of detente. Regardless of the growing uneasiness about Soviet conduct and its underlying motives, the aftereffects of Vietnam and Watergate inhibited American action. Against its better judgment, the administration acquiesced in Moscow's *fait accompli* in Angola. It proceeded to enhance both American and Soviet security by concluding the Vladivostok agreements and SALT I. But these undertakings failed to induce Soviet moderation—as the events first in Ethiopia and eventually in Afghanistan persuasively showed.

Soviet assertiveness abetted by American forebearance did not alone undermine the fragile edifice of detente. More important—and not directly related to American policies—

was what happened to undermine the other assumptions on which Moscow based its calculated risk. High among them was long-term stabilization in Eastern Europe as a result of the acceptance at Helsinki of the order that the Soviet Union imposed in the area since World War II. To safeguard that order once and for all, the endorsement by Moscow of the apparent platitudes of "Basket Three," with its improbable phrases about respect for human rights, seemed a negligible price to pay for helping the West save face.

The institutionalization of detente at Helsinki further promised the Soviet Union easier access to much-needed Western technology without paying a political price. Indeed, if the West's problems got worse while the East's got better, that price might instead be exacted from the West Europeans by making them more dependent on Soviet-controlled supplies of energy and raw materials and thus loosening their ties to the United States. Never before had Moscow allowed its economy to become so enmeshed with the capitalist one. But never before had it seemed in a better position to control the terms of the relationship.

If the Soviet concept of detente meant that East-West relations could be made to follow a relatively stable course that could be turned gradually but irreversibly to Moscow's advantage, it might well provide the means of gaining the upper hand in the competition of systems and ideas. The Soviet leaders might long ago have lost a genuine commitment to Marxist doctrine, but they have certainly not lost their desire to extend their power by impressing on others the superiority of the system from which they derive their power. At issue is their ability to continue to project the image of the Soviet Union as the force of the future to which other nations had better accommodate.

The deterioration of Soviet-American relations since 1975 has been a symptom rather than the cause of the evanescence of detente, which reflects the erosion of internal conditions on which the Soviet leaders based their assumptions about detente and their commitment to its maintenance. To begin with, the coveted consolidation of Eastern Europe did not take place. The ink had hardly dried on the Helsinki Final Act when the seemingly innocuous provisions of "Basket Three" assumed political substance by giving impetus to dissent in Eastern Europe and in the Soviet Union itself. Repression subsequently decimated opposition in some parts of Moscow's empire but not in others. In 1976 riots again broke out in Poland. Four years later, when dissent voiced by individual intellectuals merged for the first time with the mass discontent of Polish workers, this cornerstone of the empire was shaken to its foundations.

The infusion of Western technology facilitated by detente did not reverse the declining rates of growth and falling productivity in the Soviet Union and most of its dependencies. Instead, the closer relationship with the stronger capitalist economies made the weaker ones more vulnerable to disturbances of the world market. Inflation increased and the standard of living began to decline. The Soviet leaders derived little comfort from the knowledge that the West had to cope with many of the same problems, for its performance demonstrated its better capacity to do so. As the Polish example most vividly showed, the political fabric of the communist system could not withstand the strain. The massive influx of foreign funds into Poland not only failed to forestall the crisis but actually precipitated it by exposing the regime's singular incompetence in putting the borrowed money to productive use. For the first time anywhere in the Soviet bloc, economic change forced political change—an ominous development for its Marxist chiefs.

The attractiveness of the values exemplified by the Soviet system has declined throughout the world. Hardly anywhere is the system still regarded as a desirable model—a dramatic change compared with the worldwide prestige it enjoyed in the days of Stalin. The "Helsinki process" initiated by Moscow turned against it in Europe; ideologically and politically on the defensive, the Soviet Union seems unable to make lasting gains anywhere on the Continent. It tried hard but unsuccessfully in Portugal. Meanwhile, within its own empire, the Polish developments challenged the foundations on which the whole system of Soviet control traditionally rested. The effective end of the Communist party's monopoly of power in Poland testified instead to the abiding strength of the Western values of pluralism.

As the prospects waned for achieving by detente the favorable "correlation of forces" that Moscow envisaged,[16] so did any incentive to reduce its reliance on its military might that had enkindled the desire. Even without a decision to keep arming beyond the level of approximate parity, the mere absence of a decision to the contrary sufficed to produce the same effect, causing growth to continue by its own momentum and further undermining the stability it was meant to foster. Unwarranted by any reasonable security need, the result has been a runaway military machine in search of a purpose—the last reliable vehicle for achieving the "external expansion of an internally decaying regime."[17]

Has the American policy come to grips with this momentous transformation of Soviet imperialism? By making human rights its preeminent concern, the Carter administration rightly addressed at least one major internal determinant of Soviet security. But the concern never coalesced into a consistent policy with clear operational objectives. It did not preclude, although it hampered, efforts at accommodation, which often conveyed to Moscow an impression of weakness. Unable to sort out its inconsistencies, the administration slowed down its human rights drive while increasing its military expenditures enough to make the Soviet leaders more insecure but not enough to make them more accommodating. In the end, the administration reaped the disadvantages

of both the "soft" and the "hard" line without deriving any
advantages—a unique consequence. The outcome was remi-
niscent of the similar vacillation that had failed to prevent
the cold war and not surprisingly raised the specter of its
revival. On neither occasion did American policies create the
conflict that emerged from the dynamism of the Soviet system, but they managed to aggravate it.

Ever since the Bolshevik revolution, the Soviet challenge
to the United States has been more political than military. It
was negligible as long as Soviet leaders were unable to match
their revolutionary fervor with adequate means to project
their power abroad. Even after Stalin made imperialism the
central concept of Soviet policy by linking it with security
and backing it with the force of arms, United States' military
superiority and Moscow's sensitivity to cost could contain
the challenge. Only under Stalin's successors has the Soviet
military threat grown to the extent that it may override political considerations if the perception—accurate or false—that
superiority is shifting to the other side is permitted to take
hold. This should give the United States the rationale for
sustained efforts to redress the tilting balance through its
own buildup. But restored military balance, although indispensable for stability, will not alone create a satisfactory relationship, for barring a war that both sides want to avoid,
Moscow's choice between assertion and accommodation will
be predicated on traditional determinants that consist of a
much wider range of factors.

In the past tough American policy did not always make
the Soviet leaders more accommodating; by adding to their
external insecurity, it sometimes produced the opposite effect. Neither did a greater sense of internal security make
them necessarily more conciliatory; it often led to greater
aggressiveness. But whenever an American policy of strength
coincided   with   mounting   internal   problems,   more

forthcoming Soviet positions invariably ensued. At the beginning of 1981, the inauguration of the reputedly-tough Reagan administration against the backdrop of the lingering Polish crisis again seemed to engender Moscow's greater willingness, despite previous disclaimers, to negotiate arms-control agreements irrespective of the fate of SALT II. It is unlikely that the established pattern of assertion and accommodation will change unless the Soviet system changes.

The implications for American policy are evident. It is not enough, although it is exceedingly important, to impress on the Soviet leaders the limits of Western tolerance to contain their external aggression. Beyond this goal, an effective American policy cannot avoid addressing the more fundamental problem of internal insecurity that breeds the impulse. At the very least, the policy cannot convey any vested American interest in the integrity of the system that maintains Moscow's empire. In a more positive sense, it needs to encourage such pressures for change that are compatible with the Western notion of a stable international order based not only on peace but on justice.

If it is accepted that a measure of Soviet insecurity is in America's interest, the resulting policies may occasion increased tension in the short run. Moreover, there is probably a limit beyond which a rising feeling of insecurity would generate a violent Soviet reaction leading to unpredictable consequences. But within that limit, such a feeling creates the necessary frame of mind conducive to seeking accommodation on a higher level of stability in the long run.

NOTES

1. *New York Times,* January 1, 1980, p. 1.
2. Kennan to Bohlen, cited in Charles E. Bohlen, *Witness to History* (New York, 1973), p. 175.
3. Milovan Djilas, *Conversations with Stalin* (New York, 1962), p. 114.

4. *Khrushchev Remembers: The Last Testament* (Boston, 1974), pp. 295-296.

5. Quoted in Ronald Steel, *Walter Lippmann and the American Century* (Boston, 1980), p. 447.

6. Karel Kaplan, *Dans les archives du comité central: Trente ans de secrets du bloc soviétique* (Paris, 1978), pp. 164-166.

7. See Malcolm Mackintosh, "Three Detentes: 1955-1964," in Eleanor L. Dulles and Robert D. Crane (eds.), *Detente: Cold War Strategies in Transition* (New York, 1965), pp. 103-120.

8. William Zimmerman, *Soviet Perspectives on International Relations, 1956-1967* (Princeton, 1969), pp. 173-174.

9. Entry for October 11, 1958, Veljko Micunovic, *Moscow Diary* (Garden City, 1980), p. 431.

10. *Khrushchev Remembers* (Boston, 1971), p. 520.

11. Pierre Hassner, "Cold War to Hot Peace," *New York Times,* October 16, 1973.

12. Quoted in Charles Gati (ed.), *The International Politics of Eastern Europe* (New York, 1976), p. 13.

13. *Idem,* "The Forgotten Region," *Foreign Policy* 19 (1975): 135-145.

14. *Facts on File,* 1972, p. 396.

15. *New York Times,* March 2, 1976, p. 12.

16. As expressed by Leonid Brezhnev at the 25th party congress in February 1976, Leon Goure, *War Survival in Soviet Strategy* (Coral Gables: Center for Advanced International Studies, University of Miami, 1976), p. 3.

17. In Richard Lowenthal's felicitous phrase.

III.

Toward an
Open-Society Bloc

GEORGE SCHWAB

After Detente

The Soviet occupation of Afghanistan, unabated Soviet adventurism elsewhere in the Middle East, in Africa, and in other regions of the world, the expansion and the modernization of Soviet warmaking potential, the United States hostage crisis in Iran, among other problems, and the apparent inability of the United States to respond effectively to such challenges have forced an ever-larger segment of the American foreign-policy public to ask whether there is something fundamentally wrong with the foreign policy of the United States. If, for example, the Soviet Union is at liberty to redraw lines of demarcation and if, for example, a country such as Iran is able to thwart United States foreign policy, the question to ask is: What course is America to take after detente?

Leaving aside reasons why the United States finds itself in this predicament, it may be well to recollect the so-called policy of detente that several administrations pursued for more than a decade. Notwithstanding the late Hans Morgenthau's occasional ambiguities in analyzing detente, he pinpointed how the Soviet Union reinforced the muddled thinking of a good segment of the foreign-policy public about detente, a segment that confused the "substance of policy" with the "end result of policy."[1] Detente, according to Morgenthau, "does not deal with foreign policy as such. It deals with the possible, and you may say desirable, results of such a policy."[2] Reinforcing the confusion between the substance and the end result of policy, Morgenthau argued, has "become one of the secret, or perhaps not so secret, weapons with which the Soviet Union has opposed our interests as well as the interests of the world, and of the policies best suited to support these interests."[3]

Having come to the conclusion that militant Marxist-Leninist ideology is bankrupt and therefore nothing but rhetoric, a good segment of the American foreign-policy public came to understand the Soviet Union as a state of the traditional type whose foreign-policy aims are limited in scope. Given this assessment and because of the new nuclear dimension in warfare, a considerable number of American foreign-policy specialists also concluded that global war had become highly unlikely. There was thus little from the perspective of American foreign policy that stood in the way of detente.

As is well known by now, the Soviet Union's utilization of detente as a tactical device was at odds with Washington's understanding of it. The perceptions of detente entertained by a majority of the American foreign-policy public have had far-reaching repercussions in the domain of defense. Their unrealistic judgment of the character of the Soviet state was translated into neglecting the United States security equation. By permitting its military arsenal to decline in relation to that of the Soviet Union, the United States played into Soviet hands.

Having correctly evaluated the impact that detente had on the United States, the Soviet Union, at a near zero risk of provoking a Soviet-American military confrontation, did not hesitate to invade Afghanistan, a country not far from the strategic oil jugular of the world. The successful Soviet attempt to draw a new line of demarcation in a largely gray area in Southwest Asia has revealed once again that power has its own logic. Emasculating the power component in diplomacy leads to the erosion of the leverage needed to pursue interests of state. It is in this context that one needs to be reminded that diplomacy without power is poetry or rhetoric, not politics.

Because detente has contributed to destabilizing the global arena of states, the free world stands at a watershed in history. Although we are not faced with the prospect of a Soviet military conquest, its rapidly expanding military capability is finally enabling the Soviet Union to project its power globally. Notwithstanding defense needs deriving from the existence of a hostile China, unreliable satellites in Eastern Europe, the existence of NATO (however vulnerable it may be, NATO is still considered worthy of notice by Moscow), and so on, by arming itself to such an extent, ostensibly to achieve legitimate strategic security, the Soviet Union can achieve absolute military superiority, which in turn can be translated into global military hegemony. Achieving such a superiority would tidily fit into the Marxist-Leninist framework within which the Kremlin operates. The neutralization and Finlandization of a good part of the globe (that may be compounded by self-neutralization and self-Finlandization as result of the realization that Soviet power is so overwhelming that it cannot be checked short of nuclear war) are, after all, preconditions for the realization of their quintessential ideological goal, especially when the only way of rescuing

Marxist-Leninist dogma may be with force or the threat of force.

Because there are indications that the United States is no longer in the position to challenge the Soviet Union alone and inasmuch as the Soviet challenge is common to the non-Soviet world in general and to the free world in particular, the only viable response is an endeavor shared by other countries.

Notwithstanding the advocates of neutralism, Finlandism, and pacifism in Western Europe and Japan, the United States should endeavor to make common cause with those countries in the free world that possess the resolve to remain free and are prepared to commit a reasonable amount of resources to that end. Working on this supposition, I began to stake out a concept some time ago,[4] one that I am now in the process of clarifying. Given the convergence of interests, on the one hand, and the lack of coordination and dynamism, on the other hand, the immediate overriding foreign-policy goal of the United States must be to forge an alliance of the open-society countries that would be anchored in a loosely knit but well-orchestrated open-society bloc.

The Open-Society Bloc

The first step in clarifying this concept must be to delimit the open-society bloc. Because countries of the free world have evolved unevenly from the perspective of their commitments to the principle of the sanctity of man and the rule of law and therefore to political and cultural pluralism and to religious toleration, the core countries of the open-society bloc cannot embrace all the countries of the free world.[5]

What about countries whose values are akin to those of the core countries but cannot enter the bloc because of their status as neutrals?[6] In view of their affinity to such countries, which stems from their fundamental commitment to positive freedoms, that is, responsible freedoms under the law, it is assumed that they will gravitate toward a well-orchestrated open-society bloc that is in the position to respond effectively to the Soviet challenge. Given their status, however, they would fall into a category of neutral but associated states. Despite the fact that their status would not permit them to enter into alliances, the countries in the core would nevertheless come to the aid of countries in this category if their integrity were challenged by the Soviet Union because of the bloc's *raison d'être* of defending the positive human values on which the open-society countries rest. At that point the status of neutral would vanish, and the formerly neutral states could be integrated into the bloc.

Because the *raison d'être* of such an open-society bloc is to defend positive human values and, in addition, serve as a model toward which nations may be inspired to gravitate, membership in the core category must be restricted. Countries that are strongly attracted to the values of the core countries but have not matured to the point of inclusion[7] should nevertheless be encouraged to join the category of associated states. As such they should also be encouraged to enter into mutually beneficial security arrangements through a revamped NATO or other forms of military alliance anchored in the bloc.

In addition to countries in the aforementioned two categories, which will form security zones at the edges of the open-society bloc, there are those that although far from embracing the values of the core countries, are closer in outlook to them than to totalitarian Russia and will, therefore, be more readily inclined to gravitate toward a powerful open-society bloc than toward the Soviet Union. Whether such marginal countries belonging to this part of the nonfree world outside the Soviet orbit[8] should be drawn into a security zone raises a fundamental question, namely, that of lines of demarcation.

Because such lines have usually contributed to stabilizing relations between and among states, as happened in the recent past in politically and militarily circumscribed Europe, for example, and because power-political vacuums contribute to destabilizing such relations, as, for instance, in parts of the nonstaked-out Middle East, there is a need to draw such lines on a grand scale. Inasmuch as East-West relations are global and in view of the fact that events occurring in particular parts of the world that relate to the overarching competition often have ramifications in other parts of the world, the lines that need to be drawn must also be global.

Such lines of demarcation should embrace countries in the marginal category, that is, those that gravitate toward the open-society bloc, not only because the bloc would be more effective in nurturing the positive human values on which the open-society countries rest and all that this may bring with it but also because of power politics. The more comprehensive the common front, the greater the chances of its success in checking Soviet adventurism. What cannot be overlooked in drawing such lines of demarcation is the possibility that in addition to this category of marginal countries, the security needs of the open-society bloc may necessitate the inclusion of countries that may not wish to be drawn in. For lack of a better term, countries belonging to such a category may be called submarginal. Whatever the lines, neither direct nor indirect intervention will be tolerated beyond the line.[9]

The Open-Society Bloc and the Soviet Union

Before the open-society countries can be expected to commit themselves to joining such a bloc, they must first be convinced that the United States is prepared to become a

full-fledged and equal partner in such a political configura-
tion, one on which they can truly rely despite the discrep-
ancy in military power. It can then be expected that the
population of Western Europe, including a segment of the
population that is now inclined toward pacifism, neutralism,
and appeasement in the face of overwhelming Soviet military
power, will face reality, that is, recognize the Soviet threat
rather than wish it away, and act accordingly. If the open-
society countries are serious about defending the values to
which they are committed, they will have to coordinate their
political and military policies toward the Soviet Union and
modernize and expand their military capabilities, especially
the conventional component in their respective security
equations.

Inasmuch as the aim of diplomacy is to resolve conflicts
peacefully, it is assumed that a well-orchestrated and militarily powerful open-society bloc will be in a better position
to deal with the Soviet Union. Confronting the Soviet Union
from a position of strength will, it is hoped, enable the open-
society bloc to contain Soviet activities to its sphere of
operations.

It is in such a context of containment that it makes
sense to involve the Soviet Union in a web of economic interdependence. But whereas during the so-called period of detente almost every open-society country hungry for profits
traded with the Soviet Union indiscriminately, the new economic policy, in addition to initiating cooperative ventures
with the Soviet Union and developing existing ones, which
would include the expansion of travel and scholarly and cultural exchanges, must be well coordinated and, most important, must be strategically selective, unlike the transfer to the
Soviet Union of much sought after technological and industrial know-how in the 1960s and especially in the 1970s that
has greatly contributed to enhancing Soviet military might.

A determined open-society bloc that has positioned

itself to hinder Soviet foreign-policy adventures can blunt the militant dynamism flowing from Marxism-Leninism. But because the *raison d'être* of the Soviet Union is messianic, it may continue on its course of undermining, dividing, and outflanking open-society countries. Depending on the severity of the Soviet thrust, a policy of merely containing the Soviet Union to its sphere of operation may then no longer suffice. To put it somewhat differently, should the Soviet Union attempt to break out of its sphere of operation with the intention of destabilizing the open-society bloc, the logic of politics will then dictate that the open-society bloc undertake appropriate countermeasures.

Although I am not prepared to formulate an overarching contingency plan, what obviously comes to mind is for the open-society bloc to embark on a course aimed at intensifying the instability of the Soviet sphere. The open-society bloc will have to find means by which to aid those forces in the Soviet sphere that are challenging the system and encourage the devolution of other centrifugal forces. However one looks at the world scene, one thing is certain: Should the open-society countries fail to act in their true interest, history is certain to find the appropriate epithet for a society that permitted itself to be dumped into the dustbin of history.

NOTES

1. "Detente: Reality and Illusion" in *Detente in Historical Perspective*, ed. George Schwab and Henry Friedlander (New York, 1975, 1981), p. 77.
2. *Ibid.*, pp. 77-78.
3. *Ibid.*, p. 79
4. See, for example, "American Foreign Politics at the Crossroads: Idealism versus Realism" in *Innen- und Aussenpolitik: Primat oder Interdependenz? (Festschrift zum 60. Geburtstag von Walther Hofer)* (Bern/Stuttgart, 1980), especially pp. 227-228, and "From Quantity and Heterogeneity to Quality and Homogeneity: Toward a New Foreign Policy" in *Newsletter* (published by the National

Committee on American Foreign Policy), vol. 3, nos. 4-5, August-
October 1980, p. 4.

    5. For example, countries that are to constitute this core include,
in the Western Hemisphere, the United States and Canada and, in
Europe, England, Holland, Belgium, France, Italy, the Federal Republic
of Germany, Denmark, and Norway. In the Middle East it would include Israel and, in the Far East, Japan. Australia and New Zealand too
would fit into the core.
    6. Included in this category are Switzerland, Austria, and Sweden.
    7. Countries that come to mind immediately include Portugal,
Spain, Greece, and Turkey. For a discussion of political maturation, see
Dankwart A. Rustow, "Transition to Democracy: Toward a Dynamic
Model" in *Comparative Politics,* April 1970, especially pp. 350-363.
    8. Argentina is an example.
    9. Although it is beyond the scope of this paper to treat the
question of whether the open-society bloc would tolerate communist
governments within their realm, a word must nevertheless be said about
it. Because Lenin's version of Marx and Stalin's version of Lenin have
matured into one of the worst forms of repressive rule and because the
fundamental aim of the open-society bloc is precisely the opposite,
namely, to foster human freedoms, such a bloc cannot tolerate any
totalitarian movement that gains political power.

IV.

Petroleum, Minerals, and Foreign Policy

DANKWART A. RUSTOW

The 1970s were a decade mostly of sequels and postscripts. The withdrawal of American troops from Vietnam ended a bloody, costly, and profoundly misconceived adventure: The falling dominoes turned out to have been not the governments of southeast Asia but the internal consensus, the external resolve, and the global prestige of the United States. In the superpower triangle, Peking's new friendship with Washington provided a mirror image of its old enmity toward Moscow. In the European Community, the admission of Britain, Ireland, and Denmark (and soon of Greece, Portugal, and Spain) completed a process of continental union begun in the early 1950s. And at the United Nations, the admission of 23 members, including Vietnam, East and West Germany, Djibouti, Angola, and Western Samoa, ratified the outcome of some protracted struggles or confirmed the process of decolonization launched in India in 1947 and in Palestine in 1948.

The novelty and the drama of the 1970s were provided by the new global role of petroleum. At the start of the decade, the world oil trade amounted to 19 billion dollars and at the end to about 350 billion dollars—its share rising from about 6 percent to about one-quarter of the total. The successive oil price explosions resulted in a redistribution of current income that has dwarfed the effects of the sacking of the Aztec and the Inca treasures, of the conquests of Warren Hastings and Cecil Rhodes, of the reparations exacted at Versailles, and of the donations dispensed by the Marshall Plan. The powerful individuals presiding over the oil price spiral made a miscellaneous assemblage—including *Señor* Juan Perez Alfonso, *Shaykh* Yamani, Colonel Qaddafi, the presidents of Exxon, Shell, and Mobil, Mrs. Thatcher, and the Ayatollah Khomeini. Where but in the surrealistic seventies would such a motley group have boldly put to the test Karl Marx's implausible notion (conceived no doubt in his years as a starving refugee) that economic forces control the destiny of men?

The experiment threatens to continue through several more sessions in the laboratory, and questions of petroleum and of economic relations between north and south are likely to stay on the diplomatic curriculum for the remainder of the century. Thus it becomes pertinent to ask: What weight should we attach to questions of economic resources in formulating the principles and setting the priorities that are to guide American foreign policy in the years before us?

The question of resources can be phrased broadly or narrowly. Broadly, the volume of trade in raw materials and manufactured products indicates the degree of economic interdependence; that is, it measures the extent of the division of labor among the regions and nations of the world. The ebb and flow of that trade are closely associated with the cycle of prosperity and depression in the economies of the world and with the health or the sickness of national monetary systems and the international exchanges among them. An individual nation that mostly processes domestic raw materials for home consumption will prove more immune to such crises of international trade and fluctuations of currency than an economy with a preponderant external trade sector. If that sector consists of exports of specialized manufactures—say, transistors and computer chips—the economy will be sensitive to minute variations in the world business cycle; if the foreign sector relies heavily on exporting a single crop or mineral—say, coffee, bauxite, or manganese—it will be even more vulnerable to erratic price swings in the particular commodity market.

A sharp and a long rise in the price of a commodity such as oil brings obvious gains to the exporters but places a diffuse strain on the importing economies—and this strain will tend to accentuate the strength of the healthier economies and the weakness of the ailing ones. No wonder that the diplomatic agenda since the 1970s has featured debates on a "new international economic order" at the United Nations; extensive north-south dialogues on "international economic cooperation" in Paris; emergency missions of the International Monetary Fund to Britain, Zaire, Peru, and Turkey; and economic summit meetings of leaders of industrial nations at Guadeloupe and Venice. At its broadest, the question of resources and foreign policy encompasses all the issues of global prosperity and economic integration.

Taken pointedly and narrowly, the question becomes one of the raw materials essential to the conduct of war. This was the question in 1913, when British admirals, having ordered their fleet to burn oil instead of coal, persuaded their colleagues at the treasury to buy a controlling share of the Anglo-Persian Oil Company; in 1935, when the League of Nations skirted the issue of oil in voting its sanctions against Italy; in 1941 and 1942, when Romania, the Caucasus, and Sumatra became key objectives for Nazi and Japanese generals; in the 1960s, when a fallacious argument from national security deprived the United States of a potential stream of growing oil imports; and in 1956, when Washington's refusal to share American oil helped persuade Britain and France to evacuate their forces from Suez.

It was, of course, the attempt to use oil as a "weapon" in the war of October 1973 that so dramatically placed the question of resources at the top of the agenda of the 1970s. But did the 1973 events pose the question in its narrow, military-strategic, or in its broader, economic-financial, sense?

Over the bare facts there is little dispute. American weapons were flown to the Israeli front at Sinai beginning October 14; an oil embargo against the United States was proclaimed by Arab producers mostly between October 19 and 21; there was strong American pressure on Israel to accept a cease-fire; and there was reluctant Israeli compliance on October 22 and 24.

To the hasty observer, this sequence makes undeniable the dramatic impact of the oil embargo, and much American public comment since 1973 has kept alive such a dramatic interpretation. To Henry Kissinger in February 1974, the new 7 dollar price of oil presaged a "vicious cycle of competition, autarchy, rivalry and depression such as led to the collapse of world order in the thirties." His worries were widely shared. "Farewell to Oil?" "Can the Arabs Really Blackmail Us?" asked anxious magazine headlines in 1973 and 1974. "Our Arab Masters"; "This Time the Wolf Is Here," others glumly insisted. And by 1980, with the price of oil at 35 dollars a barrel, Walter J. Levy gravely pondered the prospect of "Oil and the Decline of the West."[1]

The situation is indeed grave; yet the Spenglerian language is inappropriate. Widespread concern about the physical security of supplies—whether of oil or of other minerals—is largely misplaced; and the popular notion of an "Arab oil squeeze" on the United States, in 1973 or since, is simply erroneous. The 1973 embargo itself had no appreciable effect except to cause a "logistical headache" for the transport divisions of some of the major oil companies.[2] Petroleum is a fungible, interchangeable commodity—aside from minor quality differences that may temporarily strain refinery equipment; its method of transport is ideally flexible—tankers can be rerouted at any point in their voyages. This makes it virtually impossible for any exporter to pinpoint its embargo against any specific importer. For example, in 1973, U.S. oil imports amounted to less than half the total non-Arab exports so that all of America's needs could readily be supplied from non-Arab sources. Even if, as in 1973, an embargo is accompanied by production cuts, the normal tendency of the market is to equalize the shortage all around, with some built-in bias perhaps toward larger customers. In 1973-1974 the United States suffered less of a curtailment in its total oil supplies than did Western Europe and somewhat more than did Japan. Our irritating gasoline queues early in 1974 were due almost entirely to government mismanagement of the crisis.

Thus there was no causal connection between the ceasefire of October 22, 1973, and any Arab attempt at "oil blackmail." The suspension of the American airlift of weapons to Israel in late October was not the consequence of any delay that an American motorist experienced at a filling station the following December or February. Instead, the weapons airlift to the Israeli front on Sinai and its cutoff a week later were logical requisites for a goal that the Nixon administration had been pursuing for five years: an "evenhanded policy" toward Arabs and Israelis. Such a policy had been advocated by William Scranton, Nixon's emissary to the Middle East, as early as December 1968; it had been vainly pressed by Secretary of State Rogers in 1969 and 1970; and an evenhanded policy was brilliantly carried out by his successor Henry

Kissinger in the shuttle diplomacy and the disengagement agreements of 1974 and 1975. Back in 1969 Kissinger identified a "stalemate" in the Middle East as "the strategic opportunity I perceived for the United States."[3] Whatever the effect of the embargo, the flow and the halt of American weapons to Israel produced the stalemate Kissinger had been hoping for.

From the oil countries' side, too, the situation was more complex and subtle than the image of a successful "oil squeeze" implies. Iraq—at the time the most vociferous anti-Israeli state among the Arabs—joined in the embargo but not in the production cuts. These cutbacks were first threatened at the rate of 5 percent for each month that Israel continued to hold the territories occupied since 1967. Yet full production was restored in March 1974, when 96 percent of those territories still remained occupied—but the price of oil had risen by about 300 percent. And, of course, all oil exporters —Arabs, Iranians, Venezuelans, Nigerians, Canadians—were happy to participate in that price rise.

It was clear from the start, moreover, that the Arab sponsors of this phase of the oil revolution took no economic risks in proclaiming an embargo, curtailing production, or raising prices. Saudi Arabia's oil revenues had risen from 99 cents to $1.77 a barrel since 1970, but (with world demand increasing, the United States lowering its import barriers, and Saudi Arabia cast in the role of the world's marginal oil producer) Saudi oil exports had also more than doubled—a clear signal that the traffic would bear a much higher price.[4] Oil producers, it would seem, are tempted to attach political conditions to their sales at times of strong upward pressure of demand, when price alone fails to clear the market.

In the specific situation of 1973, the Saudis, by brandishing the "oil weapon," achieved a number of related objectives. They used a unique economic opportunity to increase their monetary income; they rewarded Sadat for breaking Nasser's alliance with Moscow, which had caused them much anguish over the years; in the approaching fourth Arab-Israeli war, they avoided being branded as the lackeys of Western imperialists and their oil companies; instead, they could take a leading role both in inter-Arab and in global diplomacy. We shall note later what specific economic objectives the Saudis pursued with their management of the world oil price in the mid-1970s and what difficulties they encountered by 1979.

But perhaps this careful assessment of American and of Saudi motives in 1973 is beside the point. The events of the October war demonstrated the vulnerability not of the United States but of Israel. The fighting along the Suez front stopped abruptly not because the United States depended on Arab oil but because Israel depended on American weapons. As Defense Minister Moshe Dayan explained to his compatriots at the time: "I'm not sure the soldiers know it, but the shells they are firing today were not in their possession a week ago." The lesson of October 1973 is the military leverage not of oil but of weapons supplied in time of war.

There remain, of course, the much more serious and pervasive economic effects of the successive oil crises. But in this regard, too, the United States has been less vulnerable than is commonly imagined. Out of any ten tankers plying the Persian Gulf route, five are normally bound for Europe, two for Japan, and only one for the United States. The effects of the global oil price increases, like those of the production cutbacks of the fall of 1973, obviously are proportional to each nation's dependence on oil imports for its total energy. Thus Japan's total energy consumption in 1979 was 70 percent oil, virtually all of it imported, making for an import dependence of 69 percent. For Western Europe, oil was only 55 percent of all available energy, and 89 percent of that was imported, making for an oil import dependence of 49 percent. For the United States, although oil imports increased through most of the 1970s, they amounted by 1980 to only 38 percent of all oil consumed, which was only 47 percent of our total energy (the rest being mostly domestic natural gas and coal), making for an American energy dependence on foreign oil of only 18 percent. We must also consider that Americans consume more than twice as much energy per capita as do Europeans or Japanese and from 44 to 86 percent more energy per dollar of gross domestic product—in short, that much of our current energy consumption is waste that could be readily curtailed whether in peace or in war.[5]

How then does petroleum as a key resource affect the strategic realities of the late twentieth century? Oil became the major fuel for war in World War I and the exclusive fuel in World War II. It is likely to retain that dominant position for the foreseeable future: Tanks, warships, jet planes, and most missiles run on oil—nuclear submarines being the only notable exception. The two superpowers, together with Saudi Arabia, have also long been the world's major producers of petroleum. The United States was a net exporter until the late 1940s, the Soviet Union became a sizable exporter in the late 1950s, although rising consumption and exhausted fields are reducing the scale of those exports. China is one of the promising, still little explored, oil regions—and its prospects as a major power in the future will no doubt depend in part on the development of its oil potential.

Western Europe and Japan remain the world's leading oil importers, and it would seem unlikely that they will ever be able to play a fully independent role in global strategy without first securing an adequate fuel base at home. While both regions remain heavily dependent on Middle Eastern oil, their major alternative is to continue relying on American nuclear protection or to take advantage of any interlude of detente in order to attempt some sort of an independent diplomatic role.

Here in the United States, the 1980 election campaign plunged us into one of our recurrent quadrennial debates on the vulnerability or the adequacy of our defenses, focusing this time on issues of strategic arms limitation, nuclear parity, rapid deployment, and the like. One may hope that this debate will be extended before long to an intelligent discussion of problems of strategic oil storage. Thus far the strategic petroleum reserve is far behind schedule, and the storage policies of private firms generally tend to exaggerate rather than alleviate the economic dangers. Yet such issues of short-term crisis management must be clearly distinguished from the longer-term problem of the availability of strategic resources. However adequate or deficient our state of preparedness in several other regards, it seems unlikely that petroleum production (as distinct from storage) would become a major bottleneck in any future war effort, conventional or nuclear, in which we may become involved.

Under the dramatic impact of the early OPEC price rises and the 1973 embargo, there were widespread fears (or hopes) that similar price cartels would form for other raw materials. Advanced industrial countries could survive the oil shock by raising the price of the refrigerators and missiles they sold to others, including OPEC nations; or else they could inflate their currencies. To one-crop economies of the third world, these solutions were not available—and it was quickly recognized that the effect of the oil price rises were most disastrous for the poorest of the developing nations, such as the drought belt of tropical Africa and Bangladesh. But if the country's export "crop" happened to be bauxite, tin, or some other industrial mineral, OPEC obviously exercised a powerful demonstration effect: Rather than remain the victims of the oil revolution, why not start a comparable minerals revolution of their own? Among American observers, it was C. Fred Bergsten, on the staff of the Brookings Institution and during the Carter administration, a member of the Treasury Department, who most insistently warned of this "Threat from the Third World."[6]

A further anxiety sometimes arises from discussions of the future of southern Africa, with its rich deposits of gold, copper, chromium, cobalt, uranium, and other metals. To what extent does unrest in Zaire, sharpening conflict over Namibia or in South Africa, or Soviet penetration of Angola or Mozambique foreshadow a threat to the global balance of strategic resources? Keeping in mind my earlier distinction between the narrower and the broader meanings of such a question, I would reply that there is little reason to worry about nonfuel minerals as a military threat and that with respect to the health of the world economy, the most serious threat remains that from oil.

Whereas petroleum is found in abundance under the tropical sands of Arabia and the icy depths of Alaska, the world's metals seem to be found mainly in the temperate zones—the United States, Canada, Europe, the Urals and other mountains of Soviet Russia, Australia, the central Andes, and parts of Brazil. The United States is the world's leading producer of copper, natural phosphates, lead, and uranium; it is second in iron ore, vanadium and quartz; and third in silver and tungsten. The leading world exporters of nonfuel minerals are Canada, Australia, and the United States in that order. In the bauxite trade, Australia and Jamaica account for about half of world exports. Tin is the only major industrial metal that is produced mainly in third-world countries (Malaysia, Thailand, Bolivia, Indonesia), with Southeast Asia as clearly predominant as is the Middle East in petroleum. Correspondingly, tin is the only industrial metal whose price in the 1970s as much as quadrupled—others, such as bauxite, barely keeping up with the general rate of inflation of commodity prices.

The major reasons why metals and other nonfuel minerals are less likely than oil to become crucial bottlenecks in time of war or levers for unhinging the world's economy in time of peace are five: recycling, storage, substitution, seabed mining, and low cost.

1. *Recycling.* Metals can be reclaimed for repeated use, and the international trade in scrap iron, copper, aluminum, and so on already amounts to about one-third of the value of the trade in the new ore. The cost of recycling thus sets an effective ceiling on price increases for the new metal. Once a metal becomes as precious as gold, we no longer speak of "scrap" or "recycling"—instead, the dentist carefully extracts one filling and reshapes it in the mouth of the next patient. Such recycling is, of course, impossible for fuels: Having done their duty as sources of energy, petroleum and coal become air pollution. (Only hydropower is subject to recycling with a little help from the sun and from gravity; and fissile uranium in breeder reactors is self-generating.)

2. *Storage.* Storage is a major factor in the economics both of agricultural products and of metals. Agricultural producers must make their harvests last until the next season and anticipate occasional crop failures. Hence stockpiles corresponding to several months' or years' consumption are normal, and government subsidies to farmers, both in the United States and in the European Community, have made the silos bulge and the butter mountains pile up even more. In World War II and later years, the United States General Service Administration found it easy to accumulate stockpiles of several metals corresponding to a normal year's supply for the American market.

By contrast, petroleum, being flammable and liquid, is convenient to transport but difficult and dangerous to store. About one-tenth of the world's annual petroleum output is likely to be en route at any given moment in a pipeline, a barge, or an oceangoing tanker; a few days' supply is kept in tanks near the pipeline terminal, loading port, or refinery to compensate for traffic jams among tankers caused by high seas or among fuel trucks caused by other vehicles; and a small amount is needed as working inventory in the complex tubing of a refinery. Unfortunately, this oil en route or tied up in transport or in the production process is sometimes counted as storage. There is also some genuine seasonal storage of petroleum products: It would be very expensive to close down refineries for a major overhaul twice a year to allow them to produce more gasoline in the summer and more fuel oil in the winter—let alone build separate refineries for summer and winter use. Instead, refiners keep to an average product mix all year, storing the excess gasoline in the winter and the excess fuel oil in the summer. Beyond this, governments of importing countries have undertaken (or have required oil companies to undertake) storage programs against the possibility of supply interruptions; the size of these emergency reserves in September 1979 ranged from the equivalent of 52 days of imports for Japan and 63 days for the United States to 95 days of imports for the Netherlands.[7]

3. *Substitution.* There are few uses that are unique to any one metal. Electric wiring can be produced from copper or aluminum, kitchen vessels from clay, tin, copper, iron, glass, or aluminum. In the building trades, metals, wood, cement, glass, and a variety of petroleum-based plastics actively compete. Hence a cartel that tries to drive up the price for a single metal is likely to find itself not with a corner on the market—but without any market at all. When the exporters of mercury sharply raised their price in the early 1970s, they found that their major customers had shifted to substitutes and could not be lured back even with discounts below the earlier lower price.

4. *Seabed mining.* In the future many metals are likely to be produced not only from mines underground but from ore nodules dredged up from the bottom of the sea. The complex problems of international law surrounding this possibility of seabed mining seem by now well on the way to

resolution. Not surprisingly, American (along with European and Japanese) companies are among the leaders in this future seabed-mining technology, which thus must be counted— along with competition from recycled metals, from metals in storage, and from potential substitutes—as another restraint on the operation of a would-be cartel on the OPEC model.

5. *Low cost.* If we are to gauge accurately the importance of the resource problem both in its military and its economic sense, we must keep in mind the basic dimensions. Most of the world's trade is in manufactured goods and in services rather than in raw materials, and the tendency, at least until 1973, was for the raw-materials sector to diminish in relative value with time. Thus in 1973, before the first oil price explosion, nearly two-thirds of all the world's trade was in manufactured products, and the remaining raw-materials sector in turn consisted of three roughly equal subsectors: One-eighth of total trade was in food and other agricultural raw materials, one-ninth in fuels (petroleum, coal, and a small amount of natural gas), and one-tenth in nonfuel minerals, among which iron, copper, nickel, zinc, natural phosphates, clays, and bauxite were the only sizable ones. Even before the 1973 OPEC revolution, petroleum was by far the leading raw material in world trade, its value being more than double that of all nonfuel minerals and more than seven times that of iron ore. (Similarly, petroleum accounts for considerably more than half the tonnage in international shipping.)

The sheer dimensions of the petroleum trade thus dwarf that in tin, bauxite, or vanadium. The gains that might lure third-world governments into organizing an OPEClike cartel are at best very slight. Consumers fighting the cartel's price gouging or governments of importing countries guarding against an embargo would face no great expense in mobilizing alternative supplies from the four sources just listed: recycling, storage, substitution, and perhaps, in the future, the ocean floor. The damage that nonoil cartels could do either to a U.S. economy at war by cutting off supplies or to the global economy by constipation of the flow of money in time of peace would at worst be slight.

Early in 1975, Secretary Kissinger conveyed an oblique warning to the countries of the Middle East, which, a year before, had imposed an oil embargo against the United States. In the future, the secretary reflected, America could not exclude the "use [of] force. But it is one thing," he quickly specified, "to use it in a dispute over price, it's another where there's some actual strangulation of the industrial world. . . . The use of force would be considered only in the gravest emergency."[8] Kissinger's statement reflected a distinction that seemed to be drawn instinctively by most Americans in the crisis of 1973. There was much apprehension over the (largely imaginary) possibility of a physical cutoff of supplies: "Arabs' New Oil Squeeze: Dimouts, Slowdowns, Chills," as *Time* magazine vividly put it in anticipation. There was much less concern—indeed, there was almost a sense of relief—when the net result turned out to be a mere increase in price.

I have argued in this essay that this sense of concern and of relief is misplaced. Americans have very little reason to worry about resources and foreign policy in the narrow, military sense. No potential enemy, singly or in groups, has the power to cut us off from essential supplies of oil, to deprive us of raw materials essential to our national defense or to our status as a world power. Such problems as we do face could readily be resolved by a more effective stockpiling program in time of peace and by a modicum of rationing in time of war.

On the contrary, Americans have worried far too little about the serious threat posed to the economic future of our country and of other industrial nations by the oil price rises of 1973-1974 and 1979-1980 and of those almost certain to come in the future. And this danger is all the more serious because—unlike a military blockade or Kissinger's dramatic image of "some actual strangulation"—the threat cannot easily be averted by any quick, neat application of force. The problem we must address, therefore, is not the hypothetical economy of war but the real economy of peace. As Professor Adelman has insisted, the real problem is not supply but price[9] —and the price explosion has been caused by a reversal in regional relations. The Middle East became politically independent of the West in the early 1970s, just as the industrial countries of the West, along with Japan, became economically dependent on oil from the Middle East. (The British withdrawal from the Persian Gulf early in 1971 and the phasing out of United States' oil-import restrictions in 1971-1973 were among the crucial developments.) The Middle East contains about two-thirds of the world's proven oil reserves and contributes more than half the oil in international trade. Situated at the junction of three continents and two oceans, it is also the point of intersection of many global and regional tensions. The net effect has been a series of political crises that have led to temporary curtailments of the flow of oil and to more durable rises in its world price.

1. *1970/1971: The Qaddafi Round.* A coup in Libya in 1969 brought to power Colonel Muammar al-Qaddafi, a young man of 26, with an austerely Islamic and virulently anti-Western outlook. Qaddafi skillfully exploited the bargaining situation bequeathed to him by his royal predecessor: concession agreements with a score of rival oil companies, rapidly-mounting financial reserves, and Libya's geographic proximity to Europe in a tightening oil market. But he used those advantages not, as the king and other Middle East governments had done, to increase production at constant or falling prices; instead, he exploited them to threaten a shutdown of production and to drive up the price. Venezuelans, Saudis, Iranians, and others quickly emulated his actions. The cartel was fast learning to let each member pursue its favorite device for squeezing more income from the international oil

companies and to insist that all members benefit from any device that should prove successful—a method known as OPEC's "best of current practices" doctrine.[10]

2. *1973/1974: The Yamani Round.* We have already reviewed the circumstances in which the Saudis, joined by other Arab and non-Arab producers, used the occasion of the October 1973 Arab-Israeli War to drive the price from 3 dollars to 7 dollars and to 10 dollars per barrel.

3. *1974/1978: The First Interlude.* There followed an interlude during which Saudi Arabia used its excess production capacity (nearly 4 million barrels per day in 1974) to enforce its price preferences on OPEC and the rest of the world market; and those preferences were based on the 1974 price. Specifically, the Saudis chose to let the oil price remain steady (that is, decline in real terms) at times of global recession and to let the price keep up with inflation (that is, remain steady in real terms) at times of recovery. The 1973 price revolution had allowed the Saudis to become the fastest accumulators of financial reserves—and their purpose in rising to the top of the world economy was to enjoy its fruits, not destroy its basis. By insisting on only a 5 percent price increase early in 1977, when most OPEC members were set to increase the price by 10 percent, the Saudis dramatically asserted their pricing power to this effect.

4. *1979-1980: The Khomeini Round.* In the mid-1970s, Saudi Arabia's spare capacity had been larger than the total exports of any country except Iran. But it was precisely Iranian production that was disrupted by the revolution in that country, with exports totally halted for two months early in 1979. The temporary shortage created a panic on the spot market, which caused oil companies to bid up the price and raise storage levels to all-time highs. OPEC's medium-sized producers (Libya, Nigeria, Kuwait, Venezuela) did their best to keep prices at those higher levels, reducing their production accordingly. The net result, as in 1973-1974, was a

ratchet effect: A curtailment of supply (deliberate in 1973, accidental in 1979) raises prices; OPEC members enforce those new price levels, letting their production be determined by demand at the new prices. Although Saudi Arabia tried to arrest this new price spiral, the Saudis instead were forced repeatedly to match the hawks' price increase of 2 dollars, 4 dollars, or 6 dollars. From the end of 1978 to the middle of 1980, their own price went up from $13.30 to $32.

5. *1981—A Second Interlude?* By 1981 high prices on the world oil market and decontrol of United States' domestic prices were slowing down consumption. The oil industry had accumulated inventories of record size and thus was able to avoid a new panic on the spot market as a result of the Iraq-Iran War that began in September 1980. The Saudis continued their production at maximum levels, hoping to take advantage of the temporary price glut in order to reestablish their earlier control over world prices. If they succeed, there might be a second interlude, comparable to that of 1974-1978, with prices declining in real terms at times of recession and keeping pace with inflation at times of recovery. Yet it should not be forgotten that this potential price stability would be established at a level more than double the previous ones.

The situation at the time of writing in mid-1981 remains precarious. A renewed Arab-Israeli conflict, perhaps resulting inadvertently from Israeli and Syrian involvement in Lebanon; a second, more serious flare-up between Iraq and Iran; a conflict between Egypt and Libya (resulting perhaps from Libyan involvement in Chad); Khomeini's death in Iran leading to renewed turmoil or perhaps a Soviet takeover; a military coup or a revolution in one of the Arab countries on the Gulf: These and other developments could send oil prices off on their fourth upward spiral. For the price of oil to remain at its mid-1981 level of about 34 dollars, almost everything would have to go right; for the price to explode once again, only one of many things would have to go wrong.

                     * * *

    Must the industrial world helplessly stand by while this nefarious connection between Middle-East turmoil and the world price of oil continues to threaten our prosperity and material progress?[11] Some of the easy remedies promised from various quarters in the last decade plainly will not work. Oil finds in the last decade or two in the North Sea, Alaska, and Mexico have limited the world's dependence on oil from the Middle East but not reversed it. The magnitude of the new finds is not enough. Production in each of the locations has been 2 mb/d or less. (The 1980 figures were 2.1 mb/d for the North Sea, 1.9 mb/d for Mexico, and 1.5 mb/d for Alaska.) By comparison, Arab countries in 1973 cut their production by 4 mb/d, and Iran's exports between 1978 and 1980 fell by about 3.6 mb/d. Nor are any major new oil finds likely to be made suddenly: If new oil finds were to rival one of the major Middle East producers before the end of the century, exploratory drilling would have established their presence by now.

    Substitution of other fuels for oil is well under way and is likely to help reduce the world's dependence on the Middle East gradually. Electricity generation can be shifted from oil to coal or nuclear power—but only at the cost of sizable investments. A shift of residential and commercial heating from oil to coal presents even greater difficulties. Any increased use of coal requires further large investments in public transport. Investing in synthetic fuels—that is, the conversion of coal or shale into oil, such as was planned in the last years of the Carter administration—would very likely be a costly mistake: The price estimate for synthetic oil has suspiciously risen in tandem with the price of oil itself—from about 6 dollars or 7 dollars a barrel in the early 1970s to 35 dollars or 40 dollars a decade later.

By contrast, the price elasticity of demand would seem to be one of the most effective factors in reducing oil-import dependence. Through most of the 1970s, price controls on petroleum products in the United States shielded the consumer from the full impact of world prices, fostered the illusion of cheap oil, and encouraged rising consumption. Conversely, the removal of price controls, combined with the Khomeini round of price increases, brought about a long overdue adjustment. U.S. oil consumption rose from 14.8 mb/d in 1971 to 18.4 mb/d in 1978; and with production declining over the same period, imports rose even more sharply—from 3.7 mb/d in 1971 to 6.3 mb/d in 1973 and to as much as 8.8 mb/d in 1977. Then, from 1979 to 1980, imports declined sharply, from 8.4 mb/d to 6.7 mb/d. The shift to more efficient, high-mileage cars, which by now is well under way both among car buyers and manufacturers, promises to reinforce this downward trend; gasoline, it should be remembered, accounts for about 42 percent of U.S. oil consumption, or more than the total petroleum consumption of West Germany, France, and Great Britain combined.

Meanwhile, the Middle Eastern political scene continues to offer major hazards, any one of which (as we just discussed) might set off a new round of price increases. Yet here too there may be major long-range gains. The Washington peace treaty between Israel and Egypt of March 1979 has not brought about overall peace between Israel and its neighbors. Indeed, by taking Egypt out of the common Arab front, it may make the settlement of the remaining Palestinian issues more difficult. Yet without Egypt, a major new Arab-Israeli war is impossible. Hence the treaty has allowed Middle Easterners to shift their attention from the injuries of the past to the dangers of the future. And in facing those dangers, it has made both Egypt and Israel potential allies of the West.

What some of those dangers are is made clear by the Russian invasion of Afghanistan, the Khomeini revolution, and Iraq's attack on Iran. But there is every prospect that the United States will be less vulnerable to the effects of such crises and in a better position to counteract them. By further reducing our oil imports, we can make ourselves immune to price rises paced by events in the Middle East. By building up our Strategic Petroleum Reserve, we can overcome temporary crises of supply; perhaps, as our imports are phased out, such a reserve can be used as a buffer stock to help moderate price fluctuations on the world market. Meanwhile, we can begin to build up the Rapid Deployment Force for the Middle East, about which there has been so much talk and so little purposeful action. The result may be the kind of "consensus of strategic concerns" about which Secretary of State Alexander M. Haig, Jr., spoke in March 1981. By standing ready to help our friends when they ask for help against external attack, we can resolve or prevent some of the political crises that may continue to drive up the price of oil for our friends in Europe and Japan.[1,2]

NOTES

1. The quote is from Kissinger's opening address to the Washington Energy Conference, February 11, 1974. The articles cited appeared in *Commentary* (May 1974), *The New York Times Magazine* (September 23, 1973), *The New Republic* (March 30, 1974), and *Foreign Affairs* (April 1973 and summer 1980); "The Arab Oil Squeeze" was the title of *Newsweek's* cover story of April 9, 1973.

2. Federal Energy Administration, *U.S. Oil Companies and the Arab Oil Embargo,* a report to Senator Frank Church's Committee on Multinational Corporations, January 23, 1975, pp. 2 and 5 (the writers of the report evidently were enamored of the phrase). The best assessment of the embargo's impact is Robert E. Stobaugh's article, "The Oil Companies in the Crisis," in Raymond A. Vernon, ed., *The Oil Crisis: In Perspective* (New York, 1976), pp. 179-202. On the federal government's mismanagement of the shortage, see Richard B. Mancke, *Squeaking By* (New York, 1976).

3. Henry A. Kissinger, *The White House Years* (Boston, 1979), p. 360 f., commenting on a statement made by Egyptian Foreign Minister Mahmoud Fawzi in April 1969.

4. For the setting of OPEC's 1973 revolution and specific export and revenue figures, see D. A. Rustow and John F. Mugno, *OPEC: Success and Prospects* (New York, 1976), esp. pp. 128, 134.

5. For detailed comparisons of energy consumption, see Joel Darmstadter et al., *How Industrial Societies Use Energy* (Baltimore, 1977), and Joy Dunkerley, ed., *International Comparisons of Energy Consumption* (Washington, D.C., 1978).

6. See especially C. Fred Bergsten, "The Threat from the Third World," *Foreign Policy* 11 (summer 1973), and "New Era in World Commodity Markets," *Challenge* (September/October 1974).

7. See E. N. Krapels, "Focus on Emergency Oil Reserves," *The Petroleum Economist*, February 1921.

8. Kissinger in a *Business Week* interview published January 13, 1975, but widely reported by late December 1974. See Rustow and Mugno, *op. cit.*, p. 53. The *Time* article appeared November 19, 1973.

9. M. A. Adelman, "Is the Oil Shortage Real" *Foreign Policy* 9 (winter 1972/1973).

10. The "best of current practices" doctrine is contained in Article 10 of OPEC's Resolution no. 90 of June 1968; see Rustow and Mugno, *op. cit.*, pp. 21ff, and 166ff.

11. See my book *Oil and Turmoil: America Faces OPEC and the Middle East* (New York, 1982).

12. See my article, "Reagan, Mideast, and Oil," *The New York Times*, January 12, 1981.

V.

New Directions
in American
Foreign Economic Policy

WILLIAM DIEBOLD, JR.

This paper might have been called *New Directions in Our Trade Policy,* the title of my first book, published 40 years ago in the spring of 1941. Today we are concerned with more than trade policy, and that is at least partly because during the intervening years, the United States did in fact move in new directions, departing from its historic trade policy of protection, a change that affected both the country itself and the rest of the world. The question we face today is whether the pursuit of new goals again requires changes in American policy. We may conclude that the main need is to pursue known methods and measures more effectively irrespective of whether our goals have changed. Thus my subject is a facet of a larger theme: continuity, change, and consistency in foreign policy.

That theme was one of the most controversial and therefore the most stimulating in the work of Hans Morgenthau to whose memory we dedicate these proceedings. Associated with the much debated question of the place of morality in relation to national interest are questions about the definition of national interest. What endures despite changing circumstances? Properly pursued, that line of thought transcends the oversimplification of the concept of national interest that has been derived from Hans's doctrines. Questions of continuity and change are relevant to Hans's views about public issues in which theory blended with subjective elements, including personality, convictions, and passion. I am happy to have played some part in bringing Hans to the Council on Foreign Relations for a year. We all benefited from his stay. I wish he were with us today.

Energy and Raw Materials

My first task is to comment on Dankwart Rustow's paper. At the risk of not doing justice to a complex and subtle line of thought, I shall focus on only part of his rich analysis. Middle Eastern policy I shall leave aside in spite of the fact that it presents such splendid illustrations of the interrelation of economic and other factors, the clash of ends in American foreign policy, and the difficulty of acting on a balanced view of the national interest in any consistent and constructive way when that concept has to be applied in a field of force where the interests of many other nations operate. That leaves for comment our energy future and the place of other minerals in U.S. policy.

With regard to energy, I agree with the main line of argument articulated in the Rustow paper. I have picked out a few points to underline or embroider.

The decade of the 1970s was indeed a time of oil partly because of the economic "success" of the world in the 1950s and the 1960s. For many reasons—including the American pursuit of the foreign-policy goals we are calling into question today—the world became a richer, more productive place during the postwar period. To a degree it floated to that position on a sea of oil. Recall what a considerable transformation was wrought—and at the time it was thought to be "progress"—in shifting the main energy base of the industrial countries from coal to oil. It was, we told ourselves, the truly modern fuel—at least until the time came to switch to nuclear power. As we get used to living with OPEC, we forget, I think, the shock of discovering how open to exploitation by a handful of countries the world economy, especially the industrial countries, proved to be. After all, if one wanted an example of the power of private capital that escaped from the controls of even the most powerful governments in the world, one could cite the big multinational oil companies. How often did analysts maintain that the miscellaneous group of countries in which the oil is located could not work closely together and, it was projected, certainly not over a long period of time? The prediction proved true in some respect; how often have only two members of a cartel been at war with one another? Nevertheless, OPEC has brought about a major shift in the control of the oil supply and in the flow of payments for the rents—as economists call them—that derive from this activity. Part of the explanation relates to the pervasiveness of oil itself: As consumer good, industrial fuel, and raw material, it generates the power to wreak exceptional political and economic dislocation.

We walked right into this situation in spite of the fact that it was known that sometime in the not too distant future oil would be relatively scarce. Part of our miscalculation flowed from our assumptions about nuclear power (and I missed a discussion of the future in the Rustow paper). One may well ask to what extent the U.S. oil policy of the 1950s contributed to our long-term blindness. In those days we limited imports on the theory that we needed to maintain domestic production for security purposes. (Today we realize that we would be far more secure if the oil were still in the ground.) Or was that only an exercise in cynicism?

Some key characteristics of the energy problem pertain as well, although in a different mix, to a number of other aspects of foreign economic policy. The domestic and the foreign components of the oil issue are inextricably tied together both in their impact on our lives and in constituting possible ways out of our difficulties. The old question of whether the oil companies had become so powerful that they were usurping the government prerogative of shaping American policy has been supplanted by the question of whether government and business can work together in ways that are unprecedented in the United States, at least in peacetime. Another characteristic of the oil problem relates to the fact that the great shifts in the control and flow of payments pose problems in adapting the structure of the U.S. national economy and indeed of the whole world economy on a scale that outruns our experience, at least in terms of conscious policy choices. Instead of being offered the incentives of rewards for good adaptation, we are presented with the need to limit damage. Gains may lie ahead, but the costs are considerable and immediate. The repercussions go beyond the energy industry; automobiles and petrochemicals are only the most obvious examples.

Although the energy problem is common to the industrial world, we have experienced the utmost difficulty in dealing with it on that scale. Different countries are affected differently, and differences among them may be exacerbated by energy shifts. In the past external forces sometimes pushed countries together to deal with a common problem, but the energy problem has proved divisive for the industrial world. If there were space, I would trace the sequence by which each industrial country, anxious to ensure its oil supplies to the best of its ability and looking for ways to pay for its supplies that would not impinge too heavily on its other needs, tend to work out preferential relations with one or another set of oil producers. The continued use of such methods (and results) will increase divisions within the industrial world and add to the other forces breaking down the system of multilateral economic cooperation into a series of special, more or less bilateral deals.

For the United States, it can be argued, the biggest problem in accommodating changes in the energy structure of the world involves living with a dependency that we cannot control. There was dependency in our past, but in modern times there has always been a sense (perhaps unconscious) that we could either do without or in the end find some way of managing. For most of the world, however, this kind of dependency, not only in energy but in many other things as well, has been the normal situation. The U.S. reaction—in this case a proper one I believe—is to reduce dependency. But assuming that can be done in the case of energy, is it the proper approach to other problems? What would be the consequences for us and the rest of the world if we were to think primarily in such terms?

This question brings us to the third of Dankwart Rustow's subjects, other minerals.

I agree with his emphasis on no other OPECs. We know what was wrong with the Club of Rome's analysis. Nevertheless, do we not have to add a cautionary word or two? Even if there were to be no more effective cartels (although there was one in uranium, and bauxite producers have managed to work together reasonably well), a shift has occurred that has strengthened both the control over raw materials exercised by producing countries and the flow of rents to them. (Despite this change, quite a few things can be achieved by a national government acting alone and putting pressure on foreign producers [that are to a degree captives] or in asking for better terms from foreign customers.) Partly as a result of this apparent shift in the balance of power, there is occurring an extensive process of change in the structure of the raw-materials industries. As occurred in oil, nationalization has broken up vertical integration in a number of cases, and even measures short of nationalization may produce that effect. How serious is the economic loss? How significant is the change in bargaining power? We have not been able to project answers to these questions so far as I can tell. Probably different answers apply to different minerals, just as the economic rationale of locating processing near the source or near the market varies according to the commodity and the national economies involved. The implications of these choices for bargaining power and the security of the supplies of consuming countries vary accordingly. Finally, the shift has yielded higher costs for most mineral raw materials as a result of the need to mine poorer veins in more remote places of the earth. Although we may not be approaching as predictable a situation as we faced in oil, more exploring remains to be done. Heavy investment costs as well as uncertainty about markets and the political climate in producing areas tend to favor security at higher costs. Deterrents to current investment may hold down the level of production some years from now, thus exacerbating basic problems.

One result may well be that raw materials will be accorded a greater prominence in both economic and political analyses in the next 10 or 20 years than in the period before OPEC. Although it signals a change in recent priorities, focusing on raw materials is really nothing new. When I studied international relations in the 1930s, a large part of the study was made up of two subjects: The League of Nations and strategic raw materials. Two of the first four or five books published by the Council on Foreign Relations were about "ores and industry" in Latin America and Asia. When the Second World War ended, paying attention to raw materials seemed natural. The Charter for an International Trade

Organization—surely the most comprehensive international economic agreement ever proposed by the United States—contained a whole chapter on commodity agreements drawn up in part because the economics of raw materials were considered different from those of manufacturing and often differed from one mineral and vegetable product to another. Cartels were also a big worry then, and one of the aims of those agreements was to ensure that consumers had a voice. We did not need to recall that Herbert Hoover had considered one of his chief achievements when he was secretary of commerce to be effective action against the raw-material cartels that were then organized not by third-world countries but by Britain, France, and Holland.

After the ITO failed, the Paley Commission in the early 1950s looked intensively at the problem of the security of supply for raw materials and decided that it was primarily an economic problem to be coped with by substantial investment, a fairly free flow of trade and payments, and the development of substitute resources. After that things quieted down apparently because no one was particularly worried about the current or the historical problem of the security of supply. Stockpiling—always a controversial issue—faded from attention, and quite a few of the stockpiles were sold. After OPEC there was a burst of concern and many discussions about how to secure access to raw materials. Should GATT rules be strengthened, better bargains be struck with producers, mechanisms such as the proposed—but abandoned—International Resources Bank be devised? To a degree talk has subsided again, but I do not think that is because the problems have been solved.

The United States has often been protectionist with respect to some of its mineral production. Now Americans seem to be more concerned with the environment, and that preoccupation is having an effect on both mining and processing. We have produced substitutes for raw materials and in at least one case—the synthetic rubber industry—showed a good adaptation to the problems of efficiency and competition. Thus there is a lot of experience to study but little evidence from which to infer the direction national policy on raw materials is likely to move—or be pushed. The problems do not strike people as urgent, but then neither did the oil problem ten years ago.

Past, Present, and Future Goals

It is unusual to be able to cite documents setting forth a panoply of a country's goals in foreign economic policy and even rarer to find them partly consistent and more or less focused. But we can do that for U.S. policy at the end of the Second World War. To a considerable degree national objectives with respect to a new international economic structure were embodied in policies and even some international agreements while the war was being fought. The characteristics of those policies and aims are too well-known to need summarizing here, but it is important to underline the fact that the most important national objective of U.S. policy was the creation of an international economic order with certain salient characteristics. Contrary to what people may be learning from reading quite a few of the books in circulation today, this combination of national and international objectives was not chosen because the United States thought it was in a hegemonic position and could impose terms with which the rest of the world would have to live. Perhaps that was the case, but it was not the position that Americans at the time understood themselves to be in. And even if Americans possessed that power in some respects, they could not use it to achieve the goals they were seeking for the international economy. American military power, great though it was, could not produce the economic results that were sought in the proposals for international economic cooperation even though they assumed a security system that was at first expected to be dependent on the United Nations and then on cooperation among countries that continued to be "like-minded." The interrelation of American concepts of the economic order and the political and social objectives it was meant to achieve is too complex for systematic analysis here. Instead, I shall sketch a different picture from the one painted in much of the received wisdom of today.

The object was to create an international economic order that would avoid the worst errors of the interwar period. That, it was believed, could only be accomplished if the United States behaved in a manner different from the way it had acted between the wars. Therefore, one of the important objectives of the advocates of this approach was to make sure that the main lines of American policy were set in the right direction and that the U.S. government could not depart from rules and obligations because it was convenient to do so. In other words, the concept of American national interest embodied in this approach was diametrically different from what would be expected by someone who believed that a hegemon should act hegemonically, selfishly, and mercantilistically in order to attain the main objectives of immediate material gains and the maintenance of power. The formulation of this broad concept of the national interest was essential for achieving an international economic system that was to be built on a high degree of cooperation among governments. That system also called for the creation of more international economic organizations than had existed before. Such organizations could work only with the consent of sovereign governments. Even if the United States had been disposed toward imposing conditions during a period of relative weakness in Europe, the consequences would not have been acceptable once other nations regained their economic strength. If they had failed to recover, American policies would have failed. Consequently, negotiation and compromise were the necessary methods for attaining American economic goals, which meant that for a considerable period after the war the United States pursued a double standard that permitted other countries to restrict trade and payments and do things that the United States refrained from doing not as a sacrifice but in pursuit of its redefinition of the national interest.

Although the importance of the United States in the new economic world order was certainly not underestimated, the picture of the world economy that most people had in mind was one in which Europe remained very important not only as the center but as the pivot of world trade. In particular, the position of the United Kingdom was considered essential for attaining the "triangular" pattern of world trade that had been described in some major studies undertaken by the Secretariat of the League of Nations when it was at Princeton during the war. The position of Japan was underestimated, but it was understood that if that country reduced its territory to the densely-populated home islands and was not to be aggressive in the future, there had to be established a world economic environment that permitted decent living and expanded production. China was thought of as the big developing country that would finally live up to the promises of Sun-Yat Sen. India would be close behind, but for other countries decolonialization was thought of as a process that would last for some decades. The idea that the United States could dominate a world economy with such players did not occur to many people. The real task was to work out acceptable arrangements for long-term cooperation that would combine a necessary mix of firm obligations and flexible arrangements (when necessary).

We smooth history in retrospect and can easily forget what a hard struggle it was to bring about even the limited part of the new international economic order that was set in place. American bankers opposed the creation of the International Monetary Fund. The British loan got through Congress partly on anti-Soviet grounds; it may well be true that a more generous arrangement would have been wiser, but it was not acceptable. GATT commitments involved negotiations to remove barriers to trade; no one ever spoke of "free trade" as the goal. Until the bargains were struck, no one was sure how far the United States or any other country would go along that road. If there was a use of power that was more hegemonic than I have been claiming, it was expressed when American negotiators had to tell their foreign counterparts that this or that arrangement would never work because it would not be accepted by Congress. Nevertheless, if one looks at what was done compared to the accomplishments of any preceding period of American history or if one asks whether the same things could have been accomplished during the last fifteen years, one may well conclude that the 1940s and the 1950s were an extraordinary period in the history of international economic cooperation. That is an important point to bear in mind when we discuss reconsidering the goals of American policy today.

If the present day's received wisdom about U.S. foreign economic policy at the end of the Second World War is distorted, it does not follow that those who tried to create an international economic order had perfect vision. There were indeed blind spots; the job of European reconstruction was not adequately foreseen, and that was why the Marshall Plan had to be invented. European integration was not taken seriously, and even its early forms—the European Payments Union and trade liberalization within the OEEC—presented problems of accommodation to what was essentially a global multilateral approach emphasizing a large number of independent nation-states that accepted the principle of equal treatment. The extraordinary turnaround of Germany and Japan and the extent to which they became the recipients of

especially benevolent American treatment, were not anticipated. England proved unable to occupy the strong, central
economic position that had been ascribed to it.

The postwar monetary system based on the dollar as the
key medium of international transactions was not the one
that was designed at Bretton Woods, although it managed
reasonably well to make the rules of 1944 work for a period
of time. The failure of the ITO seemed ominous; who could
imagine the system working without the "trade leg"? But
then GATT, intended as an interim measure, proved not only
durable but effective. The development issue, which was
recognized as a real and continuing problem, erupted much
sooner than anyone anticipated and proved to be of a size
that did more to shape the problems of the world economy
than expected. For quite a while the response was to emphasize foreign aid, while leaving the developing countries out of
other activities, notably, trade negotiations and the management of the monetary system. That response accounts for
some of the difficult problems we face today, which involve
not only giving the developing countries a greater voice but
persuading them to accept more obligations.

There is no need to trace here the history of how the U.S.
goals and policies of 1945 were adapted to the changing realities of the postwar period. What needs to be done is to cite
some of the times and places in which elements came into the
picture that pushed the United States toward what I regard as
more conventional views of the national economic interest.
These elements did not necessarily challenge the broad concept of the national interest but individually and cumulative-
ly produced a shift in emphasis.

When President Kennedy came into office, he thought
that the balance of payments was a problem comparable to
that of atomic war. It was not, but his reaction was sympto-
matic. The assumption of greater burden sharing by the allies
has been an American preoccupation through most of the

postwar period. To the original emphasis on military expenditure was added concern for the management of the world economy and the accommodation of the economic needs of the third world and Japan. The East-West division might have pushed some measures of cooperation within the West farther than they would otherwise have gone, but it also gave rise to a number of events concerning which the United States felt itself more or less isolated in the pursuit of political goals vis-à-vis the Soviet Union, while its allies were more interested in pursuing "business as usual." The disarray of the monetary system became apparent by the mid-1960s, and what looked like a choice between approaches to reform turned out to create clashes of views between the United States and other countries, notably, the members of the European Community. Whether true national interests were involved is a matter for debate, but there was certainly doubt about whether the dollar's role as an international currency was a burden to the United States or an unfair advantage, and whether necessary changes could be made by phasing out the dollar and substituting in its place a truly international unit or whether sharp and radical measures were necessary to effect change. In the fifties and the sixties there were repeated expressions of doubt about whether trade liberalization had gone "too far" and overtaxed the ability of the United States to adapt to change or to compete in new circumstances. The devices resorted to by a number of countries to shape the growth of their economies were increasingly judged by Americans as forms of unfair trade practices that justified protection if not retaliation. By the beginning of the 1970s resentment over unfair trade, inadequate burden sharing, and concern over the loss of American competitiveness as well as the strains exerted on the domestic economy produced widespread support for the measures of economic nationalism associated with the name of Secretary of the Treasury John Connally.

In the early 1970s stagflation was thought of primarily as a domestic problem, much of it attributed to the way we misfinanced the Viet Nam War. But the impact of oil and the realization that stagflation and slow growth were general phenomena in the industrial world—although not uniform in all countries—and that neither national measures nor miscellaneous efforts undertaken to coordinate international economic policy were producing good results laid the groundwork for what could yet become another surge of economic nationalism, as I indicated in connection with energy.

That recounting brings us to the present day. Instead of starting off in another direction, I shall try to round out the discussion by comparing the present state of affairs, which has led us to ask whether we need new goals for our foreign economic policy, to the state of affairs in the 1940s when we found such goals. We do not now have a picture of the world economy we want. This lack is especially important because the old picture is out of focus. Although it is wrong to conclude that we should scrap the old system and put a new one in its place, it is difficult to decide what should be kept and what dropped, what can be adapted, and what needs to be added. The discussion of what should constitute the world economy of the future has remained the province of a surprisingly small number of people.

The second big difference is that we are far more dependent on the world economy than we ever were before. Trade in relation to the gross national product is more important than people realize (because they remember out-of-date figures). It is particularly important in a number of sectors whether measured by import dependency or the share of national production allocated to exports. Production by American companies abroad and the profits thereof constitute a major part of our involvement with the rest of the world, a relationship that is not usually reflected in our concepts of the national interest or even of the national economy. Although it is commonplace to say that we are living in a far more interdependent world than we used to, it is not always realized how intricately we are enmeshed in the international division of labor, how difficult it would be to get out of it, and how burdensome it would be to lose the benefits that flow from it.

The world economy has changed; the diffusion of power is well-known. However, we do not really know how to mobilize such diffuse power to carry out the functions that the United States performed in its so-called hegemonic past. The issue is no longer limited to Western Europe and Japan but involves other countries as well. This new world is one in which comparative advantage shifts from country to country more rapidly than ever before. The problem of accommodation therefore has become more intense and more difficult. If, as is generally believed, we face a period of slow growth, then everything else will be harder. We confront the paradox that the efficient use of resources has become much more important than it was when growth was rapid and much more difficult politically and socially because shifting burdens and advantages require changes in the status quo. In these circumstances the apparent built-in pressures for protectionism and economic nationalism in democracies will intensify and prove more difficult for governments to resist. Perhaps the natural economic state of man is mercantilism and the degree of interdependence that has developed is at least in part the result of a kind of artificial civilization.

Distinctions between the domestic and the foreign are more blurred than ever before. Foreign investment, whether at home or abroad, is an example. Ownership and control are old problems that have assumed a new look. Foreign trade involves domestic industrial organization; it always did, but the scale and the visibility of the connection are greater than ever before. Capital movements in a sense are freer and elude national controls while exerting a major effect on even very large economies as the money moves in or goes out. Every effort to cope with national economic problems, including those relating to structural change and improving the quality of life in the old industrial centers, produces repercussions abroad that are not adequately dealt with by the structures of international cooperation built up during the last 30 years. Clashes are increasing, and the structures are imperiled.* Domestic mechanisms, at least in the United States, have proved to be not much more effective.

We are led then to a few key questions. Are we prepared to take international competitiveness as the standard for our economic performance at home and abroad? The adoption of such a standard would entail continuous adjustments to maintain competitiveness in changing conditions. If not, can we pay the price exacted by the inefficient use of resources? But if we accept the challenge, what do we have to do to meet it? Do power, security, and foreign policy help very much in this matter? Would a failure to meet economic standards undermine our ability to maintain our power and security? Is there a contradiction between concentrating our talents, resources, and political will on economic problems and staying ahead of the diplomatic game? Can the United States still lead others toward devising collective solutions to common problems? Can we enlist any followers if we lead? Who would we accept as leaders? If we cannot generate an adequate international movement, what can we do? Should we act unilaterally, bilaterally, or with a few friends, and if so, which ones? The basic question is by what view of the world will we be guided? That view was clear in the 1940s and perhaps has never been so clear since then. It is certainly obscured now.

*I have tried to explain this process in more detail in *Industrial Policy as an International Issue,* McGraw-Hill for the 1980s Project of the Council on Foreign Relations.

VI.

The United States and the Third World: From Dialogue to Differentiation

N. A. PELCOVITS

From the outset of its tenure in office, the Carter administration faulted its predecessors for being "overly pre-occupied" with the Soviet challenge and for forgetting that the "struggle for world influence is being played out in the third world."[1] By the heightened attention paid the United Nations, the administration also consciously expressed the growing importance of the third world in the multilateral arena. Among the benefits to be derived from the shift was the projection that life would become easier for the United States in the UN. As Stanley Hoffmann later put it, to the vision of detente Carter added "the dream of convergence between United States deed and third world aspirations." President Carter told the audience at the Notre Dame commencement on May 22, 1977, that policy "must respond to the new reality of a politically awakening world." National security adviser Zbigniew Brzezinski echoed this sentiment two years later. Realism demanded a policy responsive to the "global pattern of redistribution of power" and to the assertive demands of the developing world for "global political and economic arrangements that reflect these new realities."[2]

Until its last year in office, the Carter administration made a declared and a determined effort to come to grips with these "new realities." It was accepted as axiomatic that the prime concerns of the third world were to bring political independence to colonial vestiges in Africa, Asia, and the Caribbean and to establish a new international economic order (NIEO). The principles and the programmatic objectives of the new order were codified in certain basic documents, mainly the declaration and the program of action adopted at the Sixth Special Session of the General Assembly in May 1974 and the Charter of Economic Rights and Duties approved by the 29th General Assembly that fall.[3] Tactically NIEO was to be achieved through a global north-south "dialogue" within the UN system and other multilateral arenas. The essence of the third-world agenda—to which the West, it was argued, had to be responsive if policy was to be in line with the new realities—was a dual transfer of power: of resources through massive development aid and supporting programs (trade preferences, technology transfer, debt relief) and of decision-making power in international economic institutions.

An adequate response made by the West, as spelled out most recently by the Brandt Commission,[4] must aim at overcoming global inequities by increasing development aid, policing multinational corporations, technology transfers on liberal terms, the "rescheduling" of debt, eliminating legal restraints on the expropriation of foreign direct investment, commodity stabilization, and changing trade rules to give preferential and nonreciprocal access to markets.

The Ford administration had not been totally insensitive to these claims. In the General Assembly in September 1975,

Kissinger and Moynihan dramatically unveiled a program of cooperative action on commodity prices, aid, trade, energy, food, and monetary stability. Certain institutional changes were proposed, notably, a facility within the International Monetary Fund (IMF) to stabilize export earnings, an international energy institute, a world grain reserve, and what later became the International Fund for Agricultural Development (IFAD). This program was adopted in the consensus resolution on development and international economic cooperation (Resolution 3262: S-VII, September 16, 1975). But the Carter administration questioned the adequacy of this response and criticized its predecessor for failing to follow through.

Above all, a new philosophy emerged based on the principle (although often uneasily expressed in policy) of the justice of the south's demand for revolutionary change in the structure of the international system in order to alter the balance of decision-making power in its favor, particularly in multilateral lending institutions such as the World Bank and the IMF. Some were also sympathetic to the south's demand for overcoming the constraints of domestic politics in donor states through "automaticity," that is, empowering international institutions to collect revenues through international taxes to finance third-world development and exports. In some of the established specialized agencies of the UN system, such as WHO, the third world used its voting advantage to assess members for programmatic activities—notably, technical assistance—to an extent that appeared to many to violate unwritten restraints in the political compact under which these agencies had been set up.

Without swallowing whole either doctrine or program in the formulation of U.S. policy during the seventies, certain presuppositions were held about third-world motivations and priorities in the north-south relationship. In the first place, the drive to achieve the new economic order (NIEO) was

considered the core of the south's agenda. This certainly was
and largely remains the conventional view around the UN.*
[*Thus when it was revealed that *Le Monde* and other pres-
tigious newspapers had received hidden subsidies from the
UN for supplements giving the UN's official view on aid to
the third world, its director, Jacques Fauvet, justified the
practice on the ground that "it is desirable to support the
north-south dialogue." In one article Bhaskar P. Menon of
the UN's Division of Social and Economic Information de-
plored the fact that NIEO had not been enacted. He had not
bothered to explain its elements but simply characterized it
as the "decolonization of the world economy." B. Rossiter,
"UN Gave $432,000 to the Foreign Press to Publish Its
Views," *The New York Times,* May 28, 1981.] Unless they
were satisfied on this score, it was assumed that fruitful diplomatic relations with individual third-world nations could
not be expected. Although bilateral issues were naturally of
concern—particularly because such issues affected their security—it was presumed that in third-world chancelleries particular national interests and goals were subordinated to the
overall aims of the south.

Moreover, it came to be accepted that the structure of
the relationship with the third world differed materially from
the classical diplomatic pattern in which bilateral modes prevailed. The central axis of the relationship, it was presumed,
revolved around a process of "global bargaining" in the multilateral arena designed to alter norms governing trade and aid
in order to shift economic power and benefits to the LDCs
and to transfer decision-making power in their favor in established institutions such as the IMF and emerging ones such as
the International Seabed Authority.

From the presumption that in the policy calculations of
third-world leaders collective and coalition interests outweighed national goals, American policy strategists assumed
that moderates could not be readily coopted or diverted by

appeals to their particularist national interests. The converse was accepted: If the political and the economic agendas of the south were accommodated, particularly on systemic issues of "structural reform," third-world leaders would accommodate the United States on bilateral concerns. Although no explicit equation was drawn, the implication was that if the West made concessions on, say, Namibia or the makeup and the distribution of power in the council of the International Seabed Authority, Brazil and India would be more tractable about nuclear programs, Mexico about oil, migrants, and fishing rights, and Algeria about the price of liquid gas. It need hardly be pointed out that none of this was ever proved when put to the test. Mexico's radical posture in multilateral encounters—for example, at the New Delhi meeting of UNIDO in February 1980—in no way influenced bilateral negotiations with the United States.

Also affecting policy toward the third world during the 1970s was a broader world view—that complex interdependence had ushered in an era in which the classical power balance was giving way to a mutually-perceived need for cooperative action on global issues. From this perspective, the new era heralded the transcendence of economics over power politics. And it was presumed that third-world leaders shared the vision of the planetary bargain. Creative diplomacy in the era of interdependence called for a new structure of international norms and institutions ranging from generalized codes of technology transfer to an international regime to govern the exploitation of seabed minerals. The assumption was that transnational or global issues, such as the control of nuclear energy and the protection of the environment, were as organic to the north-south agenda as, say, development financing and commodity stabilization.

What confounded policy planners in the West, however, were indications that third-world leaders did not necessarily share their world outlook or their sense of priorities about

such issues as the environment, terrorism, or nuclear proliferation. More startling was the realization that growing interdependence had been accompanied by greater, not less, concern in the developing world with power relations and reliance on military force.[5] In a remarkable replay of Europe in
the time of nation formation, the paramount concern of
third-world leaders was the protection and the integrity of
the state and its governing class against threats from its neighbors and subversion within. Nevertheless, the myth prevailed
that this concern was an aberration. If only the third-world
could be helped in its drive to eradicate the last remnants of
colonialism and to achieve economic growth and status, its
leaders would soon cease wasting their substance on arms and
cooperate in trying to fulfill the agenda of the new world
order.

In sum, downgrading security concerns in a world of
complex interdependence and focusing on the collective concerns of the third world in the north-south relationship added
up to a presupposition in official circles of the West that the
road to productive policy toward the developing countries
and regions lay in being responsive to the agenda of the south
as a whole.

Misgivings Emerge

A certain uneasiness emerged almost immediately. The
Carter administration had difficulty in coping with the NIEO
construct and the NIEO agenda. At the ECOSOC meeting in
the summer of 1977, Andrew Young, U.S. representative to
the UN, endorsed the "concept" of NIEO but cautioned that
"no single blueprint" could solve the problems. Young reiter-
ated that the United States continued to have serious reserva-
tions about the 1974 resolutions defining NIEO that had led
to U.S. abstentions. The United States "will not be able to

join [in supporting the concept] when we are asked to endorse or implement the provisions of the Sixth Special Session resolutions as a whole. . . ."[6]

American policymakers and thinkers were bothered by the apparently reductionist fallacy implicit in trying to deal with the complexity of relations with third-world countries through the generalized and idealized goals of the north-south dialogue. Could the specific concerns of particular nations be satisfied through a wholesale policy toward the third world and conducted most productively through multilateral negotiations in multilateral institutions? One might concede that the salience of certain north-south issues in the UN was unlikely to fade. Achieving self-determination for the few remaining colonial dependencies, redefining human rights to ascribe primacy to racial equality, or increasing aid to the least-developed countries evoked unshakable solidarity. Did it logically follow that America's important business with third-world countries over the range of bilateral dealings would be or should be centered in the UN arena and on "collective" north-south issues?

Actually the erosion of the doctrine of the centrality of the dialogue and its corollaries about NIEO as defining the authentic agenda and "interdependence" as transforming the classical pattern of diplomacy could be discerned toward the end of the Carter administration. Although no open abandonment ever took place and in many quarters the doctrine of the dialogue reigns supreme (reinforced by the findings in the Brandt report), a marked shift in the premises of policy toward the third world became perceptible in 1980.

1980: A Watershed

The broad geopolitical concerns that impelled Washington to shift gears must be understood, for they are still operative and help explain why the Reagan policy strikes a responsive chord. Partly the change in direction and second thoughts about the primacy ascribed to the relationship with the third world resulted from the perception that America's world position was declining and the imperative to restore the military balance. Access to the oil fields of the Persian Gulf was elevated to the top rung of American priorities. A search for reliable strategic partners in the third world followed the shock of the fall of the shah and the obsessively anti-American direction taken by the Khomeini revolution. Disenchantment with detente followed the Soviet invasion of Afghanistan in December 1979. At the beginning of the New Year (1980), President Carter confessed to Frank Reynolds of ABC-TV News that "my opinion of the Russians has changed most drastically." The entire tone of the interview contrasted embarrassingly with the declaration three years earlier that "we are now free of that inordinate fear of communism which once led us to embrace any dictator who joined us in that fear."[7]

American policymakers began to view relations with third-world countries from an altered focus. The north-south agenda could no longer be the centerpiece of relations with third-world countries. Enlisting their support in the UN for measures to counter the Soviets in Afghanistan or at least legitimize those taken by the United States against Iran and against Soviet action in Afghanistan became a prime objective. Some pointed to third-world support on these issues in the UN as evidence of a payoff for a more forthcoming posture on the part of the United States on southern Africa and in the dialogue. Perhaps. But the main conclusion drawn was that in the larger scheme of things, the policy of accommodating the south on the agenda of NIEO had to be subordinated (at least for a time) to the urgent need to build up American military power and enlist security partners selectively among third-world countries to help counter the Soviet threat.

Another reason for subordinating the north-south relationship to other foreign policy goals during the last year of the Carter era was the lowering of domestic tolerance for foreign aid. When the Reagan administration came to power, some observers remarked about a "new reorientation that places a heavier emphasis upon making foreign assistance a tool of U.S. foreign policy," stressing bilateral security assistance.[8] But the shift to retrenchment had already begun toward the end of the Carter era. At the outset of his administration, President Carter promised expansion of aid "to insure sustained American assistance as the process of global economic development continues." Beyond this, he testified to the belief that "developing countries must acquire fuller participation in the global economic decision-making process." Although the rhetoric was impressive, the record was less so. By the time President Carter addressed the World Bank Group at the end of September 1980, the administration's vocal support for the sixth replenishment of the International Development Association (IDA) and for an energy development affiliate at the World Bank was accompanied by a note of caution about the need for a "strong antiinflation program of fiscal and monetary restraint . . . to revitalize our own industrial base and to accelerate productivity growth."[9] A major global policy announced early in the Carter administration was thus thrown overboard. Despite cries of anguish and warnings that such retrenchment would discredit America in the United Nations and risked global collapse as well, it became more and more difficult to build a policy consensus for foreign aid, particularly that dispensed multilaterally.

Not only in the United States but more generally in the OECD world, there arose the perception that Western economies no longer set the pace for the world economy, that Europe was in economic distress, and that a relentless shift of wealth and industry to former colonial areas was taking place. French Premier Raymond Barre warned that the West must brace itself for a decade of sluggish growth and high unemployment while it adapted to the new realities of costly energy and the migration of industry to the south.[10] Whether this Cassandralike forecast would prove accurate was politically less significant than the dampening effect it had on the declared policy of increasing foreign aid and making economic concessions to the third world.

As domestic concerns rise in importance, the problem of allocation at home is aggravated, and overseas generosity becomes less politically affordable. Equity decisions that appear to sacrifice the interests of domestic constituencies for foreigners are hardest to justify at such a time.[11] A certain Gresham's law operates in which short-term concerns drive out expectations of long-term benefits for stability and world order that might result from world redistributive politics. One result was to highlight the value of particular countries as strategic partners as against a more general concern with maintaining world order in a world of complex interdependence.[12] As I note below, this development was aggravated by the perception that the dialogue was moribund anyway and that multilateral programs had marginal uses in the U.S. quest for allies.

By the end of 1979, if not earlier, a dual effect on the north-south relationship was apparent. The United States became more inclined toward protectionist measures and receptive to a renewed, post-Vietnam readiness for unilateral action if necessary to maintain a strategic presence in areas of vital interest. Relations with third-world countries shifted toward the pursuit of specific, "possession" goals rather than systematic or "milieu" goals, following the distinction once made by Arnold Wolfers.[13]

Disenchantment with Nonalignment

Fueling growing pessimism about possibilities of entering into a healthier relationship with the third world was the growing evidence that the south's professed nonalignment was suspect as it came under Cuban and other radical sway. Despite the new "understanding" of U.S. policies that some U.S. representatives at the UN discovered among third-world moderates, the conviction that the nonaligned movement meeting at Havana in the fall of 1979 had become captive to Moscow suggested to many observers that the policy of accommodation had not perceptibly changed the ideological tilt of the Group of 77. The message at Havana was clear. Western "imperialism" was to blame for the third-world's perilous economic state and for remnants of world colonialism; Soviet aid to liberation movements proved Soviet benign intentions when it intervened in Angola or Ethiopia. (Although some claimed that the United States was winning points at the UN because of its softer policy, as manifested by the defeat of Cuba's bid for a Security Council seat in the wake of the Soviet invasion of Afghanistan in December 1979, on most issues that really mattered to the United States, such as support for the Camp David process and budgetary restraint, the voting scores showed no appreciable gain as compared to General Assembly sessions in the pre-Carter period.)

For many the implication of Havana for U.S. policy toward the third world was that a posture accommodating the third-world agenda on southern Africa or NIEO did not help win hearts and minds. As Fouad Ajami observed, Havana demonstrated that true nonalignment had been corrupted, and many third worlders, while blaming the West, were actually suffering from self-inflicted wounds.[14] The gap between utterances of rulers at world conferences and the daily realities of their societies demonstrated that declaratory policies at international conferences were hardly likely to solve their problems and thus did not provide a sound basis for the formulation of U.S. policy.

Disenchantment with the Dialogue

Disenchantment with the process of the dialogue was growing. The premises on which it had been initiated were called into question.[15] Although certain negotiations, notably, on the law of the seas, showed possibilities of realistic compromise on matters of concern to the third world, the overall NIEO agenda as it unfolded in global conferences continued to be dominated and politicized by the radical leadership. A conspicuous encounter that soured many and presaged the failure of the "global negotiations" in the fall of 1980 took place at the third conference of the UN Industrial Development Organization (UNIDO III) in New Delhi early that year.[16] A handful of radicals (led by Mexico, Iran, Algeria, and Cuba) steamrollered through a patently non-negotiable proposal, conceived at the Havana nonaligned conference the previous September, to create a separate global fund of 300 billion dollars of "new and additional" money to help build up the industrial sector in third-world countries. The United States, backed by other Western delegations, opposed it as politically unrealistic, unnecessary, duplicative of the work of the World Bank, and totally unacceptable in its administrative structure, for the fund would have been under the control of the recipients and not subject to established practices of accountability. Many observers at New Delhi were convinced that in rejecting any realistic compromise, the radical leaders were deliberately pursuing a confrontationist strategy to solidify the G-77 behind the militant policy to be advocated at the forthcoming "global negotiations" session in September. The experience at UNIDO III convinced many in the administration that the dialogue had become a power game played between the first and the third worlds (with the second nervously cheering the third world from the sidelines). The stakes were the control of world institutions through "restructuring" so that the G-77 could dictate new rules of trading and the massive and automatic transfer of resources.

NIEO Under Challenge

Both the philosophy and the programmatic premises of NIEO came under increasing challenge in the West on grounds of political feasibility and economic good sense. The premise that external factors were mainly to blame for the plight of the LDCs or that their problems were amenable to the remedies offered in the dialogue was judged as only marginally plausible. It was unrealistic to base policy toward the third world on a generalized approach in multinational forums, for this did not address the intrinsic and particularistic causes of poverty. As Lincoln Gordon pointed out,[17] many of the components of NIEO were either of dubious relevance to development or so contrary to the north's interest that they were considered unnegotiable. For example, the indexing of commodity prices would freeze relative prices against changes in the supply of technology or the structure of demand; the generalized rescheduling of debt would impair the credit of middle-income LDCs; the need for technology could not be met by a generalized code of technology transfer.

The marginal relevance of what transpired in multinational forums on the realities of life in third-world societies could not escape notice. It became increasingly clear, as Rothstein noted, that the view from third-world capitals had always differed from the policies espoused by G-77 spokesmen in Geneva and New York. Officials in LDC capitals knew

little about the substance of the negotiation and perceived
the dialogue as essentially symbolic—a search for status and a
place in the sun—from which few tangible benefits for their
countries could be expected.

Nor could NIEO—and the Western response to it—
usefully serve as the organizing principle of U.S. policy toward a third world divided over what it wanted out of the
"new order." Did the road to the new order lie in increasing
self-reliance or in a strategy of collective bargaining with the
West (mixed with confrontation)? How was the West to respond to generalized demands for economic and social equity? Whose equity was to be served as the gap between elites
and tradition-bound masses widened?

But the main difficulty with basing policy on an overall
accommodation with the NIEO demands voiced by the south
is the great diversity among third-world countries[18] that im-
pels them to pursue sometimes parallel, sometimes conflicting national interests. Thus governments in the third world
differ markedly in their policies toward multinational firms.
Some host governments collaborate to achieve tangible economic goals, such as maintaining employment. It is the
south's own leaders who in other contexts plead with the
West to recognize economic and political diversity and criticize undifferentiated policies. Thus Mexican officials fault as
woefully inappropriate a single hemispheric policy "toward
such a heterogeneous region," for, noted a Mexican official,
Washington should realize that "it cannot even have the same
policy toward, say, Mexico and Brazil because they are so
different."[19]

The Breakdown of Global Negotiations

Whatever the cause, the north-south dialogue was
perceived as having reached an impasse by the end of 1980.

Especially did it become clear that the main thrust of the south's politics—structural change in the decision-making power in international institutions—offered little room for bargaining, for it posed a threat to the integrity of such institutions as the World Bank in which Western influence was predominant.

This is not to say that on the plane of declaratory policy, of elucidating overall third-world aspirations, the global approach was written off. Even the Reagan administration felt it necessary to pay obeisance to a policy that would "offer hope and aid to the developing countries in their aspirations for a peaceful and prosperous future" but with due attention to the priorities of restraining the Soviets and reinvigorating the Western alliance.[20]

The gulf between the West and the south was made dramatically clear when the UN Special Economic Session of the General Assembly to prepare for "global negotiations" in September 1980 ended in disarray and attempts to reach a compromise at the 35th General Assembly that fall proved fruitless. On the surface, the battle was over the forum and the procedures for bargaining. The fundamental issue was "which institutions and nations will have ultimate control over the process of reforming the world economic order."[21] The Group of 77 wanted to centralize the negotiation in a "central conference" linked to the General Assembly with authority over existing specialized agencies, the World Bank, and the IMF in policymaking and the allocation of funds. The United States, joined by Britain and West Germany (the rest of the OECD acquiesced but was fearful of taking an openly antisouth position), insisted that the power of decision must stay with existing institutions in which industrialized nations have the dominant voice. The G-77 model would have meant, for example, that in theory the "central conference" could direct the IMF to distribute reserve assets and undermine the weighted voting system. The integrity of the existing system and of special institutions such as the International Monetary Fund was at risk. The G-77 proposal was viewed as a threat to the integrity of the specialized agencies and the structure of the international system.

Although in much of the press the United States was depicted as a spoiler,[22] the confrontation over global negotiations exposed a fact that many refused to face—the entire process was stalemated. As an Arab oil-producing representative remarked to Bernard Rossiter of the New York Times (December 2, 1980), the gap could not be bridged in six months or six years, for the West, led by the United States, could hardly negotiate on the basis of a revolutionary shift of power in the international system.

The Reagan administration thus rode into office after the curve of the north-south relationship had shifted. The new direction was compatible with its own predispositions. It remained only to accelerate the momentum. Although the rhetoric and the mind set of the new administration were quite different from its predecessor's, in the main the policy line it adopted toward the third world was to accelerate and adapt shifts already underway. The point should not be overdone: On Namibia and the Law of the Seas, for example, President Reagan and Secretary of State Haig moved to reshape policy altogether. But in essential aspects the new administration speeded up a course already set in the last year of the Carter era.

It was not only that the Reagan administration considered preoccupation with the north-south relationship as diverting attention from the reality and the persistence of the East-West conflict in which the third world was assigned a derivative role as "strategic partners." Beyond this the historical premises on which the 1970s policy had been based (articulated most recently in the Brandt report) had come under serious challenge as less and less in consonance with the realities of the north-south relationship and of U.S. interests. The

Reagan administration was ready to view the collapse of the "global negotiations" exercise as indicative of the bankruptcy of the policy of the 1970s.

True, out of deference to Western allies and to the Mexican host, President Reagan agreed to participate in the summit meeting at Cancun, Mexico, in October 1981, which was aimed at reviving the north-south dialogue. The letter of invitation to Cancun stresses that a key objective of the summit is to reach a meeting of minds on the "global negotiations" and to reactivate the commitment to progress in north-south relations. But the occasion is more likely to mark the end of the effort at grand multilateral diplomacy on north-south issues and usher in an era of more differentiated economic diplomacy.

Economic and humanitarian aid and the vision of a cooperative north-south relationship command an important constituency in Europe. Cooperation with the third world on development is supported across party lines. There is wide awareness of European dependence on third-world sources of raw materials and energy. Some European leaders are convinced that the West must overcome the impression of waning interest in the dialogue and believe that LDC leaders are themselves becoming more pragmatic about their economic needs and expectations. The Brandt Commission report enjoys considerable popularity because it expresses underlying European attitudes toward the third world. The election of Mitterand and the perception that the Eurosocialists have gotten a new lease on life have further fed the impulse to devise a policy of accommodating the developing world. Although governments are not likely to commit themselves to generous new resource transfers, which the African, Caribbean, and Pacific states discovered to their dismay during the renegotiation of the Lomé Convention, the appearance of a positive attitude toward the third world is good politics in Europe. The Reagan administration thus considered it prudent to join in what was in essence a European initiative to declare sympathy for the south and re-affirm the Brandt policy.

The Trend Toward Differentiation

If anything, however, in terms of practical results for the developing world, the summit at Cancun is likely to underscore the inevitability of a differential policy toward the third world. In a world of economic distress that has given substance to the perception that the tide of economic progress is no longer running in Europe, the pressure for bilateral deals and "special relationships" may be irresistible.

Actually certain groups of LDCs have always been treated selectively. The European Economic Community (EEC) has special trade and aid relationships with 58 African, Caribbean, and Pacific countries, which are codified in the Lomé Convention. Also, under the EEC's "Community Association Policy," preferential access to markets is given to "associates" within the general system of preferences.

Another path to differentiation is the revival of moves toward regional "collective self-reliance" partly out of frustration with the north-south dialogue. Thus without in any way absolving industrialized countries of responsibility for advancing toward NIEO, the regional development plan adopted at the Montevideo meeting of the Economic Commission for Latin America emphasized internal and regional measures for cooperation in trade and investment.[23]

Another regional pattern is emerging in the Reagan administration's plan for directing resources to third-world areas to achieve specific goals in specific areas. The first of these plans was unveiled in May 1981 in a long-term trade and aid plan for economic, political, and military assistance to the Caribbean and Central America into which the richer countries of the hemisphere, such as Mexico and Venezuela, would be drawn. Bilateral trade, aid, and investment agreements with specific developing countries would be coordinated into a mini-Marshall Plan that could then serve as a model for regional and cooperative programs in other areas of the third world.[24]

The U.S. Strategic and Economic Stake in the Third World

America's strategic and economic stake in the third world, often cited in support of a policy of "cooperative efforts" and the need to sustain the dialogue, actually underscores the wisdom of a differential policy.

Regional conflicts and structural political instability are endemic in the third world, which, since 1945, has been the scene of repeated eruptions, regional wars, social, tribal, and religious struggles inside nations, coups d'etats, assassination, and genocide. In the last decade alone a few that come to mind are the breakup of Pakistan; the Yom Kippur War; communal strife in Cyprus; the sanguinary dictatorship in Uganda that was overthrown by the Tanzanian invasion; the civil war in Chad "settled" by Libyan intervention that could provoke resistance from Chad's neighbors; the civil war in Nicaragua and its functional equivalent in El Salvador; social turmoil in the Caribbean; revolution in Ethiopia and a frontier war with Somalia that precipitated intervention by Soviet-supported Cuban troops; war in Angola and on the borders of Namibia; civil strife in Lebanon; and a full-scale war between Iraq and Iran.[25]

For U.S. policymakers it would appear that two cardinal lessons can be derived from this recital. One is that an American response to the threat that local conflict poses to American interests and world stability cannot usefully be defined in terms of an overall accommodation with the third world. Being responsive to the third world's demand for economic and social justice in the aggregate will not promote peace if for no reason other than that the sides in the conflict are third-world nations.

The other lesson is that the root causes of and the issues associated with those conflicts are essentially local, and U.S. influence can usually be exerted only if the United States is willing to become directly involved. Only by sustained support for one side in the Ethiopia-Somali conflict, for example, could we hope to exert decisive influence on the outcome, as Moscow has amply proved. As American national interests in third-world areas are redefined in the 1980s, the "stake" in local conflicts must be measured by judging how outcomes would affect U.S. interests in particular cases and by an assessment of America's capacity to intervene directly or indirectly.

Nor are such conflicts necessarily amenable to UN intervention or other kinds of "preventive diplomacy" (such as "regional solutions") so often suggested. UN peacekeeping has been productive, as Professor Finger notes, in a few cases in suppressing or containing postcolonial disputes in the Middle East and Africa. UN peacekeepers helped insulate the Congo (Zaire) from great power confrontation and helped restore order in Cyprus and Lebanon. The UN was also called in by third-world champions as a device to halt the fighting when their friends or allies were losing, as in the four Arab-Israeli wars.

But the curious and significant thing is that with few exceptions, neither UN nor regional peacekeepers have been enlisted in local conflicts between card-carrying nonaligned states, such as Ethiopia and Somalia or Iran and Iraq, or in internal conflicts in third-world states. Although the UN role is often thought to be particularly constructive in settling such disputes, the record indicates that nonaligned states are not eager to involve the UN (or regional organizations) in their quarrels. Since the installation of UNMOGIP in 1949 to police the Kashmir line, there has been no pure case of a conflict of nonaligned country versus nonaligned country in which an international peacekeeping mechanism was productively invoked. To some the failure of the UN to become involved in the Iran-Iraq quarrel exposed the UN's "dirty little secret," that it averts its gaze from disputes between third-world countries.[26] Similarly, the hollowness of pleas for "regional solutions" was exposed in the recent Chad conflict. An effort to enlist OAU peacekeepers to pacify Chad was rapidly aborted when it became clear that despite OAU resolutions, neither a political consensus nor the requisite institutional resources could be mobilized to counter the Libyan intervention in December 1980.

Any decision concerning U.S. involvement cannot be based on a blanket preference for nonintervention or the vain hope of supporting regional action but on a case-by-case determination of American interest and capacity to effect an outcome that is important to our strategic, political, or economic aims.

Similarly, the argument that America has an economic stake in the third world needs to be examined differentially. Our exports to third-world countries have indeed tripled in the last five years; they supply many vital raw materials; and investment by multinationals is expanding.* [*Peter Drucker observed in 1974 that even in the aggregate, for the typical multinational engaged in manufacturing, distribution, or finance, "developing countries are important neither as markets nor as producers of profits." See "Multinationals and Developing Countries: Myths and Realities," *Foreign Affairs,* October 1974.] Aggregate figures, however, conceal the reality that the south as a whole, especially the Nigers and the Bangladeshes, is not becoming a significant trading partner. Instead, trade with non-OPEC developing countries has been highly concentrated among a small number of such countries. World Bank figures for 1977, quoted by Rothstein, show that seven countries—many not classical third worlders—accounted for two-thirds of U.S. exports and took 58 percent of imports: Mexico, Korea, Brazil, Taiwan, Hong Kong, Israel, and Malaysia.

Figures compiled by the International Monetary Fund on the direction of U.S. trade in 1979 show a similar pattern of concentration. Non-OPEC developing countries of the third world (i.e., excluding South Africa and the less-developed European countries) in the aggregate took 27 percent of U.S. exports ($50 billion out of $182 billion), but two-thirds was accounted for by about a dozen advanced LDCs in Asia and Latin America: Mexico, Korea, Brazil, Singapore, Hong Kong, Argentina, Israel, the Philippines, Egypt, Colombia, India, Thailand, and Malaysia.[27]

Again, the significant lesson for U.S. policy is not the conventional and superficial insight that the "third world" is important to the United States but two propositions on the basis of which policy for the 1980s must be reformulated: Some third worlders are more important than others—an importance manifested in a variety of ways; the real challenge to U.S. foreign policy is to distinguish areas and issues in which the operative relationship is with the south or the nonaligned or LDCs as a unity from those in which the operative relationship requires differentiation and disaggregation of policy and treatment.

Disaggregation and a Differential Policy

Given the pause in the dialogue and the reassessment of U.S. interests that every new administration undertakes as a matter of course, the new direction of policy should point toward disaggregation of the third-world coalition and a differentiation of interests.* [*The Reagan administration deliberately adopted a policy of "disaggregation" which Jeane J. Kirkpatrick, as the newly-appointed U.S. representative to the UN, defined as "breaking down a term like the third world" into its component nations. (See her speech to B'nai B'rith in New York, January 7, 1981.)] It should not be inferred that a split in the Group of 77 should be sought or would be desirable in itself. In fact disunity may be destablizing; unity provides discipline and order in bargaining. But realism suggests that the coalition will hold together mainly on a few collective issues and on symbolic matters and that its solidarity will not be readily transferrable to negotiation on most tangible matters of specific interest. In some cases the calculation of self-interest or the strength of ideology may sustain G-77 unity because the poor LDCs have no place else to go, because the Group of 77 provides an arena for asserting the leadership of the more advanced countries, or because they see opportunities in LDC markets or seek political help in achieving their national goals. But the main lesson of the impasse is that diversity will impel the more advanced third-world countries to negotiate on specific matters more directly, that is, not through the coalition, and to isolate their national diplomacy from the agenda and the politics of the coalition.

The outlines of a differential policy are emerging. It is made up of two key features. First, breaking down the notion of political geography so that policy objectives and diplomatic strategy can be adapted to the interests and the outlooks of nations or special groupings. A corollary is predicated on the assumption that as far as the more advanced LDCs are concerned, the balance of diplomacy will tilt toward bilateral contacts and will often require "special relationships." The inclination will be to isolate bilateral dealings from the regional and global agenda.* [*During President Lopez Portillo's visit to Washington in June 1981, a

Mexican official stressed to reporters that it was important to "isolate" issues involving the two countries, such as trade, migration, and fishing rights, from regional and global issues.] Second, a policy of differentiation requires defining or redefining the "collective" interests that still agitate the third world and distinguishing the authentic north-south agenda from transnational issues more properly termed *global* because they concern wider world interest.

Disaggregating Political Geography

Even those who accept the doctrine of differentiation have paid little attention to developing criteria that would enable policymakers to draw distinctions among the advanced or semideveloped LDCs that deserve special policy attention because they affect America's strategic, historical, or economic interests. Traditional U.S. aid policy has favored military and ideological allies, but aid has also been given for moral or prudential reasons. What new criteria may guide policy in the 1980s? The development of such criteria will reflect the perception of the place of third-world countries in the world and America's changing strategic and economic needs. Rothstein[28] has identified approximately thirty-two crucial countries based on economic, political, and strategic criteria. Adapting his list (by adding Senegal and Israel), one arrives at the following array of crucial countries. In Latin America: Mexico, Brazil, Argentina, Venezuela, Chile, Peru, Bolivia, perhaps Colombia, perhaps even Jamaica; and defining crucial as the ability to command America's strategic attention, Cuba. In Black Africa, Nigeria is the primary crucial state, followed by Kenya, the Ivory Coast, perhaps Zaire (resources and potential economic performance), Zambia, Ghana (in the hope of a renaissance in the 1980s), and Senegal and Tanzania (presumed political influence on the continent). Zimbabwe is a candidate for the list if Mugabe can sustain his charisma and political skills. In North Africa, Algeria, Morocco, and Libya and in the Middle East, Egypt, Israel, Saudi Arabia, Iraq, and probably Iran belong on any list of influential states in the 1980s. In South and East Asia, the list would include India, Indonesia, Malaysia, the Philippines, Pakistan, South Korea, and Taiwan.

Another approach, informally discussed in Washington during the past few years, would rank countries in terms of their capacity for exerting a "significant impact" on the United States. "Resource" power and the propensity toward and the capability of destabilizing the international environment in a manner that would affect U.S. interests would be weighed. One variant measures national capabilities (nuclear program, defense spending, oil production, GNP, population, strategic location, critical mineral exports, and foreign exchange reserves); the nature and the extent of relations with the United States (troops stationed, military students, bilateral treaties, U.S. direct investment, economic and military aid and sales, U.S. exports, debt to the U.S. private sector, size of the U.S. diplomatic mission, proximity to the United States, tourism both ways); and its obverse—the nature and the extent of relations with the Soviet Union (technicians, economic aid, Soviet bloc troops, military sales, size of mission, and so on). The scores of states rated of "significant impact" would reflect a combination of weighted factors applied to these three categories.

Omitting China, Israel, and South Africa from the calculation, some two dozen LDCs would appear to exert significant impact on U.S. interests: Mexico, Brazil, India, Saudi Arabia, South Korea, Iran, Venezuela, Egypt, the Philippines, Indonesia, Libya, Morocco, Thailand, Argentina, Colombia, Iraq, Peru, Taiwan, Panama, Afghanistan, Pakistan, Jordan, Algeria, Nigeria, and Syria (as of the end of 1980).

Whether these criteria make sense from the standpoint of policy or are realistically weighted, some formula for differentiation among third-world countries in terms of their significance for U.S. policy interests needs to be developed for the 1980s. Unlike the criteria used in the fifties and the sixties, which favored ideological friends and allies, distinctions will need to be based on an assessment of the capacity of third-world countries or groups to affect U.S. strategic and resource interests.

At the very least, a sensible policy for the 1980s would distinguish, both in substance and in institutional mechanisms, from the rest of the third world,[29] the three dozen or so countries whose actions can exert significant impact on American interests.

Distinguishing North-South from Global Issues

Difficult tasks for the 1980s will involve determining what parts of the classical collective agenda will continue to influence the politics of the third-world coalition and learning how to distinguish "global issues" from "north-south" issues. Confusion about the north-south relationship has been caused by the conventional tendency to consider all multinational issues—whether development or seabeds or telecommunications or population or the environment— "global" matters or issues involving "interdependence" and by a strange logic to ascribe them on the north-south agenda.

There are two sets of collective issues. One is the "global" so designated because this set affects the wider "world interest." These matters range from adjusting the international monetary system to allocating radio frequencies to assuring the world's public services of air safety and the control of epidemics. Many of the newer interdependence functions, such as environmental protection, engage multilateral processes in the same way as do the operations of the functional programs of such old-line specialized agencies as the World Health Organization and the International Telecommunications Union.

Global issues have filled the agenda of the UN system as the generation of technology has created political and legal problems. These issues, not north-south issues, as is often imagined, account for the fact that approximately two-thirds of American diplomatic effort goes into multilateral diplomacy. The Outer Space Committee, for example, is concerned with limiting the dissemination of primary data sensed by satellites without the permission of the targeted country. The World Administrative Radio Conference (WARC) in 1979 revised the table of radio-frequency allocations and adapted regulatory procedures for international notification of frequency assignments and satellite orbit locations. IAEA has formulated rules for and managed the safeguards system against the diversion of nuclear materials to weapons use.[30] In the 1970s world conferences (most initiated through the General Assembly) projected onto the world scene a set of global issues arising from the impact of new technologies.

It is problematic, however, whether most transnational issues should be addressed as part of the north-south agenda. Not only the developing nations are concerned about their proprietary interest in geological data collected by earth resource satellites and in protecting their airwaves from "culturally-intrusive" transmissions via direct broadcast satellites. The desire to reserve radio frequency bands and seabed mining sites from being grabbed by technologically-advanced nations may be of special concern to the less developed, and they have been most vocal about a perceived threat. But they are not alone, and no hard and fast line can be drawn between the interests of the "developing" south and the rest of the world, much of which is concerned about the technological head start enjoyed by a few. In any event such "global" issues by and large transcend the north-south relationship and need to be separated from the north-south agenda.

Actually such global issues raise other concerns about the trend of the Reagan administration's policy not toward the third world but toward the uses of multilateral norms and institutions in advancing U.S. purpose in the world. A negative attitude toward the World Bank and other multilateral lending institutions is a case in point. Beyond this, certain multilateral issues need to be addressed in the context of America's broader moral and political purposes. Take, for example, human rights and the law of the seas. All postwar administrations subscribed to the value of "internationally recognized human rights" even before national sanctions were legislated against countries with records of gross violations. There is no gainsaying Finger's conclusion that "the moral position of the U.S. and the practical realities of world politics require an active position on human rights in the UN and the world." Any retreat on this score would not only betray our tradition but weaken a vital source of America's strength in the world.

Similarly, reneging, as the administration appears to be doing, on the bargain negotiated over the past six years on the draft treaty governing use of the seas and their resources could damage America's position in the world. In the package bargain, the interests of coastal states in the economic zone, of maritime and military powers in the broadest definition of freedom of navigation on the seas and through international straits, of technologically-advanced nations to unfettered access to mining of seabed minerals, and of developing nations to sharing in exploitation and revenues were delicately balanced. The perception that the administration means to block early completion of the treaty could seriously damage the U.S. position in the world. Whether this is a north-south issue is immaterial; the United States cannot renege on the bargain without sustaining serious costs in relations with allies as well as the third world.[31]

What Is Left of North-South Issues?

The other set of "collective" issues remains relevant to the north-south relationship. It consists of the drive for self-determination and racial equality and what is left of the development agenda. With the independence of Zimbabwe—and leaving aside the Palestine dispute as a residue of the postwar redrawing of the political map of territory relinquished by former colonial powers—Namibia remains the sole significant case on the postcolonial agenda. How to weigh the moral, strategic, and economic interests in Black Africa against America's "vital interest in the survival of South Africa as a Western ally" is likely to remain at the center of the Reagan administration's African policy. As of the end of May 1981, the administration had concluded that although Washington and Pretoria may continue to differ on apartheid, the United States "can cooperate with a society undergoing constructive change." Bilateral ties, it was argued, can be improved in exchange for cooperation in countering Soviet influence in southern Africa and in achieving a stable settlement over Namibia by amending the UN plan to accord constitutional guarantees to the white minority.[32]

There are limits to deviating from the negotiated plan. Sooner or later the Reagan administration will find that it cannot come to terms with the problem of stability in southern Africa except through a settlement that does not depart in any substantial respect from the Western-negotiated plan for UN management and policing of an orderly transition to independence for Namibia. Once this is accomplished, the era of decolonization will have come to an end.

A New Pragmatism

What part of the development agenda will remain for north-south negotiation? The impasse reinforces the realization that the diversity among third-world countries rules out any unified solution.

If a differential policy is to be effective, not only will the idea of structural change have to be set aside but international institutions will have to devise more pragmatic and more flexible approaches to the problems of third-world countries. Officials of the IMF, for example, have adopted a more flexible operational code governing the use of the pool of currencies to help nations with balance-of-payments problems. New windows for borrowers, with multiples of quotas and extended terms of repayment for the neediest, have been set up. New rules governing conditionality mandate that the fund pay "due regard to domestic social and political objectives."[33]

A less doctrinaire outlook in international institutions would signal a more pluralistic and differentiated approach to the problems of the third world. More important, it would reflect the realization that given the squeeze on world resources, those channeled through multilateral institutions would have to be concentrated on the needs of the poorest and the least developed. In the 1980s, whatever the symbolism and the rhetoric, the substance of north-south negotiations will center on the problems of the least developed and on a humanitarian agenda (refugees, emergency relief). Concessional aid through international institutions, the application of a preferential policy regarding loans, trade, and basic human needs will constitute the substance of multilateral business between the third-world coalition and the developed nations. A consensus is emerging that equity requires targeting aid programs to the least developed countries and to the poorest of the least developed.

The development agenda of the 1980s will unfold not in the extravaganza of "global negotiations" but more likely along the lines set forth in Robert McNamara's farewell address to the Board of Governors of the World Bank on September 30, 1980. His theme was that in the interests of world order, international financial aid must zero in on rescuing the 800 million "absolute poor" through programs of "human development." Global economic distress has visited particularly severe penalties on the poorest LDCs. OECD nations and the capital-surplus OPEC nations should now consider "what measures they take to increase concessional assistance to the poorest nations" through international financial institutions, whereas the middle-income developing countries will need to continue to "depend on external capital flows from commercial banks *throughout the decade*" (my emphasis).[34]

An attempt to revive the north-south dialogue on the old terms by focusing on generalized pleas for increasing aid to the "third world" according to the agenda of NIEO[35] will deflect attention away from the goal of moving along the McNamara line of concentrating on practical measures and resources available in international agencies to confront the immediate needs of the 1980s.

One means of achieving success would involve equating decision-making power and real power. Serious business flowing from according attention to priorities and achievement is more likely to take place in such institutions as the World Bank and the IMF (or for that matter small institutions such as IFAD) in which there is some correspondence between voting power and the ability to get things done. Thus it is puzzling that an administration that purports to be pragmatic as well as selective in its multilateral diplomacy has seen fit to move all multilateral options to the end of the policy line. A sensible policy would involve strengthening American influence in such institutions as the World Bank and the IMF that serve a selective policy. Yet in cutting foreign-aid programs, the administration has been reluctant to press Congress to authorize the sixth replenishment of the World Bank's soft-loan affiliate (IDA) and has apparently been persuaded to stretch out over six years the amount that had been pledged to be paid over a three-year period. This apparent reneging on an American commitment has led to a decline of American influence in international financial institutions.[36] What might have been an opportunity to "differentiate" became a liability. A signal conveying the lack of American interest in third-world problems was transmitted at the time the United States was attempting to reassert its leadership in certain parts of the third world. Not blanket rejection but selective engagement of multilateral processes in international institutions that have the capacity to be effective in achieving foreign-policy goals is the quintessence of a differential policy.

NOTES

1. Address by C. W. Maynes, who had only recently resigned as assistant secretary of state for International Organization Affairs, to UNA-USA National Convention, New York, April 18, 1980.

2. Carter's speech in Department of State *Bulletin*, vol. 76/621, June 13, 1977; Brzezinski's address to the International Platform Association, August 2, 1979, Department of State, Current Policy Series #81.

3. UN General Assembly, Sixth Special Session: Declaration on Establishment of the New International Economic Order (Resolution 3201-S-VI), May 1, 1974, and Program of Action (Resolution 3202-S-VI), May 1, 1974; and 29th Session of the General Assembly, Charter of Economic Rights and Duties (Resolution 3281-XXIX), December 12, 1974.

4. North-South: A Programme for Survival. Report of the Independent Commission on International Development Issues under the Chairmanship of Willy Brandt (Cambridge, Mass., 1980).

5. See E. A. Kolodziej and R. Harkavy, "Developing States and the International Security System," *Journal of International Affairs*,

Special Issue on International Relations of Developing Countries, Spring/Summer 1980, Columbia University, New York, vol. 34/1, p. 60.

6. See account in *United States Participation in the UN: Report by the President to the Congress for the year 1979*, released December 1978, Department of State #8964, p. 86. For NIEO resolutions, see Note 3.

7. Text of the interview in *The New York Times*, January 1, 1980. Notre Dame address in Department of State *Bulletin*, vol. 76/621, June 13, 1977.

8. D. T. Shapiro, "Strings aid: the politics of persuasion," *The Interdependent*, March 1981.

9. The first statement was in the address to the UN General Assembly on March 17, 1977, (Department of State *Bulletin*, vol. 76/321, April 4, 1977); the second in Department of State *Bulletin*, vol. 80/2045, December 1980, p. 1. See also C. H. Farnsworth, "Aid to Poor Countries," *The New York Times*, Sec. E., October 5, 1980.

10. Paul Lewis, "The West v. OPEC," *The New York Times*, November 30, 1980. British, German, and other economists were saying that Europe was in the most severe recession since the war, according to E. J. Epstein and J. Steingarten, "Europe: The End of a Miracle," *Atlantic Monthly*, July 1981.

11. See Lester C. Thurow, *The Zero-Sum Society*, (New York, 1980), pp. 16-17.

12. Some argued that the United States had become an "ordinary country" without the margin of power to take on special responsibility for maintaining the international system. Anxiety about growing vulnerabilities, especially on assured access to oil supplies, did not allow the United States the amplitude to pursue systemic goals at the cost of immediate national goals. See R. Rosencrance (ed.), *America as an Ordinary Country: U.S. Foreign Policy and the Future*, (Ithaca, N.Y., 1976), p. 11.

13. Arnold Wolfers distinguishes possession goals (i.e., specific and tangible aims) from "milieu" goals (i.e., supporting the world system). The former aims at enhancing or preserving specific values (territory, membership in the Security Council, tariff preferences); the latter aims at shaping a world environment compatible with America's long-range interests. See his *Discord and Collaboration: Essays on International Politics*, (Baltimore, 1962), pp. 73-74

14. Fouad Ajami, "Fate of Nonalignment," *Foreign Affairs*, Winter '80/81. See also J. A. Graham, "The Non-Aligned Movement After the Havana Summit," *Journal of International Affairs*, Special Issue . . . Spring/Summer 1980, vol. 34/1, pp. 153-160.

15. See R. L. Rothstein, "The North-South Dialogue . . .", *Ibid*, pp. 1-17.

16. "UN Conference on Poorer Countries Ends in Discord," *The New York Times*, February 10, 1980. This account is also based on off-the-record interviews with the American delegation to the conference.

17. Lincoln Gordon, *International Stability and North-South Relations*, Occasional Paper #17, Stanley Foundation, Muscatine, Iowa, June 1978.

18. See P. T. Bauer and B. Yamey, "Against the New International Economic Order," *Commentary*, April 1977, and "East-West/North-South," *Commentary*, September 1980. They argue that there is no monolithic south anymore than there is a monolithic north. In culture the south varies from the most primitive to the most advanced and sophisticated civilizations (India, Indonesia, Nigeria, Mali). There is a continuous range in income. It makes no sense to lump together such a heterogeneous collection of mankind who live in widely different physical and social environments with different governments and economic structures.

19. Alan Riding, "Reagan and Latin America," *The New York Times*, February 13, 1981. On collaboration between developing countries and multinational firms, see C. Fred Bergsten, "Economic Tensions: America versus the Third World," *Foreign Affairs*, October 1974.

20, Secretary of State Alexander Haig's address to the American Society of Newspaper Editors in Washington, D.C., on April 24, 1981. Department of State, Current Policy no. 275, April 24, 1981.

21. See D. B. Ottaway, "U.S. at Odds with Third World on New Economic Order," *The Washington Post*, September 19, 1980; also B. Nossiter's piece in *The Washington Post*, September 2, 1980.

22. See the Ottaway piece cited in Note 21 and M. J. Schultheis and J. V. Blewett, "The United States and the North-South Dialogue," *America*, November 22, 1980.

23. E. Schumacher, "Latins Stress Self-Help in Charting a Course for '80s," *The New York Times*, May 18, 1981, and "North-South by South," *The New York Times*, Sec. E., May 31, 1981.

24. See B. Gwertzman, "U.S. Is Said to Study Long-Term Aid Plan for the Caribbean," *The New York Times* May 24, 1981, and follow-up piece on June 4, 1981. Alan Riding reported from Mexico City that despite the unexpected agreement by President Reagan and Mexican President Lopez Portillo to work out a joint economic aid package for the Caribbean Basin, the initiative faced formidable

political difficulties. Nevertheless, the World Bank, the Inter-American Development Bank, Venezuela, and Canada were expected to join the United States and Mexico in financing and implementing the plan. *The New York Times*, June 23, 1981.

25. See C. W. Yost, *History and Memory*, (New York, 1980), p. 213.

26. Stephen S. Rosenfeld, "The UN's 'Dirty Little Secret,' " *The Washington Post*, November 24, 1980. For a superb analysis of the kinds of cases that do and do not lend themselves to UN peacekeeping intervention, see J. A. Finlayson and Mark W. Zacher, "The United Nations and Collective Security, . . .a background paper for the UNA-USA Project on the UN System at 35, April 1980.

27. International Monetary Fund, *Direction of Trade, Yearbook of 1980*, pp. 378-380.

28. R. L. Rothstein, *The Third World and U.S. Foreign Policy: Cooperation and Conflict in the 1980s* (Boulder, Colorado, 1981), p. 239.

29. Senator Daniel P. Moynihan discovered when he was U.S. permanent representative to the United Nations that roughly two-thirds of third-world countries centered their diplomatic efforts in the multilateral arena. Most U.S. ambassadors to these countries had little bilateral business to conduct; the core of diplomacy at Ougadougou had to do not with bilateral affairs but with how Upper Volta aligned at the UN. For most their UN missions are the centers of their diplomatic action. For these countries a differential policy would involve concentrating our diplomatic relations with them in the UN framework. D. P. Moynihan, *A Dangerous Place*, (Boston, 1978), pp. 106-110.

30. See, as a sampling, accounts of specialized agencies and international conference proceedings in *United States Participation in the UN: Report for the Year 1979*, Department of State Publication 9138, released October 1980.

31. G. F. Seib, "U.S. Blockade of Law of the Sea Treaty Will Continue, . . ." *The Wall Street Journal*, June 5, 1981. For a revisionist interpretation of the "common heritage" concept that defends the Reagan administration's policy of renegotiating the LOS treaty, see R. A. Goodwin, "Locke and the Law of the Sea," *Commentary*, June 1981.

32. See J. Ritchie, "U.S. Offers Terms for Closer Ties with South Africans," *The Washington Post*, May 29, 1981, and Anthony Lewis, "Conservative Reality," *The New York Times*, June 11, 1981.

33. Bernard D. Nossiter, "New Pragmatism at the IMF," *The New York Times*, February 5, 1980.

34. *Address to the Board of Governors* by Robert S. McNamara, President, World Bank, Washington, September 30, 1980, pp. 17-27, 42-43. This is not to say that Brazil, for example, will not have recourse to the IMF for loans, for it faces a deficit of 60 billion dollars. But it is in a position to shop around for other deals, and its situation is no different from that of Poland, which is not part of the third world. On the other hand, Bangladesh and Burundi have no other options.

35. Arriving at a workable policy toward the third world is complicated because of pressures to which the United States is being subject from its European allies to demonstrate more "sympathy" to "calls in the third world for a greater global redistribution of wealth [and] increased no-strings Western aid for its development plans," which observers noted during French Foreign Minister Cheysson's visit to Washington in June 1981. John M. Goshko, "French Aide Ends Talks," *The Washington Post,* June 7, 1981.

36. See articles by Hobart Rowan in *The Washington Post,* February 3, 1981, May 20, 1981, June 4, 1981, June 7, 1981; Leonard Silk, "McNamara Warns U.S. of Perils in Reducing Aid to World's Poor," *The New York Times,* June 21, 1981, and R. J. Samuelson, "Global Economics: The Go-It-Alone Spirit," *The Washington Post,* March 10, 1981.

VII.

The United States, The United Nations, and the Third World

SEYMOUR MAXWELL FINGER

The notorious Willie Sutton was once asked why he robbed banks. He replied succinctly, "that's where the money is." For similar reasons I am concerned about U.S. relations with the third world. In my view that is where the action is and is likely to be during the next decade, barring a nuclear holocaust.

Let us look at the American stake in the third world.

A. Strategic. U.S. and NATO defense capabilities make it unlikely that the Soviets would mount a frontal attack across Europe. Much more tempting for the Soviets are soft spots in Asia, Africa, and Latin America where instability can be exploited at comparatively little risk; for example, Afghanistan, Iran, Pakistan, the Persian Gulf, Ethiopia, Central America, the Caribbean, and, eventually, South Africa. Soviet domination of trade routes, oil, or other vital raw materials could upset the balance of power drastically and bring on serious economic decline in the West.

B. Economic. Third-world countries buy 37 percent of our exports and supply many vital raw materials, for example, oil, chrome, nickel, tin, copper, cobalt, bauxite, and uranium. U.S. exports to third-world countries have tripled in the last five years. They now take a greater share of our exports than either Europe or Japan.

C. Resource management and ecology. With an exponential increase in world population and rising expectations, Malthusian predictions of widespread famine now appear all too realistic. Cooperative efforts with third-world countries to deal with that problem as well as with the energy crisis, threats to global environment, peaceful uses of outer space, and management of the resources of the seas and the seabeds are essential.[1] The record of the past 35 years shows that chaos and instability are dangerous for the West and offer opportunities to the Soviets.

Strategic Concerns

The 1980s will be a dangerous decade. The greatest risk appears to be in Asia, the Middle East, Africa, Central America, and the Caribbean. The Soviet invasion of Afghanistan and its intervention, with its Cuban and East German allies, in Angola, Ethiopia, and South Yemen testify to the extensive reach of its armed forces and to its appetite and potential for exploiting opportunities in the third world.

There is no single, simple answer to these threats. American strength, resolve, and reliability are clearly important, but unilateral intervention in every unstable situation would be unwise and unrealistic. Concerted approaches with our allies are desirable whenever and wherever feasible but very difficult to achieve with respect to third-world areas where perceptions and interests differ. As demonstrated in the Congo in 1960 and the Middle East in 1973, U.N.

peacekeeping can be most important in dealing with dangerous situations that threaten to bring about superpower confrontation. But because the United Nations has no power
except what the member states choose to confer, it was unable to counter the Soviet invasions of Hungary, Czechoslovakia, and Afghanistan or even stop the wars between
Morocco and the Polisario, Ethiopia and Somalia, and Iran
and Iraq. In a disorganized world the United States must be
prepared to act through a variety of instruments and organizations, depending on the situation and—equally important—
not to act at all in situations in which the utility of American
intervention is dubious.

A flexible, pluralistic approach is appropriate to the
diversity among third-world countries and the great variety of
situations that obtain in the developing world. At his confir-
mation hearings Secretary of State Alexander Haig stressed
the need to recognize variety among third-world nations and
not lump together nations as diverse as Brazil and Libya,
Indonesia and South Yemen, Cuba and Kuwait. He also criticized "our propensity to apply to these emerging states
Western standards, which resolutely ignore vast differences in
their social cultures, political developments, economic vital-
ity, and internal and external security."[2]

Haig's criticism was obviously directed at the Carter
administration's policies in Iran and Nicaragua. It might better have been directed at those who aligned us with oppres-
sive regimes in the first place. Yet his general proposition—
that the United States endeavor to understand local situations and local standards rather than intervene because of our
own standards—could form a reasonable basis for American
policy. It could mean a rejection of knee-jerk anticommunism or antisocialism as a basis for foreign relations. United
States support for a peaceful settlement in Zimbabwe and
subsequent relations with Robert Mugabe, an avowed Marxist, constitute a good example of adapting policy to local

conditions. Zimbabwe's relations with the United States are better than with the Soviet Union. An opposing policy of support for Ian Smith, Abel Muzorewa, and their South African backers in the name of anticommunism would have resulted in continued bloodshed, worsened relations with other African states, and, in all likelihood, the emergence through military victory of a virulently anti-U.S. regime.

In Africa, generally, the United States must continue to follow the approach developed over the last five years of basing its policy on a realistic appraisal of long-run trends in Africa and the perceptions of the Africans themselves. For Namibia, the last significant problem of decolonization, the U.N. Security Council has approved a plan worked out by the United States, the United Kingdom, France, the Federal Republic of Germany, and Canada after extensive and exhaustive consultations with the African parties concerned.[3] In essence it provides for elections supervised by the United Nations to determine the regime that will prevail in an independent Namibia. The Southwest Africa People's Organization (SWAPO), the main guerrilla organization, has accepted the plan. South Africa has also accepted it but continues to stall and raise new conditions. Any weakening of American resolve in support of a plan for which the United States bears a major responsibility could encourage South African intransigence, prolong the fighting, and have adverse repercussions on U.S. relations with other African countries.

A negotiated settlement in Namibia might open a new chapter in Angolan-American relations. The departure of South African forces from the Angolan border would afford that government the opportunity to send Cuban troops home if it wants diplomatic relations with the United States. Despite the Marxist regime in Angola, both countries would have much to gain through improved relations.

I do not suggest for a moment that Marxist regimes are better than private-enterprise nations; in fact, I am convinced of the contrary. But it is not the proper role of the United States to determine the government of another country. What should concern us is the *external* behavior of a government, particularly as it affects our national interests. We have working relationships with China and Yugoslavia as well as with Japan and France. Why not apply similar criteria in the third world? The West, with its pluralistic traditions, can accommodate better than the Soviets the diverse political aspirations of developing countries. And notwithstanding the anti-Western rhetoric so often heard at the United Nations, it is the West that can do the most to help developing countries of various political persuasions move toward their goals. It is the West that has the capital, the markets, and the technology they need. How wisely the West uses these assets in dealing with developing countries will be a crucial factor in the course of events there, a strategy more enduring than the fruits of military intervention or subversion.

Perhaps the most critical and complex area in the 1980s will be the Middle East. Robert Tucker has pinpointed the Persian Gulf along with Western Europe as "the two most critical areas of concern for the United States" and contends that "there is no substitute for American power in the Gulf."[4] He considers the search for an American surrogate or alignment with the West through a regional arrangement or collective alignment utterly vain. In light of the intense rivalry among the Gulf states and their instability, I agree with Tucker. As he has also noted, the fall of the shah and the Iraq-Iran war have had only the most peripheral relationship to the Palestine issue. Thus settlement of that issue, as important as it is for other reasons, will not solve our problems in the Gulf. Tucker advocates a policy of moderate containment, "concentrating on the Gulf and Western Europe, while being prepared to make compromises and concessions in other parts of the Third World."[5]

Tucker's idea of nonideological, moderate containment

appears more reasonable than the containment policy advocated by Norman Podhoretz.[5] At least it limits the areas of potential American intervention to two instead of making containment global. Yet the question of essentiality to American interest may well be a matter of gradation rather than sharp distinction. Who is to say that Korea, the gateway to Japan, is unimportant? Can one consider Africa expendable? Or Mexico, Brazil, or Argentina? Or China? Perhaps selectivity should be based on national interest and a general caution about intervention rather than geography. Certainly oil is the most critical raw material today, and the West must be prepared to protect its supply. But if the Gulf is so unstable and difficult to defend, would it not be more prudent for the United States and its allies to reduce their dependence on Gulf oil by conservation, exploration, and development of alternative sources?[6] During the transition, of course, there must be sufficient American power and the will to use it in order to prevent a Soviet stranglehold coupled with pragmatic, understanding diplomacy and improved intelligence about the situation in each country. Again, our basic concern must be with oil and external policy, not with the regime or its professed ideology.

A peace settlement between Israel and its neighbors is also important. Consequently, the United States must firmly resist efforts by any party to undermine U.N. Security Council Resolution 242. That resolution, accepted by Israel and its Arab neighbor states, embodies principles that form the only agreed basis for peace negotiations. Its principles have been applied to the peace treaty between Egypt and Israel. They include recognition of the right of Israel to live in peace within secure and recognized boundaries and of the principle that territory shall not be acquired by conquest, either direct or creeping (through settlements). Still to be negotiated are the rights of the Palestinian Arabs living on the West Bank and in Gaza, whether to autonomy or to a greater degree of self-determination, and the secure and recognized boundaries of Israel to be established on the West Bank and the Golan Heights. Negotiations are bound to be protracted and difficult, but they must not be made impossible by undermining the only agreed basis for them.

For similar reasons the United States should continue to support U.N. peacekeeping forces on the Golan Heights and in southern Lebanon for as long as security considerations require. By helping restrain violence that could escalate into war, such forces buy time for the arduous process of negotiating a stable, secure, and just peace.

In Latin America and the Caribbean, too, the United States must think in terms of selectivity, national interests, and a general caution about intervention rather than expect an overall policy for the area to fit all situations. Some countries *are* more important to the United States than others, for example, Mexico for its proximity, size, and oil; Venezuela for its oil; Argentina and Brazil for their size and economic importance; Panama for its canal. Even in those countries, their external policies rather than their internal situations are of concern to the United States. We should, however, be careful to avoid actions that threaten the internal stability of governments with which we can have reasonably cooperative arrangements. In many situations in which there is a repressive oligarchy, there will be revolutions, including violent revolutions in some cases. It is not the job of the United States to oppose such revolutions or to promote them. Of course, where there is significant Soviet or Cuban intervention, the United States may need to counter it, but it should not hasten to intervene merely because some local dictator or American company alleges that there is outside communist intervention. Here, as in Africa, the West has the aces; that is, the capital, the technology, and the markets that third-world countries need. Unless pushed toward the Soviet Union, as Castro was, their natural economic partners are the countries of the West, particularly the United States. Because some of the regimes that will be overturned have had links with the United States, revolutionary regimes may be anti-United States in their rhetoric and even some of their policies. But if the United States uses a combination of patience, firmness, and understanding, such regimes need not be pushed toward the Soviet camp.

With the growing importance of Mexico, Brazil, Argentina, and Venezuela, the United States should find it prudent to consult with them on regional security problems. Central America and the Caribbean are of little economic importance to Mexico, Venezuela, or the United States, but all three share a security concern about the Panama Canal and any Soviet or Cuban encroachment in those areas. In formulating our positions we should take into account the views of these key countries and the Organization of American States (OAS).

Naturally, prudence suggests that we take into account the views of our NATO allies and Japan on situations in the third world that affect their vital interests as well as our own. If the sharing of views leads to the sharing of burdens, so much the better. Consultation does not mean that the United States must always act on the basis of consensus among allies, which rarely develops because of differences in their situations and viewpoints. At times there must be American action, or there will be no action. Nevertheless, it is wise to consult them beforehand, reassess our own position when there are significant differences, and undertake unilateral intervention only when a vital national interest is at stake and there is no feasible alternative.

The United Nations can be most useful in dealing with third-world conflicts in which there is a danger of superpower confrontation. As Vietnam showed, unilateral intervention can be both costly and dangerous. In the Congo (now Zaire) in 1960-1964 and the Sinai in 1973, U.N. peacekeeping operations staved off Soviet-American confrontations and paved the way for developments acceptable to the United States. Yet the cost of these operations to the United States would have paid for only a few weeks of the war in Vietnam, leaving aside the enormous cost in human life and suffering. U.N. peacekeeping forces cannot be used in all situations because they can function only with the consent of the contending parties. Thus they could not be used in Vietnam, Cambodia, Hungary (1956), Czechoslovakia (1968), or Afghanistan. The strong opposition of either superpower precludes U.N. peacekeeping. But where it can be used, U.N. peacekeeping is an important instrument of international peace and security, especially when it is combined with determined efforts to arrive at a negotiated, peaceful settlement, as at Camp David.

In this connection the United Nations offers an unparalleled opportunity for private negotiations, particularly in the early fall when prime ministers and foreign ministers congregate for the annual general debate. Discussions can take place without fanfare, protocol, or the glare of publicity. Such private discussions and negotiations can be particularly useful when there are no formal diplomatic relations, as between the United States and Angola, Cuba, and Vietnam. Discreet, private contacts at the United Nations were helpful in ending the Berlin blockade in the 1940s, obtaining the release of American fliers from China in the 1950s, opening negotiations for the release of the Pueblo crew from North Korea in the 1960s, and fostering cooperation between Angola and Zaire in the 1970s to deter dissident groups based in their respective countries from launching attacks across the border. The first steps toward a peaceful resolution of the Zimbabwe conflict also originated in private discussions at the United Nations.

Arms Control and Disarmament

Because of mutual distrust and problems of verification, there has been no disarmament since the United Nations was established. Indeed, arms expenditures have increased to over 500 billion dollars per year, draining scarce resources and making the world less secure. There has, however, been some limited success in arms control.

The United States has been both a stimulator and a legitimizer of the various international arms control agreements, notably, the partial nuclear test ban, the nuclear nonproliferation treaty, and treaties banning the placement of weapons of mass destruction in outer space or in the seabeds. The United Nations has also encouraged the negotiation and the ratification of a treaty banning the use of nuclear weapons in Latin America, and it has discussed similar proposals for other areas, for example, the Middle East and the Indian Ocean. The establishment of additional nuclear-free zones is in the interest of world peace; consequently, although the initiative is likely to come from countries in the region, it is in the interest of the United States to support and encourage such initiatives in the United Nations. It is also in the United States' interest to encourage continued U.N. support for the international nuclear nonproliferation regime.

There is little hope for further U.N. contributions in the area of global arms control. On the other hand, there would be great interest in arms *reduction* if the United States were to take the initiative. Balanced and verifiable arms reduction would mean not only enhanced security for the United States but the release of enormous resources to stimulate economic growth and productivity, combat inflation, and improve living conditions both at home and abroad. The United Nations would be an excellent forum for the United States to rally support from our allies and third-world countries and thus put pressure on the Soviets to engage in negotiations on balanced and verifiable arms reduction.

Human Rights

Another issue related to peace and security is foreign policy on human rights, a problem of extraordinary complexity. The Carter administration made a particular point of emphasizing human rights as a major issue of foreign policy and was criticized by both the left and the right. Some critics argue that detente has been hindered by publicly-expressed U.S. concern with human rights violations in the Soviet Union and Eastern Europe. Others, notably, Jeane Kirkpatrick, the new U.S. permanent representative to the U.N., charged the Carter administration with invoking double standards; she argued that the United States had undermined friendly dictatorships in Nicaragua and Iran by stressing human-rights violations there, while ignoring violations in Marxist dictatorships.[7] (It is not at all certain that the shah and Somoza could have remained in power no matter what the United States did.)

What the various criticisms demonstrate unquestionably is the difficulty of maintaining an active human-rights policy that is both fair and consistent because human rights are only one aspect of total American foreign policy. In any serious conflict between human rights and major economic or national-security interests, it is clear that human rights will be, at best, third in the hierarchy. For example, the United States will not forgo cooperation with China or South Korea because human rights are violated in those countries. Consequently, an active human-rights policy is bound to be inconsistent as a result of conflicts with major strategic and economic interests.

In these circumstances some might be tempted to conclude that the best policy would be to ignore human-rights issues abroad. Such a policy would have the virtue of simplicity and consistency. Yet throughout its history the United States has expressed concern with the rights of foreign peoples, for example, in Czarist and Soviet Russia, in Latin American dictatorships, in Africa, in the Habsburg Empire, and more recently in South Africa, Uganda, Cambodia, and South Korea. The Nuremberg trials, the U.N. Charter, the Universal Declaration on Human Rights, in all of which the United States played a major role, have anchored in international law the principle that serious violations of human rights are matters of international concern. Despite the provisions of Charter Article 2 (7) about nonintervention in "matters which are essentiality within the domestic juris-diction of any state," 35 years' of practice since 1945 have created ample precedent for voicing international concern about serious violations of human rights. The Helsinki agree-ments have placed human-rights violations in Europe on the agenda of follow-up conferences. It would be unseemly, to say the least, for the United States to abandon a historical position of championing human rights. Moreover, it would hand our adversaries a propaganda bonanza. Despite com-plexities and inevitable inconsistencies, the moral position of the United States and the practical realities of world politics require an active position on human rights in the United Nations and abroad.

In the United Nations the United States and its friends face an uphill struggle. The emphasis of the majority con-tinues to be focused primarily on three areas: South Africa, Chile, and territories occupied by Israel since 1967. In recent years the United States has sought, with a measure of success, to call attention to egregious violations in the Soviet Union, Uganda, Cambodia, and elsewhere and has been joined in this effort to apply human-rights standards consistently by both Western and developing countries. The tide has not yet been turned, but surely the struggle must continue. The United States' position would be improved significantly if the Senate would ratify certain important human-rights instruments, notably, the Genocide Convention, the International

Convention on the Elimination of Racial Discrimination, and the International Covenants on Economic, Social, and Cultural Rights and on Civil and Political Rights.

The United States and the United Nations

In 1961 a newly-elected John F. Kennedy launched at the U.N. General Assembly a proposal for the U.N. Development Decade. This proposal, triggering a major increase in the operational activities of the U.N. system, symbolized the position and attitude of the United States at that time: sure of its economic and military strength; compassionate toward the goals of third-world countries; and confident in the effectiveness of the United Nations and most of its specialized agencies.

In 1981 the picture looks starkly different. Militarily the United States is under serious challenge by the Soviet Union. Although its economy is still the world's largest and most productive, it is plagued by serious and persistent inflation, a declining dollar, huge budget deficits, and stagnating productivity. Moreover, it has witnessed an enormous growth of expenditures in the U.N. system, for which the United States pays the largest share of the bill. Meanwhile, there has been disappointment with the inability of the U.N. Security Council to prevent or stop most aggressions and wars, the flawed operation of some specialized agencies, and the injection of extraneous political issues into functional agencies and conferences in ways that distract them from their objectives and weaken the fabric of international cooperation.

In these circumstances it is tempting to turn away from the United Nations in frustration or disgust, to withdraw, or minimize United States' participation. It may also be emotionally satisfying to vent our spleen and maintain a tough combative posture, as Moynihan did.[8] In my view, a great power such as the United States must resist these temptations. Our stake in a more stable world, peace, and survival does not permit such luxuries.

Third-world countries are important to the United States, and the United Nations is their chosen forum. It would be folly to abandon the field to our adversaries or to show so little involvement with or concern for the problems of these countries that we forfeit any chance of obtaining their cooperation. This does not mean that we should let the majority dictate to us; under the U.N. Charter, they cannot. It does mean that we should listen to their concerns and take them seriously as we formulate policy.

Nor should the United States deal with third-world countries exclusively through the United Nations; that would serve neither their interests nor American. As noted above, there is great diversity among third-world nations and the problems they face; consequently, the United States must have a flexible, pluralistic approach. Some situations can be dealt with in the United Nations, whereas others lend themselves to bilateral or regional approaches.

Where the United Nations can be particularly useful is in calling the attention of governments and peoples to world problems and in multilateral bargaining on issues that are ripe for the development of international law; for example, the law of the sea and outer space. It was at the United Nations that world attention was first focused on the race between population growth and food supplies and threats to the environment. The important *actions* were taken by governments, but it was the United Nations that provided the forum for governments to be alerted and to educate and persuade each other.

The General Assembly, grandly called the Parliament of Man, is much less than that. It cannot legislate through the process of majority voting and the use of titles such as

Declaration or Charter; however, international law may be developed by consensus if the text is carefully worked out and meaningful. The Assembly's main impact, positive or negative, is on governments that alone have the power to give effect to its resolutions. Indeed, although hundreds of Assembly resolutions have been ignored by governments, some have had a significant impact on national attitudes or action, for example, resolutions establishing the U.N. Development Program, the U.N. Environment Program, UNCTAD, and UNIDO. There are also instances in which discussion without the adoption of a resolution may have more significant impact than the putative resolution. There was, for example, the Fifth Emergency Special Session of the General Assembly in the summer of 1967, at which neither major resolution on the Arab-Israeli issue received enough votes for adoption. Yet the debates at that session led to the widespread recognition among third-world countries that Israel could not be expected to withdraw except in the context of peace and secure and recognized boundaries—a profoundly important change in attitudes that resulted in the unanimous adoption of Resolution 242 by the Security Council on November 22, 1967. Similarly, debates over the notions of an international soft loan fund, compensatory financing, and nonreciprocal tariff concessions for developing countries led to a U.S. reassessment and then important changes of position on all three issues. The result was IDA, a substantial compensatory financing facility in the International Monetary Fund (IMF) and generalized special preferences.

On the other hand, the adoption of resolutions that outrage governments, their legislators, and public opinion can have seriously adverse effects. For example, the 1975 resolution equating Zionism with racism significantly reduced support for the Decade Against Racial Discrimination. The introduction of extraneous political issues at the World

Conference on Women in 1980 resulted in a situation in which 26 governments, including virtually all the developed Western countries and the Holy See, were unable to support the Program of Action.

The United Nations has no troops and no financial resources other than those its members are willing to provide. Its greatest potential strength lies in building a reputation for objectivity, justice, and integrity among governments and peoples. If, as has happened too often, a transient majority lends itself to partisan purposes and demonstrates a blatant disregard for the principles of justice, impartiality, and moral, intellectual integrity, the damage is palpable. The result diminishes respect for the United Nations and undermines confidence in its institutions. Without integrity, morality, and public confidence, the United Nations can have neither power nor influence on solving the problems that face humanity.

Economic Issues

The goals of the New International Economic Order (NIEO) form a major part of the U.N. agenda and pose a difficult challenge to the West. Because of the importance of third-world countries in strategic, economic, and global survival terms, the United States must be deeply concerned with NIEO issues at the United Nations irrespective of whether it intends to use that forum for substantive negotiations on particular issues. Most economic issues are better addressed in the appropriate specialized agencies, such as the World Bank and the International Monetary Fund; they are more expert and have a good track record. Moreover, their voting and negotiating processes ensure that U.S. interests are adequately protected.

Regardless of the instrument chosen to deal with

specific issues—bilateral, regional, World Bank, or IMF—it is essential that the American perspective be broad rather than narrowly nationalistic. In the long run economic development in the third world is in our national interest. Such development is more likely to be achieved by specific concrete steps than by grandiose declarations or radical restructuring of economic institutions. Some of these concrete actions may be generalized to all developing countries. Others, by their nature, can be dealt with best in negotiations with particular countries or groups of countries. It may be assumed that each developing country will be guided by its own national interest and will be more interested in concrete steps than in slogans. Yet it would be a grave error to pursue tactics transparently directed at splitting the Group of 77 at the United Nations; such tactics would harden positions, embitter feelings, and promote rhetoric rather than the cooperative action that is needed.

In considering its responses, the United States should endeavor to coordinate intended policies and strategies with the other countries of the Organization for Economic Cooperation and Development (OECD). Such coordination is particularly important on measures to ensure that international trade, to the greatest extent feasible, is free and fair, in the interest of improving efficiency, increasing productivity, and fighting inflation. Consequently, the United States, in cooperation with other OECD countries, should work to stem protectionism, a particular danger during times of economic stress such as the present. Such efforts are especially important to developing countries in need of reliable and growing markets for manufactured and processed goods as well as primary commodities. Only in this way can these countries, which now take almost two-fifths of U.S. exports, continue to be part of an expanding market. The United States should think in terms of adjustment to the world market, moving from low- to high-technology industries as Japan has done.

The United States should also rethink its policy on foreign aid. Once the leader in aid, the United States is now among the least generous of the industrialized countries. Official U.S. development assistance has fallen to 0.18 percent of gross national product. The U.N. target is 0.7 percent, and a number of industrialized countries are now at or above that figure. True, there are many strains on the U.S. budget for defense and social needs, and the threat of inflation argues for budgetary restraint. Yet an American effort comparable to that of France and the Federal Republic of Germany would be a good investment in our relations with third-world countries and in sustaining the market for U.S. exports.

Threats to Global Survival

Looking ahead two decades, threats to global survival may become more serious for the United States than the Soviet threat. And it is in efforts to ensure a livable world that cooperation with third-world countries is particularly important.

John Herz, in an admirable essay in this volume, has described the threat represented by potential nuclear annihilation, explosive population growth outrunning food supplies, the depletion of resources, and environmental decay. He argues, with acute logic, that the true national interest may be global survival rather than the conventional preoccupation with military and economic competition. He concludes: "Mankind now either must decide to survive as an entirety or else it is doomed."

One may argue with Herz as to the degree of danger, but there can be no doubt about the danger itself. Nor is there any doubt that cooperation for survival requires international institutions. It was at the United Nations that the first international alarm on population growth was sounded. As Herz points out, governments are less likely to resent family-planning advice from a U.N. agency than from the United States. Current famine in some areas and the problems of increased food production, especially in the developing countries, can also be dealt with better in a cooperative international framework, using the FAO, the World Food Program, and the International Fund for Agricultural Development as a starting point. The U.N. Conference on the Environment in 1972 sensitized governments around the world to threats of environmental decay and has led to remedial action. The pressure of growing demand on finite resources has made the seas, the seabeds, and outer space increasingly important, and these issues are best dealt with in the context of an international organization. Finally, there are the issues of arms control, arms reduction, and nuclear nonproliferation that are so important to global survival.

The U.N. system, evolved over the past 35 years, can deal with most of these issues. Yet there can be no a priori assumption that a U.N. agency will always be the best institution. In recent years political attacks on functionalism in many of the agencies have raised questions about the suitability of some of them, as they now function, to fulfill their tasks.

The United States was a pioneer in sponsoring specialized agencies and conferences to deal with functional, specialized, and technical problems. The concept of the U.N. system reflects that philosophy, for example, the World Bank, IMF, GATT, FAO, ILO, WHO, UNESCO, ICAO. It was reasoned that expert representatives, dealing with clearly-defined specialties that were not part of "high politics," could reach important agreements on investment, trade, monetary policy, agriculture, labor, health, education, science, culture, civil aviation, communications, nuclear energy, and merchant shipping. It was even postulated that habits of cooperation in these specialized areas might spill over into the more politically-sensitive security area. In fact, the reverse has happened. The political quarrels of the U.N. General Assembly and the Security Council are now being replicated in many specialized agencies. This is a deplorable trend.

One should not overlook the enormous contributions of some of the specialized agencies. The World Bank and the IMF have managed to remain specialized and professional while vastly increasing contributions to the development of third-world countries. The contributions of the Food and Agriculture Organization (FAO) to agricultural development, the World Health Organization (WHO) to world health, the International Labor Organization (ILO) to labor standards, the United Nations Educational, Scientific, and Cultural Organization (UNESCO) to scientific and cultural exchange, the International Atomic Energy Agency (IAEA) to nuclear regulation, and the International Civil Aviation Organization (ICAO) to the safety of civil aviation have been notable. The Stockholm Conference sensitized governments around the world to serious environmental problems and led to the establishment of the U.N. Environment Program. The disturbing thing is that many of these efforts are threatened by the introduction of extraneous political issues that provoke friction and confrontation rather than cooperation.

As an operating concept politicization may be defined to denote three closely-related behavioral patterns: first, considering and acting on matters that lie essentially outside the specific functional domain of a given specialized agency; second, the reaching of decisions on matters within an agency's functional competence through a process that is essentially political and that does not reflect technical and scientific factors in the decision process; third, the taking of specific actions on issues within an agency's competence for the sole purpose of expressing a partisan political position rather than attempting to reach an objective determination of the issues.

A prime example is the Decade Against Racial Discrimination. Here was an issue on which the efforts of virtually all governments should have converged. Yet the injection of a statement equating Zionism with racism—an assertion that horrified a good part of the world—seriously hampered cooperation at the conference called to mobilize joint efforts and weakened the thrust of the decade, which was poisoned by this obnoxious concept.

The World Conference on Women, held in Copenhagen in July 1980, also inflicted serious damage on a most worthy cause by the injection of extraneous political issues. As a result, 26 governments, including virtually all the developed Western countries and the Holy See, were unable to support the Program of Action in a roll-call vote. Divisive issues included specific aid programs for Palestinian women to be carried out by U.N. agencies (but no mention of Somali and Eritrean women) and special resolutions on the situation of women in El Salvador and Chile, but no reference to women in Afghanistan, Argentina, Cambodia, Uganda, and Saudi Arabia. Appeals against the injection of extraneous political issues were met with the argument that women are concerned with all major issues. Yet if everything is to be discussed everywhere, what is the point of a special conference? The General Assembly can deal with these issues with less expense, less fanfare, and less pretense. Special conferences can be justified only if they are special and particularized.

It must also be questioned whether voting has any place in such conferences. Resolutions have no binding power; they are made effective only to the extent that they influence government attitudes. Outvoting governments whose cooperation is important can have only a negative impact on them. Conferences do not have the mandatory powers of the Security Council. Permitting voting at the conferences encourages the introduction of extraneous, divisive political issues. Consequently, the U.S. government should consider taking a firm position against voting at such special conferences, including the possibility of not attending and not sharing in the costs of conferences at which the prospect of divisive, extraneous issues may jeopardize the objectives. Obviously, such a position will be more effective if it is shared by other governments, particularly OECD members, who should be consulted in advance.

Similar problems have arisen in some of the specialized agencies. The recent UNESCO conference in Belgrade posed challenges to the freedom of information in the form of a New International Information Order. I believe the United States should help third-world countries improve their communications facilities, but information must not be "balanced" at the expense of freedom. UNESCO is a large, multifaceted agency that has done significant work in promoting educational, scientific, and cultural cooperation. Of late some of these activities have been seriously damaged by being subordinated to broad political objectives. The same trend has impacted on other specialized agencies. Although hasty or impulsive action should be avoided, perhaps the time has come for the United States to reassess the value of UNESCO with no a priori assumption that American support can be taken for granted. Subsequently there might be similar reassessments of other agencies. When political rot or inefficiency has seriously impaired the effectiveness of an agency in its avowed special function, alternative institutions or approaches ought to be considered.

Conclusions

In the decade ahead third-world countries will be of increasing importance to the United States for strategic, economic, and global-survival reasons. In dealing with them, the United States must not regard the countries of the third world as mere pawns in our struggle with the Soviet Union but as individual nations composed of peoples who have their own goals and aspirations. We should devote much greater efforts to understanding them and their goals and be far more cautious about intervening in situations that we do not fully understand. In particular, we should not be confused by labels, such as Marxist or socialist. The record suggests that we can find congruities of interests with countries like China and Yugoslavia and can pursue productive relations with countries like Algeria and Angola. With patience, understanding, and restraint, the West can develop good relations with third-world countries. It has the capital, the technology, and the markets they need.

Because the United Nations is important to the third world, it must also be considered an important arena for the United States. U.N. peacekeeping cannot be used in all situations because it requires the cooperation of the parties concerned, but it has proved to be of major benefit in preventing or stopping third-world conflicts that could otherwise have escalated into Soviet-American confrontations. Where U.N. peacekeeping can be used, it is certainly better for world peace and security than unilateral Soviet or U.S. intervention, especially when combined with efforts at negotiating peaceful and just settlements. Of course, where U.N. action is blocked, the United States must be prepared to use other instruments, either national or regional (NATO), but recourse to such agencies should not be hasty or frequent.

Economic goals, as elaborated in the New International Economic Order, are a major concern of third-world countries in the United Nations; they must be considered by the United States with seriousness, concern, and understanding there and in other international forums. But most of the specific, concrete steps that are the real keys to progress can best be taken in the World Bank and in the International Monetary Fund or through bilateral or regional negotiations.

Consultation with other OECD countries and a willingness to reassess U.S. positions are vital to the constructive formulation of measures to buttress a healthy world economy for the benefit of both developed and developing countries.

Cooperation is particularly important in dealing with threats to global survival, for example, the proliferation of nuclear and conventional weapons, the increasing burden of the arms race, the deadly race between an exponentially-growing world population and food supplies, energy shortages, the depletion of raw materials, and the degradation of the environment. The United Nations and its specialized agencies can be important institutions for dealing with these problems provided they are used constructively by the member states and not abused by the introduction of narrow, extraneous political interests. The United States should be prepared to use those institutions and instruments, whether inside or outside the U.N. system, that are best suited to the cooperative efforts needed to deal with these vital problems.

If we develop policies based on strength, prudence, understanding, selectivity, and consistency, we will be able to deploy the assets required to maintain cooperative and fruitful relations with the third world.

NOTES

1. See, for example, Dennis Meadows et al., *The Limits to Growth* (Cambridge, Mass., 1972), and Harlan Cleveland, *The Third Try at World Order,* (New York, 1976).

2. Opening statement by Alexander M. Haig, Jr., before the Senate Foreign Relations Committee in Washington, as published in *The New York Times,* January 10, 1981, p. 9.

3. U.N. Security Council Resolution 431, July 27, 1978. For a brief account of the negotiations, see S. M. Finger, *Your Man at the U.N., People, Politics and Bureaucracy in the Making of Foreign Policy* (New York, 1980), pp. 278-283.

4. Robert Tucker, "The Purposes of American Power," *Foreign Affairs,* winter 1980-1981, pp. 241-274.

5. Norman Podhoretz, *The Present Danger* (New York, 1980).

6. See Dankwart A. Rustow, "Reagan, Mideast and Oil," *The New York Times,* January 12, 1981, A 19.

7. Jeane Kirkpatrick, "Dictatorships and Double Standards," *Commentary,* November 1979, pp. 34-45. For a contrary viewpoint, see Stanley Hoffmann, *Primacy or World Order* (New York, 1980), p. 31.

8. See Daniel Patrick Moynihan, *A Dangerous Place* (Boston, 1978) for a presentation of his confrontationist philosophy. See also Abraham Yeselson and Anthony Gaglione, *A Dangerous Place* (New York, 1974) for similar arguments. I do not believe Moynihan was familiar with or even aware of the earlier book of the same title.

VIII.

Foreign Policy
and Human Survival

JOHN H. HERZ

I.

We always seem to be at some crossroad. Since the
United States emerged from the Second World War as one of
the two superpowers, observers and practitioners of
American foreign policy have continuously been engaged in
some "Great Debate" about which road to take and which
goal to attain. But as with so much in the world of action,
what constitutes a decisive turning point lies in the eyes of
the beholder. It is a matter of perception, of one's views of
the world. Since 1945 there has hardly been a time when the
military (on both sides) and the militarists did not perceive
some "present danger," as ours do now with respect to an
alleged decrease of America's power and influence in the
world. Cold warriors claim that the United States is in decline
and must recuperate its global role. Their "Great Debate"

concerns the question of arms, especially nuclear weaponry, of facing the Soviets from a position of strength; the issue is joined with those who emphasize balance, restraint, detente.

I shall say something about this issue in due course, but I place it next to another, overriding issue, suggesting that the present malaise in world affairs stems less from traditional problems involving nation-states competing for power and security than from a deeper dilemma.[1] Since the beginning of the nuclear age, something more fundamental than even the security of a particular nation has been at stake: the future of the human race as such. To be sure, awareness of the new power of humans to destroy themselves in omnicidal war has been part of our world perception since Hiroshima, but we have failed to draw the radical conclusion from this novel situation and thus have taken the wrong turns at various turning points—first right after Hiroshima, then, when the decision to manufacture the hydrogen bomb was made, and so on—real crossroads because a fundamental change in world conditions regarding the weapons of war had occurred. The road actually taken has led to a bipolar power concentration, East-West confrontation, and an ever-more ludicrous spiraling of the arms race, in short, conflict deadly in character because it involves the danger of mutual if not global, extinction.

The nuclear threat, however, is only the most spectacular among a number of global threats. Human survival is also in jeopardy because of some seemingly less drastic, more gradually emerging developments. They are connected with the great scientific-technological revolution of the modern era through its impact on world population, world resources, and the environment. The technological revolution has caused world population to explode; still proceeding in accelerating fashion in most parts of the world, the demographic explosion tests the accommodative capacity of a finite planet. Additional billions of people require corresponding increases in food, energy, and other natural resources, but today the earth's capacity to meet such elementary needs as food, housing, jobs, and education, not to speak of the amenities of life, is in doubt; nonrenewable resources are being depleted and in the process the biosphere—that fragile and vulnerable rim of land surface, seas, and atmosphere—is placed in jeopardy through overuse and pollution. The globe is in danger of becoming uninhabitable.

Together with the nuclear threat, this triad of demographic, economic, and ecological catastrophes poses the problem of man's physical survival. For the first time in history, the future of nature, man's habitat that has always provided succeeding generations with ample means of living, can no longer be taken for granted. And inasmuch as the maintenance of existence is the basis of all national interest, even the most powerful and richest nations must now confront the dilemma of how to place policy into the framework of securing survival. I submit that traditional political realism will lose its realistic aspect if it fails to recognize that national interest is now merged with the interests of all in global survival. We humans have become an endangered species, and when the future of the species is at stake, the issue is joined not so much between left and right, hard- and softliners, cold warriors and detentists but between parochial and global world views and approaches.

Hans Jonas, in his recent book on the ethics of responsibility, has defined the new imperative for man as actor: "Act in such a fashion that the effects of your action are not destructive of the future possibility of life."[2] This is a novel injunction for the statesman who, taking the future for granted, has always been concerned with the immediate task of safeguarding the interest of his state. Henceforth he must also act as a trustee of mankind and its patrimony; foreign policy has to ensure that there will be a future and thus must give priority to the issues that concern the future.

II.

What would such a new orientation imply for the conduct of American foreign policy? We can distinguish new goals only on the basis of a clear picture of the world in which this orientation would operate. In the confines of this paper I can merely summarize the essential conditions.[3] World population is still rising exponentially, a fact often overlooked or played down because in some industrialized countries population approaches zero growth, and in a few developing countries efforts at family planning have begun. But the opposite is true in most countries of the world that contain most of mankind, the third world. And the momentum is such that even if all or most now begin radically to control their birthrates, a flattening of the curve cannot be expected for several decades. Awareness of this basic phenomenon is of utmost importance for the development of policies and for policymakers.

But the decisive factor is that what happened in the old industrial countries—where industrialization eventually enabled increasing numbers of people to live and live even better than before—has so far failed to happen in the so-called developing world. What characterizes its maldevelopment? Whatever their geographic, cultural, political, and other differences, these countries almost uniformly present the picture of societies in which a small, urbanized, and modernized sector—businessmen, landowners, military, and politicians—enjoying rapidly rising living standards, faces a vast majority of the utterly impoverished, chiefly rural people whose fragmented parcels of land, if any, offer only starvation. Many of the poor, therefore, migrate to metropoles where, unable to find jobs, they and their armies of offspring live in slums and shantytowns, lacking even the minimal amenities of life. From an article in *The New York Times:* "Abidjan (capital of the Ivory Coast) is a sparkling city of glass and steel skyscrapers encircled by poor communities of tin and cardboard shacks."[4] This phenomenon is repeated everywhere, from Mexico City (whose population for the year 2000 is projected at 30 million) to Cairo, Calcutta, and Jakarta. Even the more advanced developing countries, such as Brazil[5] and South Korea, exhibit these developmental imbalances. Based on the importation of chiefly capital-intensive technologies, their industrialization benefits only the modern sector of the economy, thus creating few jobs. This "trickle-down" failure characterizes all modernizing countries. Few labor-intensive, light-capital technologies are introduced; no small irrigation systems are developed in the countryside; instead, in many countries agribusiness for export or luxury crops is introduced or maintained so that food for mass consumption must be imported. One-crop or one-commodity export systems that generate unfavorable terms of trade contribute to the impoverishment of the masses.[6] Even the oil countries or other countries rich in resources, instead of using their wealth for genuine development (rural, infrastructure, and so on), usually use it to fashion a Western type of life-style for the elites and/or for acquiring ultramodern weapons systems plus a police force to control the immiserating masses. They fail to build that infrastructure of self-sufficiency (from diversified agricultural production to transportation systems to schools, and so on) that enabled the older industrialized nations to develop their integrated socioeconomic systems. Instead, north-south relations are characterized by a system in which the first world's trading and investing businesses, in particular its multinational enterprises, investing for quick returns, operate hand in glove with a small segment of a third-world country to establish an economy from which the vast proportion of the population is excluded so that its effective domestic market is comprised of only 5 to 15 percent of the population; to sum up: a system of misdirected investment, misguided production, unequal and unfair distribution.

III.

Why should American policy be directed toward alleviating conditions such as these? Haven't the poor always been with us? And can't we, in the worst cases, use charity to feed the starving people of Bangladesh, or Cambodia, or the Sahel or admit, as refugees or immigrants, limited numbers of the world's underprivileged? But it is not enough to patch up famine conditions here and there. In a world in which half a billion people live in what is defined as "absolute poverty" (that is, below the subsistence level in food, clothing, and shelter), charity alone won't do. We must recall the basic feature of the situation: the rapid increase of population. It means, among other things, increasing population pressure against the rich countries: American interest is directly involved when millions of illegal immigrants swamp the United States; how shall we cope when more millions from all over descend on the rich enclaves of the world by land, sea, even air? It is safe to predict that this problem will become one of the most "pressing" among the foreign-policy issues that the developed countries will confront in the near future.[7] Obviously, the goal must be to stem the flood, but how? I submit that it can only be stemmed by the United States and the other industrialized nations doing their utmost to see to it that the overpopulated states become viable for increasing numbers while engaging in effective population planning. The same is true for problems arising from other global issues:

Resouces: Threatening exhaustion of nonreplenishable resources, such as oil, poses all the more urgently the question of their more equitable allocation among the nations of the world; it would seem that any chance of poor third-world countries improving the living standards of increasing numbers of their destitute people depends on the availability of energy for fertilizers, irrigation systems, rural electrification, building of farm-to-market roads, light industries, and so forth. But the oil countries, instead of using their oil for developing intrathird-world relationships by recycling their earnings into the third world, invest their petrodollars in first-world ventures and/or "modernize" themselves in the way of the shah, who acquired one of the world's most up-to-date military establishments, while Teheran, a city of millions bursting with jobless young people from the countryside, remained without a sewer system.

We have experienced the consequences. Here is one source of the growing turbulence of the world. We can hardly expect the stability of regimes and the reliability of allies when the expectations of impoverished masses are disappointed time and again. As for the oil-deprived countries, yes, oil from OPEC; but in principle they, like ourselves, must become more self-reliant by developing their own resources (from hydroelectric power to solar energy), with the respective technological and investment aid coming from the industrialized world. Again, the goal is to establish viable third-world units.

Ecology: We recall the somewhat plaintive statement of the Brazilian delegate at one international conference, to wit: You, the developed countries, have had your share of polluting the world; now we want to have ours! And they have it, deforesting their Amazonas valleys, turning their lands into deserts, polluting their rivers and coastlines, and, together with the industrialized countries, placing their toxic wastes into that sewer of last resort, the ocean. Continuous oil spills by supertankers contribute to its pollution. It should be the goal of the developed countries not only to clean up their own environment but to convince the latecomers that all of us share a global interest in keeping the environment livable.

IV.

What, in particular, should be American policy in the face of global threats? I say "should be" although I am aware of the possible reproach of committing political idealism. But policymakers cannot long avoid pursuing some purpose beyond immediate interests. Nor is it entirely selfless or "idealistic" to engage in a policy that would save the nation from that lifeboat or triage situation in which less fortunate ones would be condemned to a doom that we would escape only for a little while. When somebody explained to Churchill the threat of world population outrunning food supplies, the great realist is said to have remarked that if no solution were found, the situation would lead to unfortunate consequences because people would refuse to starve to death in equal measure; there would be sharp conflicts about how to divide the last crumbs. International terrorism, including even nuclear blackmail, pursued by some groups or governments might well be one of the results of a desperate situation.

Before going into some details about what the needed reshaping of U.S. foreign policy goals implies, I shall set forth a few more general requirements: First, putting the world into a shape that would enable billions of humans to live minimally well requires money, a lot of it; where is it to come from? Second, capital investments and transfers of technology will provide no benefits if they are not directed into channels quite different from the usual ones. Third, such investment steering *en gros* can hardly be the task of one country; the United States must act in concert with other industrial states and, in order to maintain a common approach and procedure, use international agencies, which, in turn, must be given improved funding and broader jurisdiction. Finally, this kind of foreign or, rather, international policy cannot be conducted without producing major impacts on domestic policies and life-styles.

The need to channel action through international organizations (whether public international agencies, such as FAO, ILO, WHO, the World Bank, the World Fund, and regional banks and funds, or NGOs, such as foundations, churches, and charitable organizations), instead of relying on individual or bilateral approaches,[8] may be illustrated by citing examples from the area of population planning to which the supranational approach is clearly preferable to attempts by specific countries to influence unilaterally the population-planning policies of countries that receive foreign aid. Conceivably, the United States could engage in a policy in which foreign aid would be made dependent on the propagation of satisfactory birth-control measures by the recipient, but the objections to exerting such unilateral pressure are obvious. On the other hand, an international agency such as WHO might be authorized to go into the field and provide the usual kinds of health services simultaneously with teaching contraceptive methods. By combining these two activities, the agency's program would demonstrate that the provision of health services, which by themselves would only worsen the demographic situation (reducing infant mortality, increasing life expectancy, and so on), would prove beneficial when combined with birth control. Also, populations would possibly resent "interference" by international medical personnel less than coercive policies on the part of their governments (the sad case of India comes to mind). True, deeply rooted prejudices might still impede such efforts; but, as the case of some developed countries (France, Italy) indicates, such obstacles can be overcome when people who still consider numerous offspring as the only guarantee of support in old age are assured of such support through systems of old-age and social-security benefits now hardly available in the third world. Thus policies of family planning are intimately connected with the overall problem of transforming maldeveloping societies into societies that provide at least minimal welfare benefits.

Similar considerations apply to food and the supply of similar basic necessities. The United States, of course, is one of the few food surplus countries, and one would assume that much of the world's food and famine problems could be solved with the assistance of the United States. But food and similar exports are controlled by the practitioners of free enterprise, that is, they are subject to speculation by oligopolist traders; when the government plays a part, as in the case of the grain embargo against the Soviet Union, it usually is for purpose of economic warfare.

The international distribution of food surpluses, instead of the artificial reduction of planting to maintain price levels, would prevent a good deal of starvation and malnutrition in the world, and an international grain reserve ("ever-normal granary") should be established for this purpose. At present only 6 percent of U.S. foreign aid consists of food assistance.[10] However, even if this amount were increased, it would not be enough. To solve the underlying problem of increasing numbers chasing food supplies, the vast regions of agricultural underproduction, or wrong production, can be made self-supporting through the importation of intermediate technologies, the buildup of the necessary infrastructures, and the training of rural populations (combined, wherever necessary, with agrarian reform). It is not likely that such a task could be performed by individual countries alone, not even the wealthiest and most advanced; they should be assisted by international agencies.

V.

For examples like these it appears that three things are needed to enable international agencies to function properly. One is the conference by member states of effective jurisdiction to the agencies, especially jurisdiction to act "in the field," that is, within developing countries. International relations may thus assume another character by nation-states yielding portions of their sovereignty and agencies becoming more supranational—a system intermediate between traditional state sovereignty and world government—the one becoming outmoded; the other remaining utopian.[11] Second, when channeling action through international agencies, priority must be given to the right kinds of investment and other projects, "right" meaning their direction or redirection into such areas as raising the productivity of rural and urban masses, distributing more broadly the wealth thus created, laying foundations for self-sufficiency through emphases on the production of mass-consumption goods, encouraging sound family size, and protecting the environment. This means favoring "basic needs" projects as practiced by Robert S. McNamara as head of the World Bank.[12]

Third, agencies need adequate financing by member states, that is, their willingness to increase their funding vastly. The United States, by slashing its budget allocations for foreign aid and development almost every year, has set a bad example for other wealthy nations. The one percent of GNP once targeted as the average contribution—a figure that by itself would probably be far from sufficient to safeguard a livable world—by now has shrunk to one-fifth or even less. The disparity between this paltry amount and, say, the hundreds of billions paid for oil imports, or the tens of billions provided for MX systems, or similar unneeded and costly defense toys is grotesque. The usual annual battle in Congress over foreign aid might be replaced by fixing budgets for longer periods, for example, five years, to enable international agencies to work out long-range plans. In inflationary times, appropriations might be indexed, as are some domestic programs such as social security.

Where is the money to come from? I shall deal with the strategic and security aspects of military expenditures shortly; here I refer to the impact of defense budgets on attempted solutions of global issues. The proportion of GNP devoted to the military establishment in the United States and in other countries and especially by the nuclear powers has grown so vast over the last couple of decades that militarism imperils the future of mankind. A reversal in attitudes and policies is needed if there is to be enough capital to create minimally-satisfactory living conditions not only among the exploding billions of the third world but also within our own developed world. Never mind current squabbles over some billions more or less in the U.S. defense budget: It is a matter of expenditures having long ago got out of hand and threatening in the near future to devour as much as now goes into the entire federal budget. Military misallocations affect domestic programs in such a way that what we observe in the third world—the exclusion of a large proportion of the population from the economic process—may well spread in this country from the now excluded "underclass" of minorities, unemployables, and others, to ever-larger strata. We shall be all armor, and nothing will be left to be protected. It is not even an issue of guns or margarine when inner cities rot and their people, especially the young, are condemned to a life of hopelessness. We shall see further deterioration of the entire infrastructure of industrial society, from decaying railroad systems to buildings, streets, bridges, and so on. Worse, the ablest are attracted to the defense industries, a new kind of brain drain endangering technological progress in the civilian sector. We shall become ever-more like communist countries where, as in the Soviet Union, all "progress" resides in the military sector, while the masses remain poor. Unless we effect a radical reduction in military expenditures, vital domestic and global problems cannot be solved.

As the military develops an unsatiable appetite for resources, the availability of vast funds encourages waste, and the investment of these funds in ever-more sophisticated and expensive weapons systems leads to the neglect of maintenance and repair of available systems, endangering military readiness. And military spending becomes a world problem when defense industries compete in the global arms market and military assistance increases constantly, enabling the rulers of developing nations to acquire the most modern military equipment (often as a means to subdue internal reformist forces), while means for civilian development are nonexistent; Iran may serve as an example and a warning. In the words of one observer, such countries become "military fortresses in a vast desert of economic misery."[13] It means that trillions of dollars go into arming the developed and the developing countries, which, in turn, means the perpetuation of the now global inflation because investing in armaments *per se* reduces the supply of consumable goods.

All this concerns not only development but also security. If we want developing countries to stay out of the Soviet orbit and instead line up with what we call the free world, we can hardly rely on those authoritarian or dictatorial regimes that our armament and development policies support. Their political, social, and economic instability renders them doubtful allies; do we want other Irans in South Korea, or Pakistan, or Latin America? Our somewhat frantic search for at least minimally stable countries to grant us bases in the Middle East (Oman, Somalia, Yemen) shows what I mean. Egypt, overpopulated and unable to provide for its masses, may prove a similar disappointment. In Latin America, can we rely on the Somoza type of regime to prevent Castroization? I suggest that we support whatever progressive regimes or mass movements exist short of communist ones.[14] By supporting them we would not only engage in policies commensurate with American moral purpose and encourage efforts to protect human rights where we have a chance to influence events; we would also have a better chance of earning the appreciation of countries whose people all too often turn anti-American because of our protection of their oppressors. And it is only such progressive regimes that can be entrusted with the task of providing for the basic needs of their people.

VI.

Discussing the contest for the alignment of the nonaligned has brought us close to the traditional problem areas of foreign policy—the armaments race, confrontation versus detente, East-West conflict, alliances, and so on. Of these I will chiefly deal with the ones connected with the other great issue of survival, that of the threat of nuclear war.

As a political realist I have always emphasized the role of power and security in a world of sovereign nation-states. I once developed a theory according to which the historical units of international action were determined by the development of the means of destruction, that is, warfare, from the small medieval castle or walled city that, in the pregunpowder age, could provide protection to small groups only in the territorial state, whose means of defense provided larger units, such as entire nations, relative security through what I called impermeability.[15] In the nuclear age not even the mightiest and the largest are safe from penetration by ICBMs and similar weaponry; once a certain level of conventional and nuclear armament has been reached, a level sufficient to ensure the destruction of any opponent, a further increase, involving overkill capacity, becomes senseless. To quote Hans Morgenthau, whose credentials as a political realist are uncontested, "once one is able, through the instruments of nuclear weapons, to destroy one's enemy even under the worst of circumstances, one has reached the optimum of armaments beyond which it is obviously senseless to go." And, again, "as long as my enemy has one gun with which to kill me, it is irrelevant for our mutual relations that he has also the finest collection of guns in town."[16] We long ago arrived at the point at which talk of "superiorities" and "inferiorities" in nuclear power does not make sense. The capacity to inflict unacceptable damage on an opponent is enough to deter him. Whether one or the other side has a couple of bombs or warheads more or less hardly matters in an excess quantity of tens of thousands.[17] But this simple consideration tends to get lost in the physics and metaphysics of so-called strategic doctrine. Distrusting one's own retaliatory capacity, one piles one system of retaliatory striking force on the other. We have at this point three: land-based ICBMs, airborne forces of the strategic air command, and the submarine-based seaborne missile force. The Soviets are in the process of building up the latter. Each might do with one or at the most two.[18]

The danger becomes imminent when one or the other side or both believe that they can strike without having to fear retaliation. As long as one of several retaliatory systems remains protected from such first-strike capacity, for example, the submarine-based one, such fear need not crystallize, but who knows what nuclear technology may have in store for us in the future? Laser-killer beams or the eradication of verifiability systems or something equally or more dreadful? After having missed the bus to arms control several times, now is perhaps the last time when agreement to halt such "progress" and step-by-step reduction of armaments may save the world from nuclear holocaust. Such agreements may also save us from further nuclear proliferation of a kind and to such an extent that nobody will know any longer whom to deter and how. But the nonproliferation treaty was acceded to by the nonnuclear states on the condition that the nuclear powers would engage in meaningful arms control. The ball is in our court and in the Soviets' field. Time is running out. Three false nuclear alerts in six months in the United States should have alerted everyone to the fact that we are at the mercy of a computer error (the computer, as *The New Yorker* pointed out neatly, "not possessing among its many talents the ability to distinguish reality from fantasy"). But the news was buried in the back pages.

Hardliners, when compelled to admit the irrationality of the nuclear arms race, tend to shift the argument to focus on political considerations, claiming that nuclear superiority (allegedly now possessed by the Soviets) enables the opponent to engage in blackmail, compel weaker states to make concessions, or to "Finlandize" them; some speak of "self-Finlandization" in anticipation of such pressure. There is an element of truth in this contention but not enough. As long as the United States and its allies are prepared to say no to expansionist demands and refuse to be intimidated, why should the threat succeed? It has not even in the case of Finland. As long as a minimum of nuclear retaliatory strength as well as a minimum of balanced conventional forces exist (as they do in present East-West relations), no such pressure need be (nor has been) successful, as the history of postwar East-West relations has shown from the time of the Berlin blockade to this day. Continuing crises can be expected, leading to the question of how, besides nuclear disarmament, tensions that lead to cold war and confrontation can be reduced.

Reduction of tensions spells detente, a term that has acquired a bad connotation for hardliners. Often sharing the ideological anticommunism of Solzhenitzyn, who claims that "to coexist with communism on the same planet is impossible,"[19] they condemn policies of detente as useless but dangerous efforts at appeasement and unilateral yielding to Soviet demands. But viewing Soviet communism as inevitably expansionistic is merely the counterpart of communists viewing the West, and the United States in particular, as inherently "imperialistic." Both attitudes derive from what I have called the security dilemma of nations that, not being under higher authority, feel responsible for defending their existence and, not knowing what the others are up to, enmesh themselves in seamless webs of distrust and fear, provoking competition for power and weapons and so on in unending circles. Both may be genuinely concerned about security, that is, concerned only with defending what they have, but, seen from the other side, may be perceived as threatening, aggressive, and expansionist.

Having barely survived the genuinely imperialistic onslaught of Nazism, Stalin felt threatened by a newly-dominant United States and built up a protective wall of satellites, which, in turn, was interpreted by the West as the first step in an attempt by the Soviets to establish world control. By putting oneself into the other's shoes, one can recognize his fears and suspicions and thus can engage in a policy of status quo. Detente then is possible on the basis of mutual agreement on delimiting spheres of influence and control and on nonintervention in such spheres. In one decisive area, Europe, such delimitation of spheres, although officially recognized only in 1975 at Helsinski, was tacitly agreed and observed during the height of the cold war.

In the Far East, too, where China is no longer in the Soviet bloc, there is now balance and relative stability. It should be U.S. policy to maintain this balance not by lining up with China but by keeping open that possibility.

As for the rest of the world, that is, chiefly the third world, including the Arab world, what are the chances for detente? Even there, despite Afghanistan (which was in the Soviet sphere prior to the invasion), Soviet policy need not be interpreted as expansionistic, not even with respect to the Persian Gulf region. Any Soviet military action there would rally the Arabs against them, and they might get stuck in their Vietnam, destroying, as we once did a village in the real Vietnam, "in order to save it," the Persian Gulf "it" being oil. As for the United States, we cannot rely on stable bases in any of the countries in the area for the reasons I pointed out before. Israel, as a stable democracy, is the exception, but establishing an American presence there would surely antagonize the Arabs, including the now friendly ones. And such a presence is not even desired by the Israelis. Where would we send "rapid deployment forces" if they were available? Would we send them uninvited, like the marines of yore? How would we react to similar action by the Soviets? The only solution, I submit, is a Western energy policy that radically diminishes dependence on imported oil coupled perhaps with multilateral agreements on the international management of oil and perhaps also of other vital energy resources, such as uranium, and commodities, such as manganese.

Back to the problem of detente in the third world: One might try to find a basis for it in an agreement between East and West to keep regions such as southern Asia and/or the Middle East free from military intervention and the establishment of military bases, as once considered for the Indian Ocean area and on the pattern of agreements on nuclear-weapons-free zones (as now in Latin America). The Soviets, "encircled" as they perceive themselves to be because of the new Western orientation of China, might be amenable to such an agreement. Encirclement is largely in the eyes of the beholder, but even imaginary danger can determine policy, and we should not underestimate long-standing Soviet fears not only of Western imperialism but also of Chinese expansionism (precisely as the Chinese fear Soviet "hegemonism": the security dilemma again!).

The most serious threat to peace in the Middle East-Asian region is not Soviet expansionism but the Arab-Israel conflict, a tragic and seemingly insoluble one because of the competition of two "rights." Even though the United States is committed to defend Israel's right to existence, this commitment should not prevent us from recognizing the legitimate aspirations to similar statehood on the part of the Palestinian Arabs. Probably all of us have our pet solutions. I have had my say elsewhere[20] and cannot go into details here. As far as other parts of the world outside the two blocs are concerned, nonalignment has often been interpreted by the United States as meaning belonging to the Western camp. Thus any turn toward the East has been interpreted as evidence of Soviet expansionism, even when, as in the cases of Cuba and Ethiopia, those turns came as surprises (and perhaps not even agreeable ones!) to the Soviets. But such developments have most often reflected reaction against American backing of colonialism (as in the cases of the former Portuguese colonies), or against racism of the South African variety, or against supporting rightist-oppressive regimes. As the case of Angola and other actual or self-styled socialist third-world countries shows, what counts is not whether property is owned privately or publicly but what use is made of it, that is, whether production is for domestic mass needs or chiefly for the world market. Only where there is a direct military tie-up with the Soviet Union can the respective unit be said to belong to the Soviet bloc.[21] All the others deserve our aid in building viable economies and societies (as elaborated before).

VII.

The foregoing sections can perhaps be best summed up in terms of that elusive concept, the national interest. As long as we live in a world of nation-states, that interest, although often couched in ideological terms or as a reflection of all kinds of subnational interests, for example, business or ethnic-group interests, can be most meaningfully defined as a unit's "security" interest in protecting its territory,

population, and independence. But for the United States, in
an age of utter nuclear vulnerability, to satisfy this interest
requires either global control, which, short of all-destructive
nuclear war, cannot be obtained, or a balance of nuclear and
nonnuclear forces, which, because of the extreme danger
involved in nuclear armament, must be established at the
lowest effective level, excluding, for instance, a triple system
of deterrence. Beyond SALT and similar agreements, the unilateral reduction of arms not necessary for deterrence should
be seriously considered; it might reduce distrust and lead to
bi- or multilateral further steps.

Distinguishing basic national interests, such as minimum
security, from the subnational interests of social, business,
and ethnic groups would also allow a more rational approach
to the problem of interests versus ideals, such as the protection of human rights abroad. Realists cannot subordinate
genuine vital interests to the latter goal, but wherever it is
possible to pursue it without endangering such interests, such
protection should be secured. Thus in the case of dissidents
under Soviet control, we can hardly go beyond protest without endangering peace and detente; but where, as in Latin
America, U.S. pressure in favor of protecting human rights
promises success without affecting national interests (as distinguished from, for example, those of multinational corporations), the choice should be clear.

As long as we possess the power of nuclear deterrence
and of defending our shores by the use of conventional
forces, we do not need even the balance of power in Europe,
as in the past. Does this assessment imply neoisolationism, a
withdrawal into "Fortress America"? From an egocentered
American security viewpoint it would seem so. Apart from
geographically-close areas such as the Caribbean, why should
we be interested in the defense of Western Europe, of South
Korea, of Africa, or the Middle East? As long as we are as
safe from Soviet (or anybody else's) attack as our arms can

render us, why worry about whether the Soviet Union or anybody else has a bit more territory or exercises control somewhere in the world? Why not, as in the case of Israel and the Arabs, say: a plague on both your houses? Why not leave, say, India, with its enormous problems and troubles, to the Russians to worry about and wash our hands of it?[22]

Most of us would react strongly against such national egoism, but why? I suggest that we broaden our definition of national interest as well as go beyond it—broaden it because, as I have tried to point out, the world as such, all mankind, confronts the triple threat of overpopulation, exhaustion of resources, and environmental decay, and it is therefore in the national interest, broadly defined, to counter these threats by all the means we can muster. But we must also conduct a foreign policy that goes beyond national interest proper. We would lose our national soul if we distanced ourselves from the fate of those with whom we share our cultural and political values, the states of the Western world and especially the countries of Europe from which we stem historically and spiritually and which, in a still bipolar world of superpowers, need our protection. Those controlled by the Soviets we cannot protect, but we can do more for people in countries in which we have military, economic, or other leverage, whether in South Korea or South Africa, Guatemala or the Philippines. We can and should ask Israel, in return for our protection, to grant self-determination to the West Bank Arabs and abstain from settling there. We can also ask our European allies as well as Japan to contribute more equitably to common defense. Above all, we must ask them, as we must ask our own people, to make those kinds of sacrifices in living standards and life-styles without which a minimally-decent life in the world of the poor cannot be secured.

A new policy of global survival will severely test the willingness of the developed world and especially the United States to engage in the required changes in policies, attitudes, and life-style. To avoid becoming a hollow warfare state where, as now in the maldeveloping countries, an ever-smaller elite faces an ever-growing impoverished multitude, capital and technologies must be channeled in ways that steer investments here and abroad away from arms and luxury goods toward the production of mass-consumption goods such as housing, toward creating or repairing an infrastructure that has been sorely neglected, and toward salvaging an environment that threatens to poison or suffocate all of us. Ours is now a world of scarcity—only we in the developed world are not yet fully aware of it. This does not imply advocating zero growth; indeed, we need all the growth still possible for the fulfillment of the needs of a rapidly increasing humanity. But for us who live in the overdeveloped world, with its wasteful, throwaway civilization, frugality, if not austerity, is in the offing, and this way of life will affect those portions of the working classes whose life-styles and living standards approach those of the traditional Western upper classes but who cannot expect their exploited third-world brethren to escape the sweatshop without bringing them closer to their own income levels. But the major sacrifices will have to come from the superrich and their hangers-on in our corporate system. The time of wine and roses is over.

If I advocate austerity, it is not because I want to be a spoilsport. I would love to see a world in which all enjoy and to the utmost as much as the world can offer, but this is a utopian wish in a world of so many billions. And instead of having a Hobbesian world in which people fight over Churchill's "last few crumbs," I would develop one in which there would be a more just and fairer distribution of the goodies. But to achieve this, foreign policy, like all policy, must become future oriented, taking for its yardstick the interests of future generations because, as Hans Jonas has pointed out, "the nonexistent has no lobby, and the unborn are powerless,"[23] all those concerned for them must become their lobbyists.

I know full well that, at least in the United States, the general trend of attitudes and policies is in the opposite direction. The concerns are with competition and strife and with readiness for war, not with common global efforts and with efforts to safeguard the peace in conjunction with the other countries of the world and especially the opponent superpower. I submit that present fears of weakness and unpreparedness, arising in part from defeat in foreign adventure, reflect an earlier stage of human development, with its urge to dominate, to be "Number One" in an arena of competition and fight,[24] a desire connected with age-old, now outdated world views and perceptions.

I shall conclude with a few statements about the more general significance, for the conduct of their affairs, of how humans perceive their world.[25] The way in which not only humans but all living beings sense or perceive their world determines whether and how they will survive. The more accurate, the more comprehensive, the more varied their interpretations the better their chances of survival. This is true not only of individuals but of the respective species. In human history this process of information and perception has grown over the millennia not only spatially (experiencing eventually the planet as a whole as a global habitat) and temporally (experiencing the world as past, present, and future) but apprehending what was needed to enable their groups to survive in terms of the organization of society and of culture. Perceiving the world as an environment in which political groupings must compete for wealth, power, and so on enabled ever-larger nation-states to thrive. Today this interpretation no longer guarantees the survival of even the strongest. Mankind now either survives as an entirety or else it is doomed. It is doomed if our perceptions perpetuate the conservative world image of previous history, an image that did not and did not have to take into account the possibility and the threat of dooming the human race. Only by broadening our world perception to comprehend the global threats that I have tried to elaborate and by acting on that comprehension in foreign and other policies will mankind have a chance to survive. I am aware that by issuing this call for radical reorientation, I join a minority, a small group of philosophers like Hans Jonas, ecologists like Barry Commoner, and practitioners like Robert McNamara. Intellectuals are professional image makers. With so many, even among intellectuals, now rallying around the flag, that is, withdrawing into nationalist if not jingoistic parochialism, the minority's interpretations and attitudes may seem utopian.[26] But under present world conditions it is self-styled realism that may well lead to doom, whereas what appears utopian may prove to be the road to survival. We truly stand at that crossroad.

NOTES

1. To avoid misunderstanding, let it be said from the outset that these traditional problems cannot be disregarded just because, like a hurricane-driven flood, global issues threaten to overwhelm us. Issues of nations' security, as of the innumerable international issues of ethnicity or similar issues—over boundaries, resources, and so on—remain of concern and shall be dealt with in this essay. The reason that issues of global survival are stressed is simply that they so often are neglected in the day-to-day or year-to-year discussions and practice of foreign affairs.

2. Hans Jonas, "Technology and Responsibility, Reflections on the New Tasks of Ethics," *Social Research* 40 (1), 1973, pp. 31 ff. (44); German version in his book *Das Prinzip Verantwortung* (Frankfurt, 1979), p. 36.

3. For a rather moderate summing up that, if anything, errs on the side of optimism, see the projections in *Global 2000 Report,* an interagency report submitted to President Carter in 1980 (U.S. Government Printing Office, Washington, D.C.).

4. *The New York Times,* May 26, 1980, or, at random, see John B. Oakes, Op. Ed. report on the Marcos dictatorship that began with

these words: "Manila. In the middle of this sprawling city of sleek new office buildings, squalid tin-roofed slums, and a million squatters. . . ." (*The New York Times,* July 4, 1980).
  5. For some details of the characteristic Brazilian situation, see Warren Hoge, "Brazil Hopes to See a Desert Bloom," *The New York Times,* May 18, 1980 (E 8).
  6. For a succinct summing up of the respective developments, see A. L. Valdez, "The Global Bracero Problem," *Proceedings* of the 73rd Annual Meeting of the American Society of International Law, Washington 1979, pp. 119 ff. (123/24).
  7. Problems of "refugees" trying to escape economic misery rather than political oppression plague those among the affluent countries that are ready to accept political refugees but not "hordes" of third-world poverty victims. Thus the problem has become acute not only in the United States, where the vast Caribbean slum tends to empty its despairing poor into the promised land, but also in countries like West Germany, where a liberal constitutional provision on asylum has permitted numerous economic refugees to gain access to the country and its welfare-state goodies (see *Die Zeit,* "Dossier," June 6, 1980). Quite generally the migration of foreign workers (who become less welcome guests in times of recession) from south to north reflects the problems created by the third-world's population explosion; see the change of ethnic patterns in the United States, Britain, France, and other countries.
  8. If "disaggregation" from acting through international organizations in favor of country-to-country dealing is now advocated by discussants of international relations, this approach may be advisable under certain circumstances but certainly not in dealing with the overall global survival issues; a collective approach is of the essence.
  9. A trend under which leaders of some industrialized countries are beginning to pay some attention to the combined overpopulation-development problem is illustrated by the following sentences from a speech by West German Chancellor Schmidt: "When I went to school I learned that there were about two billion people living on earth. Today there are well over four billion, and we are told that in the year 2000 . . . the world population will be in the neighborhood of six billion. . . . This is the most challenging problem of our time. . . . I fear, indeed, for the survival of man if the population growth continues unchecked. . . . May we hope to provide all these masses with food, shelter, energy, jobs? . . . I very much doubt it. . . . I favor family planning because I fear for human values. . . . We must strive to raise the standard of living in the poorer countries; to reduce the economic

motives for very large families, and, at the same time, to teach family planning and make it socially acceptable" (Speech by Helmut Schmidt before the Society for the Family of Man, New York, November 19, 1980).

10. Richard Gilmore, "Grain in the Bank," *Foreign Policy*, 38, spring 1980, pp. 168 ff.

11. Again, to avoid misunderstanding, I do not advocate jumping from the present nation-state system to supranationalism in one fell swoop but rather starting from what there is gradually toward more collective action, using, as far as possible, existing institutions and processes.

12. Similar to the requirement of "environmental impact statements" in the United States, impact statements might be required from the respective agencies in regard to a project's effect on (a) demographic trends, (b) resources, in particular, energy, (c) the environment.

13. Rajni Kothari, "Toward a Just World," in *Macrocosm*, Newsletter of the Transnational Academic Program of the Institute for World Order, no. 7, spring 1980, pp. 6 ff. (7). Kothari continues: "A 'new international order' is not possible without reordering domestic societies." This agrees with FAO Director-General Saouma's view that responsibility for the solution of world poverty and related problems lies with the elites between and within the countries; in third-world countries, too, there is "luxury and obesity for the few; abject poverty and emaciation for the many."

14. That is, social-democratic ones, Christian-democratic ones, labor and/or peasants "liberation" movements, or whatever the name. Membership in the Socialist (Second) International is a useful indicator.

15. See my *International Politics in the Atomic Age* (New York, 1959), chapters 2 and 3.

16. Hans Morgenthau, "The Dilemma of SALT," *Newsletter* of the National Committee on American Foreign Policy, August 1979. That newsletter's other article (Joseph Churba, "SALT and Foreign Policy") may serve as a typical example of that "strategic metaphysics" that befuddles issues clarified in the simple and clear-cut terms of scholars such as Hans Morgenthau.

17. See some data in David Singer's enlightening letter to *The New York Times* (April 12, 1979). And it is not only a political danger and an economic waste but also a deadly threat to the environment. Huge amounts of plutonium waste from nuclear-weapons production are piling up without satisfactory means of disposal, a global danger for thousands of years (see Elaine Douglass, "The D.O.E.'s Hazardous Wastes," *The Nation*, December 27, 1980, pp. 689, 704-708).

18. This means that the defense budgets of nuclear powers (in particular, the United States' and the Soviet Unions') could be slashed by tens of billions without affecting the powers' security in the least and in this way setting free large amounts to serve basic needs both at home and in the third world.

19. Alexander Solzhenitzyn, "Misconceptions about Russia Are a Threat to America," Foreign Affairs, spring 1980, pp. 797 ff.

20. John H. Herz, "Normalization in International Relations: Some Observations on the Arab-Israeli Conflict," Middle East Review, 10 (3), spring 1978, pp. 10 ff.

21. Even in the case of Cuba, usually considered part of the Soviet bloc, economic ties with the capitalistic world economy are still strong (see Susan Eckstein, "Capitalist Constraints on Cuban Socialist Development," Comparative Politics, 12 (3), April 1980, pp. 253 ff.); they would be even stronger without the U.S. trade and investment embargo. Angola's communist regime continues the Cabinda oil ties with Western oil companies and so forth.

22. If this be called a policy of double standards or interventionism, so be it; humanitarian intervention that tries to combat the now pervasive system of government or government-sanctioned torture or "disappearance" killings (often taught third-world practitioners by U.S. police experts), for example, is morally preferable to nonintervention any time. Some examples of how much (or how little) "human interest" has been taken into consideration by American foreign policymakers are found in Robert C. Johansen's The National Interest and the Human Interest, An Analysis of U.S. Foreign Policy (Princeton, 1980).

23. Hans Jonas, loc. cit. p. 51; German version in Das Prinzip Verantwortung, op. cit., p. 55.

24. In rather un-American fashion, we never tire of claiming to be "the greatest country on earth." It is a sign of immaturity. I remember my own infantile, or juvenile, enthusiasm at the time of World War I. For me, in Germany, it was "Deutschland ueber alles." But defeat in 1918 was a lesson for Germans, at least until Hitler started to reinfect many of them with his "superior race" visions. But the Zeppelins and dreadnoughts, the playthings of the warmaking boys at that time, were nothing compared to what our generals and other military-industrial boys play around with now, recklessly risking the existence of all of us. There is insufficient awareness of the deadly threat. Americans have never suffered defeat in global war, never experienced the obscenity of the slaughter on their own soil since the Civil War; most are too young even to remember Hiroshima. Most lack the imagination to visualize the effects of even one nuclear explosion in a metropolitan area. Thus the

realization that nobody can be Number One any more on this planet comes slowly. And the realization that all we can have is a world in which nobody is mightier than oneself is distasteful to leaders who, not having had the experience of conducting foreign policy—that necessary but unrewarding, patient, and dogged plodding that is required to achieve even modest results—prefer to rely on good old jingoism.

In this connection it is interesting to recall the reactions, both expressed in commencement addresses, by two American foreign-policy leaders. That of John F. Kennedy, in his address to American University right after the Cuban missile crisis, was one of a statesman who, having looked down the barrel of annihilation, was determined to build the road toward coexistence; close to two decades later, Cyrus Vance, in his Harvard address, restated Kennedy's conviction: "It is not too late but it may soon be. . . . If we fail to act we may some day ask ourselves why we were blinded by considerations of the moment and lost a vital long-term opportunity. . . ." (*The New York Times,* June 6, 1980, A 12). Alas, his was the insight of a leader who had had to resign before the onslaught of hawkish opposition to policies of restraint and the counsel of prudence.

25. Perception is based on awareness and information. Much in the world views of policymakers depends on the range, depth, and system of information available to them. I have discussed elsewhere the failure by the American establishment to probe into what may be called the lower, or social, range of conditions, particularly those in third-world countries (see my article "Weltbild und Bewusstwerdung, vernachlaessigte Faktoren beim Studium der internationalen Beziehungen," in *Aus Politik und Zeitgeschichte,* Beilage zur Wochenzeitung Das Parlament, March 15, 1980, pp. 3-17). So little had the CIA and other intelligence agencies informed the leadership of what was going on in Iran prior to the revolution that President Carter, on the occasion of his visit to Teheran in 1979, could address the shah in these words: "Iran, under the great leadership of the Shah, is an island of stability in one of the more troubled areas of the world. This is a great tribute to you, Your Majesty, and to your leadership, and to the respect, admiration, and love which your people give to you." It was the love with which, in Brecht-Weill's Dreigroschenoper, the beggars greeted their queen. It is likely that even after the Iranian debacle, not much has been done to effect improvement in countries and societies that may prove equally unstable (see, for example, a discussion of the prevalent conditions in Saudi Arabia; Peter Lubin, "Gulf Follies," *Middle East Review,* 12 (3), spring 1980, pp. 9 ff. (11-13).

26. Not for a minute do I have the illusion that what I have

proposed is likely to happen. The new Washington administration's policy goes in the opposite direction: In the security area it tends to move toward a new arms race and ensuing expenditures that will endanger a decent life in this country, whereas in the global area it is moving toward neglect of basic needs and human rights, in this way promoting dictatorship and oppression worldwide. Quite possibly, this kind of attitude and policy will spread. The global view may well terrify the less bold among the elites, who, afraid of attacking seemingly unmanageable global problems, will tend to shy away from them and withdraw into the wonted realm of the parochial. If so, only a radical change of elites might help. Such a change to be effective globally would have to occur simultaneously in East and West and many parts of the south. This is not likely to happen either. Unless we resign ourselves to the decay (if not the catastrophe) that the present approach presages, we can place our hope only in a (however unlikely) gradual change in attitudes that might eventually open the way toward required changes in policies.

IX.

Human Survival:
Crusade or
Coherent Plan?

KENNETH AND
BEVERLY THOMPSON

No one can doubt, as Professor John H. Herz has argued, that the world stands at a crossroads. To ignore the double threat to human survival would be both irresponsible and unrealistic. On one side of history, the whole habitable globe lives under the Damoclean sword of thermonuclear annihilation. On the other side, mankind is threatened by the devastating effects of famine, overpopulation, the depletion of resources, and environmental deterioration. Men envisage the one danger in the image of a vast mushrooming cloud of total destruction and the other in the ravages of forces that slowly but irresistibly drain life from millions of people.

In some circles debates go on about what constitutes the more severe crisis. Those who declare that one threat is graver than the other or speculate about the year when mass destruction from one or the other will overtake mankind speak as seers or soothsayers rather than as students or scientists. Whatever the prophesy, who can ignore the dark warning clouds visible on the horizon? Is not the real issue the search for coherent answers to two different threats, one instant and immediate and the other long term and in the future? Is there not risk in urging mankind to confront the one and ignore the other? Can responsible leaders afford to say that the world faces only one grave peril and ignore all the others? Does not the future depend more on man's discovery for each urgent problem of a steady course and a coherent plan for meeting the challenge than on merely knowing that trouble looms?

1. A Personal Preface

Questions such as these cluster together as we begin to think about human survival. Partly they flash through one's mind because of personal experience. One of us served for nearly 20 years on the professional staff of a private technical-assistance organization. The agency's august leader fervently argued and sincerely believed that the gravest world threat was overpopulation. If he could have had his way, the organization would have committed the great bulk of its resources to turning back the rising curve of population growth. Although his father and his grandfather had confronted and overcome vast odds in the industrial world, he was convinced that large-scale material resources, not the endeavors of individuals, could be used to transform the world's social order. All of us admired his single-mindedness and dedication but doubted that any *one* of the world's urgent problems could be confronted in isolation from all the others. For example, food and population are interconnected problems in the developing world. Moreover, we considered it folly to maintain that the nuclear problem need not concern a large organization with flexible funds that had done so much in every sphere to train qualified professionals. Looking back, it is possible that the organization's retreat from supporting foreign-policy and arms-control studies for more than a decade might have contributed to the shortfall of trained personnel in these areas and helped create a vacuum into which marched the ideologues of right and left not surprisingly described as teams. A Harvard professor and president of the International Political Science Association, Karl Deutsch, wrote about the emptying of the pipelines in the 1970s of specialists in foreign policy. If Deutsch was right, one contributing factor might well have been the flight of the foundations from this field. The cause of their defection was the elevation of population control to the level of a crusade. Every other interest took second place. Literature published by the foundations described the main goal as the "conquest" of hunger or turning back population growth. Much like fund-raising indicators turned on their head in a community-chest campaign, falling birth rates were charted and displayed to demonstrate success. Whenever we read a paper that calls on the world or the nation to crusade for a worthy cause to be accomplished overnight, we are reminded of the campaign in which a private organization was once engaged to rid the world of overpopulation and hunger. To say that there was something pretentious and self-righteous about the whole enterprise is not to say that the foundation failed to make an important contribution. But it failed to define a coherent set of objectives.

2. Conquering the World Food Problem?

The 1960s constituted an era of hope, particularly in the developed world, about the "conquest" of hunger. More than in any other sector of human need (with the possible exception of the conquest of infectious diseases in the 1930s and 1940s), the international community put science to work to meet a basic human need. Programs of agricultural assistance begun in the early 1940s increased food production dramatically. Mexico, which had been using up scarce foreign exchange to import corn and wheat, became self-sufficient in the new era. The United States, which had never been considered a colonial power, exported trained agronomists, plant pathologists, and plant breeders to assist in what came to be called the Green Revolution. Because the first efforts were small—the entire research budget, exclusive of salaries, of the Rockefeller Foundation's agricultural staff in Mexico in the 1940s was 35,000 dollars—private assistance dominated the field. Those who went abroad were not intellectuals advocating functional integration but technical specialists who practiced it. Such men spoke little of "a system intermediate between traditional state sovereignty and world government."[1] Their success depended precisely on states' *not* "yielding portions of their sovereignty." Gains were closely linked with national pride. American agricultural scientists were able to make contributions because the Mexicans, not the Americans, received the credit. The Office of Special Studies was a newly-created unit that housed the Americans within the Ministry of Agriculture. New varieties of corn and wheat were given Mexican names, not international designations. As the program progressed, fellows from abroad went to Mexico to be trained by Mexicans. Throughout the world the remarkably successful program was known as the Mexican Agricultural Program, not the American or the Rockefeller Agricultural Program. Eventually, the Mexicans set out to help other Latin American countries, particularly those in Central America.

If one tries to explain why this program succeeded and why other attempts at increasing food production have faltered, one explanation is that the program became a Mexican program. Another factor was the simple, clear-cut nature of the mandate. The goal was not to help satisfy a wide variety of "basic human needs" ramifying throughout society. Instead, the aim was to increase production of a few basic food crops, namely, corn and wheat. The approach followed by the visiting scientists was to don overalls and go into the field with the Mexicans, a procedure not usually followed by trained Mexicans. The approach involved a partnership in applied science—both sides contributed human as well as investment capital. The visitors stayed, learned the language, assimilated the culture, and accepted and were accepted by the Mexican people. This kind of foreign assistance took the form of help in an area in which Americans had much to offer. The agricultural sciences in the United States were highly developed thanks to the land-grant colleges. Through institutions such as the county-agent system, new scientific findings were disseminated to the primary consumer, the farmer in the field. However conservative their politics (including international politics), the land-grant-college agriculturalists had acquired an inbred sense of service. Helping farmers abroad was a natural extension of helping farmers at home.

The visiting agricultural scientists implanted enough but not too much of their national agricultural system. They insisted on training Mexican agriculturalists "to grow a crop" because they had followed the same practice at Cornell, Purdue, Minnesota, and the Davis campus of the University of California. Wherever they went, they developed experimental farms to undertake practical agricultural exercises, sometimes drawing together unlikely combinations of plots of widely-separated land. They were more practical than the British or the French but less well-versed in the history of plants and crops around the world. Wherever the Americans went, they sought to achieve the single goal of increasing agricultural production by developing a critical mass of well-trained agriculturalists who would be able to work on various crops.

The most enduring lesson learned about methods is that programs that start small and grow big are more likely to succeed. The Mexican Agriculture Program was successful, at least in part, because it was integrated into the Mexican culture. It didn't start with a global objective, such as building a world food reserve. It was established to achieve the simple goal of increasing the agricultural production of those staples that mattered most to the Mexicans. It enlisted the efforts of doers, not conceptualizers, although the endeavor rested on such a simple axiom as "it is better to teach a man to fish than to give him a fish." The teachers were not generalists who had acquired an incidental concern for agriculture but America's best agricultural scientists.

Once a program in a single country had proved successful, others followed, appearing as spokes in a wheel. The Mexican effort began in 1943; a cooperative program with Colombia started in 1950, followed by the Chile program in 1953. Lessons learned in one country were extended to another; trained personnel from one moved to another. Needs were not everywhere the same. Ecuador sought to develop and improve its potato production. Different political systems imposed different constraints on cooperation. Some taxed imported seeds and machinery, to say nothing of the incomes of American scientists, whereas others followed more liberal and effective policies. As the spokes were completed—or nearly completed—in the wheel representing one region, wheels representing cooperative programs in Asia and Africa were added. The whole effort culminated in the establishment of International Agricultural Institutes on three continents that were modeled on the structure of the country programs but responsive to regional and worldwide needs.

What distinguished this approach from other efforts was its character as an international functional enterprise. It began with an urgent need, not a theory. Different nationalities joined together to work across national boundaries to solve a common problem. The supranational dimensions of the activity evolved from rather than preceded professional and functional cooperation. From the beginning of the project, cooperation between Americans and Mexicans was bilateral. One cannot sustain the judgment that programs undertaken by an international organization, as Herz argues, would have been more acceptable to the Mexicans. Professional competence in agriculture mattered most to the Mexicans. Unless the quality of staff members in the United Nations Food and Agriculture Organization reflected similar competence, it is questionable that they would have been better received. Empathy and sensitivity, willingness to listen and to learn, coherence and continuity are more important than an international label.

Therefore, the lessons that can be derived from successful cooperative programs in agriculture suggest that Professor Herz has taken too theoretical a view of the subject. He tells us little about what has been done and even less about guides to action other than a rather vague but unsupported preference for international organizations. The words *must, should,* and *ought* crop up so often in his text that he seems more caught up in a crusade than in a coherent and a continuing effort or a plan to improve conditions. What is true of food production is no less true of population to which we now turn.

3. Controlling World Population: A Complex Task

The urgency of attacking the problem of world population growth needs no reiteration. The present world population of 4.5 billion people is estimated to exceed 6 billion sometime around the year 2000. A United Nation's commission predicts that the world's population will increase to 10.5 billion in the next 130 years with 90 percent of the increase occurring in the less developed countries. Population growth will have stabilized by the year 2100, according to this estimate, assuming present controls are effective around the globe. On one level, the advances that have been made in population control match those in agriculture. If anything, more agencies have been involved in and more words have been written about population than about the conquest of hunger. The International Planned Parenthood Association operates in 95 countries. (One is tempted to ask whether this is a case of spreading scarce resources too thin.) Spokesmen for population agencies have opened dialogues with highly-placed leaders in countries from Canada to Brazil. World conferences have focused on population problems, the most notable being Bucharest in 1974. Within the past year, Mexico, Colombia, Brazil, and other Catholic countries sent delegations to a conference of parliamentarians held in Sri Lanka (Ceylon). Various consortia of organizations concentrating on population control have been formed and are active.

However, on a more basic level, the magnitude and the complexity of the population question surpass those relating to food. Not only is population increasing on an absolute basis, but it is concentrated in vast, sprawling urban centers. In 1960 there were 60 such cities. Mexico City, which has a population of 15 million is expected to grow to 30 million by 1985. Approximately 60 to 70 percent of Latin America's population is crowded together in explosively-unstable urban centers. From 1960 to 1970 the labor force expanded by eight million people. In the less-developed countries as a whole, the work force needing jobs equals the total number employed in all industrial countries. Population pressures are acute in sectors such as education. Although world illiteracy rates are likely to drop from 32 percent in 1970 to 25 percent in 1990, the absolute number of illiterate people is projected to increase from 884 million in 1970 to over a billion.

Population programs, moreover, have generated fewer success stories than those produced by the Green Revolution. Four Asian countries—Taiwan, Korea, Hong Kong, and Singapore—have made more significant progress in reducing population growth rates than all other Asian societies combined. It is significant that the most dramatic achievements have occurred with limited groups, such as the Military Dependents' Program in Taiwan. The sponsors have restrained their sense of urgency about population control because of religious and cultural attitudes and because famine and malnutrition are considered more serious and immediate crises. (More deaths in the third world result from malnutrition than from any other cause.) The dialogue that I recall from my technical-assistance experience with responsible leaders in African countries echoed across the continent. I was repeatedly told that representatives of private and public international agencies continuously urged these leaders to devote scarce resources to population control, whereas their most urgent and compelling problem was "clean water." They asked why external agencies were indifferent to such needs and why their countries were offered incentives or "bribes" to redirect their efforts to population programs? Was there a hidden motive verging on conspiracy by outside forces to keep down their population in order to limit their nations' power in world affairs?

However irrational such thinking appeared at the time, no serious person engaged in technical assistance could dismiss it out of hand. Population programs confronted obstacles that efforts to conquer hunger did not provoke. National pride and social practices stood in the path of successful intervention by outsiders irrespective of whether they represented the United Nations or private foundations. The presence of such obstacles led to a broadening of the approach and to the combining of indirect and direct assistance efforts. For example, the wholesale supplying of large shipments of condoms and jellies was initially considered the most effective means of controlling population growth. Stories multiplied of people using the jellies not for the intended purpose but to cover or paint their bodies. Greater sophistication was required in methods of control. Campaigns promoting sterilization worked in some cultures but caused nationalist backlashes in other cultures. In some cultures, the self-respect of males is predicated on their ability to produce offspring within or outside family structures. Concluding that all social systems are alike or assuming that family-planning practices appropriate to Americans can be transferred to other cultures proved fallacious. Indirect approaches were needed.

A prime example of the indirect approach is that linking employment and population control. Economists and social scientists have produced statistics demonstrating that population growth is inversely related to employment opportunities for women. Working mothers bear a significantly smaller number of children than women whose only social function is the production of offspring. Moreover, mortality rates are connected with population statistics. Where mortality rates are high, a large family is necessary to ensure that a sufficient number of children survive to operate family enterprises such as the family farm. When death rates decline, smaller families are able to maintain family-oriented economies. Improvements in public health, including sanitation, contribute indirectly to population control. Social acceptance of efforts designed to prolong human life was greater than support evinced for programs to reduce population through more direct methods. Linking public health and population control proved more compatible with the values of indigenous societies.

The lessons of two decades of large-scale efforts to control population suggest that a diversified approach has a better chance of success. In the same way that a coherent and a broad-gauged approach to the problem of world food has been shown to produce higher payoffs, a packaged approach of diverse efforts to achieve population control is indicated. The world food problem requires concentrated efforts to increase food production but also major attempts to improve the distribution of food products, better nutrition through the improvement of food quality, and social reforms effecting more equitable systems of land ownership. Linking economics and agriculture can lead to effective solutions. Nutrition scientists have joined with plant breeders to improve the quality as well as the quantity of food. The goal has become an integrated approach to meeting world food problems by adding the knowledge of experts from such disciplines as cultural anthropology, whose findings identify the cultural preferences for crops of a certain texture and appearance. (The original miracle rice—IR8—of the International Rice Research Institute in the Philippines was the result of cross-breeding devised to reflect the tastes of Indonesians, Thais, and Japanese.) Agricultural scientists introduced the concept of a "package of agricultural practices" to adapt to and meet the diverse needs of different cultures.

Population practices reflect the effects of two major theories of population control. The first theory, that of the developed or industrial countries, emphasizes direct efforts at population control. The second theory, which many of the less-developed countries have followed, presupposes that economic development precedes population control. At world population conferences spokesmen for the two theories, guided by two different sets of assumptions, have clashed. The division produced a stalemate between developed and less-developed countries at the Bucharest conference; the cleavage has continued to the present, although some progress has been made in reconciling the two viewpoints. The influence of economists from developed countries, who have illuminated the relationship between employment and population growth, has helped close the gap. But much remains to be done. Cutbacks in the population programs of several private agencies have shifted greater burdens of responsibility to national and international agencies, including the World Food Council. Although the shift has effected an increase in total resources, the debate over theories and policies of population control has become more politicized. It would be utopian to expect that solutions can be anything but long term given the nature of the population problem and the changing cultural and national context in which it must be worked out.

4. The Crisis of Human Survival in the Year 2000: Complexity Compounded

On May 23, 1977, President Jimmy Carter directed the Council on Environmental Quality and the Department of State, working in cooperation with other appropriate agencies, to make a one-year study and project changes in the world's population, natural resources, and environment through the end of the century. The resulting report was published in 1980 as *The Global 2000 Report to the President: Entering the Twenty-First Century.* That there looms a genuine crisis in human survival becomes clear from reading the findings in this report and more recent studies.

Population

According to the *Global 2000 Report,* the world's population will experience an enormous growth from 4.1 billion people in 1975 to a conservatively projected 6.35 billion in the year 2000. A large percentage of the population growth (92 percent) will occur in the less-developed countries, meaning that by the year 2000, of the world's 6.35 billion people, 5 billion will be living in less-developed countries, and 400 million males and females aged 15 will confront the prospect of child rearing.[2]

In addition to the projected rapidly-increasing population growth in the LDCs by 2000, the *Global Report* projects a burgeoning movement of rural people to urban areas. By 2000 Mexico City will have a population of more than 30 million, Calcutta nearly 20 million, greater Bombay, Cairo, Jakarta, and Seoul 15 to 20 million each, Tehran nearly 14 million, Delhi about 13.5 million, and Manila more than 12.5 million.[3]

This rural exodus will impose heavily-increasing demands on the cities' presently overburdened services, such as housing, food, water supplies, sanitation, fire and police protection, education, and employment. Indeed, by the year 2000 the many rural people flocking to LDC cities will be living, if they survive, below the level of what is currently termed "slum living." The majority of the population in LDC cities will be found in settlements comprised of shacks, tents, shanties, and structures offering a modicum of shelter.

The impact that this rapid population growth will exact on global per-capita income will widen the present gap between today's wealthiest and poorest nation. It is estimated that by the year 2000 industrialized countries will have a per-capita GNP of 8,500 dollars-11,000 dollars (in 1975 dollars), compared to that of the LDCs, which will average less than 600 dollars.[4] Although average annual GNP growth will be greater in LDCs than in developed countries (4.5 percent compared to 3.3 percent), ". . . the LDC growth in gross national product develops from a very low base, and population growth in the LDCs brings per-capita increases down to very modest proportions."[5] "For example, while such countries as India, Bangladesh, and Pakistan will show increases in per-capita GNP, they will show nearly zero gain in per-capita income because of population growth. In these countries GNP per capita is projected to remain below $200 (in 1975 dollars) by the year 2000."[6] Furthermore, disparities between the highest and the lowest income groups in the LDCs will widen markedly.

Environment

With a dramatically increased world population and concomitant demands for more food production and a greater supply of energy, what will be the consequent impact on the global environment: agriculture, water resources, fisheries, forests, atmosphere and climate, species maintenance?

The *Global 2000 Report* states: "Perhaps the most serious environmental development will be an accelerating deterioration and loss of the resources for agriculture. This overall development includes soil erosion; loss of nutrients and compaction of soil erosion; increasing salinization of both irrigated land and water used for irrigation; loss of high-quality cropland to urban development; crop damage due to increasing air and water pollution; extinction of local and wild crop strains needed by plant breeders for improving cultivated varieties; and more frequent and more severe regional water shortages—especially when energy and industrial development compete for water supplies or where forest losses are heavy and the earth can no longer absorb, store, and regulate the discharge of water."[7]

Deterioration of soils is occurring in the less-developed countries and is spreading desertlike conditions in dry areas and causing heavy erosion in humid ones. In fact, "Present global losses to desertification are estimated at about 6 million hectares a year (an area about the size of Maine), including 3.2 million hectares of rangeland, 2.5 million hectares of rainfed cropland, and 125 thousand hectares of

irrigated farmland."⁸ Desertification, which ultimately leaves
the land depleted of nutrients and useless for crops or
grazing, is mainly caused by overcropping, overgrazing, and
using woody plants for fuel. Particularly in the less-developed
countries, where dung is the principal source of fuel because
of the lack of firewood, the land is being robbed of its
natural fertilizers.

But the devastating problem of soil depletion and permanent land damage is not confined to the less-developed
countries: It is a global problem that the United States is also
facing particularly because of the urbanization of agricultural
land, the salinization of irrigated land, sewage, acid rain, and
the industrial pollution of water resources, the accelerated
use of inorganic fertilizers and pesticides. It is reported that
in California, for example, 17 of 25 major agricultural pests
are resistant to one or more kinds of pesticides, the natural
pest-predator population having been greatly reduced.

Global land depletion, naturally, affects water resources.
As the world population soars, so does the demand on
water's life-supply systems. The *Global 2000 Report* shows
the increasing destruction of coastal ecosystems that will
negatively affect 60 to 80 percent of commercially-valuable
marine life, a high-protein component of healthful human
diets. Not only will the marine-life supply for human consumption be destroyed by industrial-commercial pollutants
but by pollutants caused by high-yield agricultural technology such as irrigation, commercial fertilizers, and pesticides.
Another heavy contributor to the pollution of water resources will be the conversion of agricultural land to urban
uses as the world's rural population, unable to maintain a
subsistence level, flees to the cities in the vain hope of finding
some means of feeding, housing, and supporting itself. Whereas water pollution in the less-developed countries is expected
to increase, developed countries are already facing the grim
problems resulting from diminishing supplies of water and

increasing volumes of polluted water. The United States, a chief producer of the world's food, is feeling the pinch. A special report, "The Browning of America," in *Newsweek* stated: "Most alarming of all, vast underground reserves of water, deposited over thousands of years, have been seriously depleted in a matter of decades. All water comes as rain from the sky, but 92 percent of it either evaporates immediately or runs off, unused, to the oceans. One-quarter of the water that irrigates farms and bathes America is taken from an ancient network of underground aquifers. In 1950 the nation took 12 trillion gallons of water out of the ground; by 1980 the figure had more than doubled, and each day 21 billion more gallons flow out than seep in. Water from the great Ogallala Aquifer, which stretches from west Texas to northern Nebraska, is being used up, as irrevocably—and some would say as wantonly—as the oil that lies beneath it. 'It varies, depending on where you are,' says Nebraska water planner, Michael Jess, 'but there are some people projecting that as early as the year 2000, there will be parts of Nebraska with their water supplies so depleted that farming may never return.' "[9]

As the pressures of growth continue to exert pressure on land and water resources, so will they exert increasing pressure on forests, atmosphere, climate, and species—the acceleration of a trend that will affect the world's ability to produce food. For example, in South and Southeast Asia today about ". . . one billion people live in heavily farmed alluvial basons and valleys that depend on forested mountain watersheds for their water. If present trends continue, forests in these regions will be reduced by half in 2000, and erosion, siltation, and erratic stream flows will seriously affect food production."[10] Moreover, in many tropical forests, soil and landforms are in a state of imbalance; and if the extensive cutting of timber should occur without replacement planting, which is the practice today, ultimately the soil will produce neither trees nor weeds, despite the application of advanced technological procedures.

Throughout the world, particularly in urban areas in both less-developed countries and developed countries, air quality has deteriorated far below levels considered safe by the World Health Organization. It is expected to deteriorate further as greater amounts of fossil fuels, especially coal, are burned, causing a greater concentration of carbon dioxide in the atmosphere. Of special concern is the warming effect on the earth caused by the increased accumulation of CO_2 and the probable consequence of diminished world agricultural production that is projected to occur shortly after 2000. The result could also change global patterns of precipitation, and a 2°-3°C rise in temperatures in the middle latitudes and an increase of 5°-10°C in polar temperatures could lead to the eventual melting of the Greenland and Antarctic ice caps, causing a gradual rise in the sea level and the abandonment of affected coastal cities.

The *Global 2000 Report* states that "Even a 1°C increase in average global temperatures would make the earth's climate warmer than it has been any time in the last 1,000 years."[11] Such rapid changes in climate would cause grave problems to all forms of human adaptation, including agriculture. An additional threat to the earth's atmosphere and a global danger to humans and crops would be the depletion of the stratospheric ozone layer protecting the earth from devastating ultraviolet rays that would result in a high incidence of skin cancer and a ray-burning of crops. Principal offenders in the burning off of stratospheric ozone layers are chlorofluorocarbon emissions, nitron-oxcide emissions from both organic and inorganic nitrogen fertilizers, and, it is believed, the effects of fuel emissions from high-altitude aircraft flights. To date few countries other than the United States have made efforts to control fluorocarbon emitted from aerosol cans.

Closely related to the problem of contamination from fossil-fuel combustion is that of safely disposing of radioactive materials from nuclear power plants. To date it has not been demonstrated anywhere in the world that high- or low-level nuclear wastes can be safely stored or safely disposed of, despite the fact that nuclear power plants are supposed to be operating under controlled conditions. It would be realistic as well as prudent to consider the immediate and the long-term effects of recent accidents in nuclear power plants. The *Global 2000 Report* states that "some of the by-products of reactors . . . have half-lives approximately five times as long as the period of recorded history."[12] And "several hundred thousand tons of highly radioactive spent nuclear fuel will be generated over the lifetimes of the nuclear plants likely to be constructed through the year 2000."[13]

Each of these sources of pollution will effect the extinction of species if present trends continue. The *Global 2000 Report* suggests that the loss of plant and animal genetic resources will mean the extinction of 15 to 20 percent of all species that contribute to human survival as food and/or fuel. Some of the most severe losses will involve the extinction of subspecies and varieties of cereal grains. "Four-fifths of the world's food supplies are derived from less than two dozen plant and animal species. Wild and local domestic strains are needed to break resistance to pests and pathogens and transform such species to high-yield varieties. These varietal stocks are rapidly diminishing as marginal wildlands are brought into cultivation. Local domesticated varieties, often uniquely suited to local conditions, are also being lost as higher yield varieties displace them. And the increasing practice of monoculture of a few strains—which makes crops more vulnerable to disease, epidemics, or plagues of pests—is occurring at the same time that the genetic resources to resist such disasters are being lost."[14]

If present trends of growth in world population and in

the use and the abuse of natural resources continue, all measures of "progress" will pose increasingly menacing threats to the survival of the "haves" as well as the "have-nots," of which 90 percent of the world's population will be comprised by the year 2000.

The problem of human survival chronically confronting the world now and acutely confronting it by the year 2000 *can* be dealt with if the world's people perceive it as one that they have created. People and their personal needs, attitudes, and/or expectations caused the problem; people and their greater concern for global welfare can provide solutions if they will to do so. We do not mean to suggest that the problem of human survival can and/or will be erased; it can and will be alleviated at some cost to private comforts and luxuries but not at the expense of national freedoms.

The key to global human well-being is control. But before control can be put into effect, there has to be manifested global concern emanating from an understanding that the world cannot continue to "grow like Topsy" and expect its depleted natural resources to support its growing, explosive demands.

5. Crusade or Coherent Plan?

The gravity and the complexity of the problems of human survival have accelerated since the 1960s. Not only has the agenda of problems pertaining to human survival been extended to include those associated with the environment, energy, and natural resources, but societies that seemed to be moving ahead in increasing food production and controlling population have failed to sustain their achievements. For example, Mexico, which became self-sufficient in corn and wheat, is now a net importer of such basic food crops.

Faced with the prospect of doomsday, planners and

policymakers in the developing countries can choose to embark on a crusade against the apocalypse or search for coherent and realistic approaches to meet their problems. Professor Herz's paper has much in common with the *Global 2000 Report*. Both foresee devastating trends that call for a far-reaching transformation of attitudes and policies throughout the world. Each seems to be proposing the development of a new man and a new international system.

Most of the evidence concerning past efforts to ameliorate urgent human problems suggests that coherent plans produce far better prospects of success than do worldwide crusades. Whatever the shortcomings and the side effects of major programs devised in the 1960s to increase world food production, they unquestionably improved agricultural systems in targeted countries and regions. Similarly, two or three decades of experience with population-control programs provide a basis for future planning. The challenge of food and population is not so much one of constructing different approaches but of adapting existing approaches to more urgent situations. It can be concluded that population control has been too successful in some countries and for certain groups; the goal should be to encourage the adaptation of successful programs to countries and groups that have experienced unabated growth.

Most difficult of all are the environmental and energy problems that haunt mankind's future. Societies must learn to think more coherently about balancing equally worthy pairs of goals, neither of which can be overlooked. Nations must pursue economic growth tempered by the need to protect the environment. Controls must be established not to thwart industrial plants but to prevent pollution. Leaders need to recognize that the depletion of resources, including water, forests, and air, can destroy man's capacity for survival. Each problem of human survival is linked to every other one. Success will not result from turning a society's resources wholly in one direction, for example, toward population control, while disregarding the underproduction of food, environmental pollution, and the nuclear threat. All must be attacked along a moving front even though one or the other may warrant priority in response to changing needs and available technology. The impending crisis of the year 2000 calls for the creation of initiatives based on lessons derived from the past. Above all, every initiative proposed should be part of a coherent plan.

NOTES

1. See the chapter by John H. Herz.
2. *The Global Report to the President: Entering the Twenty-first Century,* Figures 3, 11.
3. *Ibid.,* p. 12.
4. *Ibid.,* p. 13.
5. *Ibid.*
6. *Ibid.*
7. *Ibid.,* p. 32.
8. *Ibid.,* pp. 23-33.
9. *Newsweek,* February 23, 1981, pp. 26-27.
10. *Global 2000,* p. 36.
11. *Ibid.,* p. 37.
12. *Ibid.*
13. *Ibid.*
14. *Ibid.,* p. 38.

Conclusion

G. L. ULMEN

I

An immanent critique of the papers of the Fourth CUNY Conference on History and Politics may be the starting point for an extensive critique of United States foreign policy, but such is beyond the scope of this volume. Here we are concerned with the more immediate options and goals for the 1980s that have been brought to the fore by prior policies and recent events. Nonetheless, these papers reveal that the task of basing United States foreign policy on some fundamental principles of national interest is as much conceptual as actual and that the determination of the national interest requires a global perspective. Moreover, confusion between the national interest and the national purpose continues to hinder both the conceptualization of the national interest and the realization of the national purpose.

If, as Hans Morgenthau argued, the crisis of American politics is essentially a crisis of the national purpose, then this debate ultimately deals with the United States as a distinct moral, social, and political entity.[1] Does the national purpose precede the determination of the national interest, or vice versa? However this question is answered, the articulation of the national interest in terms consistent with the national purpose is the true test of United States foreign policy.

Walter LaFeber contends that "in the 1960s and the 1970s the assumptions of foreign policy in the 1940s and the 1950s became invalid in roughly the following order—the Western alliance cracked, the dominance of the U.S. economy began to erode, consensus fragmented (single-interest group lobbyists soon outnumbered cold warriors), and finally, U.S. strategic superiority disappeared." He further contends that the characteristics of the consensus that marked United States foreign policy in "Cold War I" disintegrated in the 1950s and the 1960s and that officials tried to resurrect them in "Cold War II" in the 1970s and thereafter. In other words, from his list of supposedly consecutive events leading to the present disarray in foreign policy, he singles out the third—consensus—as decisive. His reasoning appears to be based on Tocqueville's classic criticism that a democracy is singularly ill-equipped to formulate and carry out a long-term and consistent foreign policy because it must first solve the problem of creating a consensus to support the policy. Be that as it may, the lack of a consistent and long-term foreign policy is primarily the result of unclear conceptions of the national purpose and the national interest, which have contributed to the present decline in American power and the consensus to support it.

Speaking concretely, it was the erosion of consensus on the Vietnam War that brought an end to the policy of the global containment of communism. Detente, whether understood as a policy of retrenchment or as a legitimate attempt to limit the arms race and find accommodation with the Soviet Union, was based on a belief in the predominance of American power. It was the relative decline in American power that undermined this policy. Moreover, coextensive with the loss of American power abroad was a developing consensus at home—spurred by the Vietnam War and intensified by the Watergate affair—that the government had grown too powerful and the bureaucracy too unmanageable for effective domestic and foreign policy. This assessment is reflected in the present administration's quixotic attempt, on the one hand, to restore American military power and, on the other hand, reduce the role and thus the power of the federal government. In this connection, LaFeber does well to cite Morgenthau's reference to *The Federalist Papers* that a government too weak to control the concentrations of private power that have usurped much of the substance of public power and have grown so strong as to reduce the citizens to impotence promotes "political apathy, political violence and the search for new communities outside the official power structure."

The interlocking of domestic and foreign power and policy is a political reality of the state, whatever the ideology or ideals. The New Deal, with its goal of increasing the role of the state in society and centralizing power over private and local interests, was arguably as essential to the United States becoming a world power as it was to the attempt to solve complex economic and social problems and the conduct of the war. Although this process had its limits, it is also arguable that the attempt to reverse this process may undermine the state structure required to sustain a world power, even as it may undermine the necessary economic basis for a political consensus.

If the decline of American power vis-à-vis the Soviet Union is as much the result of United States policies as it is the rise of Soviet power, then the question of American security must be answered with reference to both. Vojtech Mastny addresses the Soviet dimension of this question; George Schwab, the American dimension. Mastny suggests that "the challenge of Soviet imperialism has always been more political than military. Even the present military build-up will not reduce the political factor." There is certainly no reason to believe that the established patterns of assertion and accommodation in Soviet foreign policy will change unless the system changes. But Mastny goes further in maintaining that "the implication for American policy is evident." What he means by this is that the United States should not only impress on the Soviet leaders the limits of Western tolerance of their external aggression but must draw the logical conclusion that an effective American policy cannot avoid addressing the more fundamental problem of internal security that breeds the aggressive impulse. Implicit in this line of reasoning is the recommendation that American foreign policymakers should encourage pressures for change that are "compatible with the Western notion of a stable international order based not only on peace but also on justice." This statement is consistent with the national purpose. But it is precisely the lack of a realistic notion of a stable international order that has led to the present debate on the national interest and the goals of American foreign policy. Mastny suggests that a measure of Soviet insecurity is in the national interest of the United States. But it is more a measure of American insecurity vis-à-vis the Soviet Union that is central to the present debate. The United States must solve its own security problem before it will be in a position to play upon Soviet insecurity.[2]

Schwab's paper addresses the American security problem in terms of the security of all "open society countries." In this vein, he singles out the Soviet Union's utilization of detente as leading to the need for collective security. As he puts it: "Because detente has contributed to destabilizing the global arena of states, the free world stands at a watershed in history." Believing that the United States is no longer in a position to challenge the Soviet Union alone and that the Soviet challenge is common to the non-Soviet world in general and to the free world in particular, "the immediate overriding foreign policy goal of the United States must be to forge an alliance of the open society countries that is anchored in a loosely knit but still well-orchestrated open society bloc." Assuming that Marxism-Leninism is the essential propelling force in the Soviet Union, Schwab seeks to find a countervailing ideological foundation uniting a limited number of like-minded countries. What supposedly would unite these countries is their "fundamental commitment to positive freedoms, that is, responsible freedoms for man under the law."[3]

It would seem that the geopolitical need for collective security would be more compelling than any ideology based on the rights of man. Indeed, it was not such an ideology but precisely a common enemy that united the allies during World War II and made common cause possible between such divergent and antagonistic societies as those of the United States and the Soviet Union. But then as now, the political reality that draws lines between friends and enemies[4] must first be perceived. Not even the Axis powers were perceived as common enemies against which to sustain a common cause of self-defense, let alone for collective security, until the Nazis attacked Poland. Even then, the United States did not enter the war until the Japanese attacked Pearl Harbor. Moreover, it was only the ideology of antifascism—against the common enemy—that sustained the Grand Alliance. At no time during the war did any such notion as the collective security of open societies prevent the United States from seeking to block the continuation of British imperialism, which President Roosevelt perceived to be at least as inimical to American interests as Soviet communism.

It is then no wonder that today the Soviet Union, however powerful its military capability and aggressive its actions, is still not perceived as a common enemy. The collective security of "open society countries" must contend not only with political reality, indeed the perception of the political reality that draws lines between friends and enemies, it must also contend with those divergent national interests that draw lines between friends. Perhaps only an ideology is capable of overcoming these obstacles, but such an ideology would of necessity have to be based on something more viable than the notion of open societies. To the extent that countries threatened by the Soviet Union, either directly or indirectly, are able to join forces, Schwab's more realistic suggestion is that lines of demarcation be drawn beyond which Soviet interference will not be tolerated.

Dankwart A. Rustow recognizes the necessity of an American military presence in the Middle East and recommends a rapid deployment force to secure that "consensus of strategic concerns" that should form the basis for any common front vis-à-vis the Soviet bloc. Although Rustow includes Europe and Japan in this consensus, his specific concern here is with the security of the United States. He thus argues that Americans have worried far too little about the serious threat posed to the economic future of the United States and other industrial nations by oil price rises. Be that as it may, the point seems moot because at different times the fluctuating world market provokes periods of scarcity and rising oil prices and at other times, like the present, a glut of oil and the possibility of either lowering prices or cutting production. Both the oil supply and oil price rises alternately pose serious threats to the oil-importing nations. In the long run, perhaps both the United States and Europe will be in a position to build up strategic petroleum reserves and rely on other sources of energy. But in the short run, despite the promise of North Sea oil, the United States is less dependent than Europe on the supply of oil from the Persian Gulf. It is precisely European awareness of the fact that their economic life would come virtually to a halt if they were denied oil from the Middle East that accounts for the increasing willingness of the affected states to accept almost any economic or political terms that producing countries may impose on them, in spite of the fact that the quadrupling of oil prices in 1973 and the large increase in 1979 propelled Western Europe in particular into a recession.

Aside from the price of oil, it is not possible to separate the issue of Western access to the Persian Gulf from the military power that the Soviet Union is able to assert in inhibiting or openly challenging Western power in the region. There is also no reason to believe that European subservience would not be accorded in greater degree to a state such as the Soviet Union that not only controlled the oil of the Middle East but also held a military position in Europe superior to that of the Western alliance. One foreign policy analyst, Robert W. Tucker, recently observed that "at issue are essentially the same security interests immediately following World War II. If the locus of the now most likely threats to those interests has shifted from Europe to the Persian Gulf, the vital interests in the Gulf will remain unchanged from the vital interests that were earlier at stake in Europe."[5] If this is true, then Europe's greater problem of oil supply is also a problem for the United States—irrespective of whether oil price rises pose a greater problem for the United States. To argue otherwise is to isolate the security interests of the United States from those of Europe in the Persian Gulf and vis-à-vis the Soviet Union.[6]

Contrary to "much of the received wisdom of today," William Diebold Jr. argues that the most important national objective of United States foreign policy following World War II was the creation of an economic world order that would avoid the worst errors of the interwar period, that this objective revived the post-World War I philosophy that economic activity was the only defensible form of American involvement abroad, and that its goals were either humanitarian or passive. This contention appears to be aimed at refuting the idea that the United States conducted a hegemonic foreign policy following World War II. However, Diebold argues that in recent times the distinction between domestic and foreign policy has become more blurred and that the United States has shifted toward more conventional views of the national interest—specifically, its economic interest. In reality, this is the economic counterpart of Morgenthau's and Kissinger's argument that the United States has been moved to recognize itself as a state among other states. Indeed, as the economy of the United States has become more dependent on the world economy, the definition of its national economic interest has narrowed to meet the competition.

But Diebold's picture is somewhat distorted by his stated decision to avoid discussion of "the interrelation of American concepts of the economic order and the political and social objectives it was meant to achieve." In spite of the fact that he is primarily concerned with American foreign economic policy, Diebold's failure to include the political dimension causes him to exaggerate the economic dimension of the national interest and to confuse the objective of United States foreign policy with the conduct of United States foreign policy. It is true that the new economic world order envisioned by the United States had its origins in schemes for a better world formulated during the course of the war and established at the Bretton Woods conference in 1944. But that conference was essentially a symbolic gesture and was in both scale and in underlying concept inappropriate even to those postwar problems that were foreseeable in 1944. Indeed, political considerations were already assuming a greater significance, even though they were postponed until the actual end of the fighting. Just as England was unable to fulfill the role ascribed to it at Bretton Woods, so it was unable to fulfill its security commitments to Greece and Turkey. The Truman Doctrine and George Kennan's Mr. X article that initiated the policy of the containment of communism in 1947 signaled a fundamental change in the objective of United States foreign policy. The Marshall Plan had at once both an economic and a political objective and the one could not be separated from the other. Whatever the genuine humanistic and other idealistic aspects of the Marshall Plan, United States foreign policy became willy-nilly hegemonic both economically and politically. It is manifestly the success of United States economic policy in Europe and the ending of its former political and military hegemony around the world that have simultaneously caused tensions in the Western alliance and the crisis of detente with the Soviet Union.

Diebold's contribution to the present debate is to draw attention to the fact that the present turning point in United States foreign policy has been brought about as much by economic as by political and military considerations and that the economic dimension of the national interest is fundamental to the view of the world that will ultimately guide United States foreign policy. Implicit in this understanding is the recognition that the actual problems confronting the United States in the world today require a new concept of the place and the role of the United States in international affairs.

Not only international energy concerns and OPEC but also the north-south agenda and third-world concerns have in recent years heightened awareness that economic policy cannot be separated from foreign policy. N. A. Pelcovits draws attention to the fact that the (U.S.) had presumed that in third-world chancelleries particular national interests and goals were being subordinated to the overall aims of the south in the so-called north-south agenda.[7] Moreover, it came to be the accepted view that the structure of the relationship with the third world differs materially from the classic diplomatic pattern in which bilateral modes prevailed. It was presumed that collective and coalition interests outweighed national goals in the policy calculations of third-world leaders. It was thought that the new era heralded the transcendence of economics over politics.[8] But it has become evident that growing interdependence has been accompanied by not less but greater concern in the developing world with power relations and reliance on military force. As Pelcovits states: "In a remarkable replay of Europe at the time of nation formation, the paramount concern of third-world leaders [is] the protection and the integrity of the state and its governing class against threats from its neighbors and subversion from within."

Recognizing this concern, Pelcovits focused his program or goals for United States foreign policy toward the third world on differentiation. He recommends that United States involvement in the third world be based not on a blanket preference for nonintervention or the vain hope of supporting regional actions but on a case-by-case determination of American interests and capacity to effect an outcome that is important to the strategic aims of the United States. Because a realistic analysis suggests that the third-world coalition will hold together mainly on a few collective issues and symbolic matters, the United States must be ready to separate the diplomacy of individual states from the north-south agenda and the politics of the coalition. The disaggregation of the third-world coalition and the differentiation of national interests require defining or redefining the "collective" interests and determining bilaterally which country or countries have the capacity to exert a "significant" impact on the United States in terms of resources and the propensity and the capability for destabilizing the international environment in a manner that would adversely affect the interests of the

United States. To the extent that aggregate interests are considered, the United States should adopt a selective policy of using multilateral processes and institutions where and when they can be effective in achieving American foreign policy goals.

Seymour Maxwell Finger accepts Pelcovits's concept of differentiation, but his argument leads in another direction. His suggestion that the United States must reject "knee-jerk anticommunism or antisocialism as a basis for foreign relations" and concern itself with the *external* behavior of a government, particularly as it affects the national interest of the United States, finds a curious parallel with Jeane Kirkpatrick's argument that the United States should not reject friendly right-wing dictatorships.[9] But the fact that the militant ideology of communism transcends national boundaries makes the character of a particular regime decisive. This is not to say that the United States should not have dealings with communist governments, but leaders charged with the fundamental task of assessing the national interest of a particular country cannot regard as irrelevant the fact that it is communist.

Although recognizing the centrality of the national interest to United States foreign policy, John Herz contends that "the national interest is now merged with the interests of all in global survival" and that the United States, as the most powerful and richest of nations, must confront the dilemma of how to place politics into a framework that would secure survival by defusing the nuclear threat and diminishing the demographic, economic, and ecological threats to the world community. His recommendation is to channel action through international organizations, which would require a great reversal in attitudes and policies. In order to make his proposal credible, he presents his credentials as a political realist. But Herz's political realism has a strong element of political idealism. He suggests that we long ago arrived at a point at which talk of "superiorities" or "inferiorities" in nuclear power makes no sense and that the capacity to inflict unacceptable damage on an opponent is enough to deter him. He attempts to obviate the political argument against this contention by stating that as long as the United States and its allies are prepared to say "no" to expansionist demands and refuse to be intimidated, Soviet threats *should not* succeed. He goes so far as to suggest that "as long as we possess the power of nuclear deterrence and of defending our shores by the use of conventional forces, we do not need even a balance of power in Europe as in the past." Herz rejects the "Hobbesian world" as he sees it and looks toward a new kind of world in which the national interest of individual states is merged with the interests of all. But political realism can only deal with the world as it is, not as it *should be.*

The Thompsons correctly characterize Herz's recommendations as a "crusade" that substitutes a belief in the ultimate effectiveness of international organizations for guides to action on the part of states. Rejecting global objectives, they propose a "coherent" plan to alleviate the problem of world hunger. Their proposal is centered on a country-by-country determination of needs and the integration of programs in local cultures. Again, differentiation, or, in the Thompsons' terminology, diversification, is the key to global well-being. Their emphasis is on control, but that goal has yet to be attained. Nevertheless, the Thompsons' attempt to find a means of dealing with world economic concerns is consonant with the political and the strategic concerns of the United States.

If no clear-cut conception of United States foreign policy has been developed by the contributors to this volume, there is agreement that the goals should be changed. Disagreement centers on why and how they should be changed. If the major issue is perceived to be the tilt in the

CARLENTLYCRITICAL

balance of power toward the Soviet Union and all that this entails, then this challenge must be met. If the major issue is perceived to be the global dangers of nuclear holocaust, famine, and ecological ruin, then these challenges must be met. In each case, the why is the measure of the how.

Any attempt to isolate strategies of foreign policy from diverse and divergent opinions is problematical but certainly warranted in the present context. Such strategies may but need not be explicit or implicit in the recommendations of one or more of the contributors and may in fact violate one principle in favor of another but nevertheless may represent the majority opinion. Three specific strategies are suggested in broad outline: one directed toward the United States and its allies; one toward the Soviet Union; one toward the third world.

Defense and Determination: on the one hand, explicitly recognizes that the security of the United States is the first and foremost priority of the national interest and implicitly recognizes that the cooperation and security of its allies in Europe and elsewhere are essential to the security of the United States and, on the other hand, explicitly recognizes that the ability of the United States to maintain its position in the world arena is dependent on a consensus of will and implicitly recognizes that the will of the United States is essential to the steadfastness of its allies.

Detente and Demarcation: on the one hand, explicitly recognizes that there is no alternative to coexistence with the Soviet Union and implicitly recognizes that there are mutual benefits accruing from contact on all levels (from cultural and academic exchanges to arms control) and, on the other hand, explicitly recognizes that the United States has no alternative other than drawing geographic and military lines beyond which the Soviet Union shall not venture without incurring penalties and implicitly recognizes that the United States must restore the balance of power to enable it to do so.

Disaggregation and Differentiation: on the one hand, explicitly recognizes that the third world is neither a political nor an economic aggregate (the "south") and implicitly recognizes that politics dominates economics even in the so-called developing countries and, on the other hand, explicitly recognizes that the United States must act independently and bilaterally in dealing with countries of the third world in accordance with its own interests and implicitly recognizes that global approaches to global problems are often illusory and international organizations limited in their effectiveness because of conflicting national interests.

II

An addendum to these strategies might well take the form of an exigent critique of United States foreign policy concentrating on the tendency to consider power and diplomacy as distinct and successive phases of foreign policy. A new dimension and thus a new urgency has been added in that a predominantly military conception of power is now linked to a still ill-defined conception of diplomacy. The restoration of American military power is expected to determine another period of international relations in general and relations between the West and the Soviet Union in particular. There appears to be little or no recognition of the fact that power can no longer be gauged in "purely" military terms. Indeed, the very character of the postwar world rules out the possibility of "purely" military, "purely" economic, or "purely" humanitarian policies. Even human survival is a political question.

Power is only as real as the willingness to use it. The potential for total destruction inherent in nuclear power has made both superpowers hesitant to use it, whatever the official pronouncements contend. The necessity of maintaining a precarious balance of nuclear power to prevent its use heightens both the tactical and the strategic importance of conventional weapons. Even more significant is the whole range of economic, social, ideological, and other factors that has become important in the power equation. Vietnam told the tale more graphically than any theory. The limits of the military underscored the transformation of power both on the battlefield and on the homefront, where the consensus supporting the war was converted to a consensus against the war. At the present time, given the administration's concentration on the military component of power, it appears that the only lesson to have been drawn from the Vietnam War and its aftermath is that the military capability of the United States must be continually enhanced or it will decline both absolutely and relatively. There appears to be little or no recognition of the equally important fact that the military is only one component, albeit the most important, in the power equation.

Perhaps the most serious aspect of the present administration's concentration on the military component of power is its corresponding disregard for information. Different from intelligence, which is primarily concerned with the gathering of secret data for military purposes, information concerns the whole spectrum of geographic, economic, social, cultural, political, and other factors about states, knowledge of which is as essential to the power equation of the United States as is economic wealth and military strength. After Japan attacked Pearl Harbor, the United States had few Asian specialists and was forced to draw primarily on the resources of the Institute of Pacific Relations, an international organization with diverse and even problematical political affiliations. Even the Office of Strategic Services, which later became the Central Intelligence Agency, was forced to draw on the services of many recent European emigres who had fled from their homelands. Finally, the actual goals and purposes of the Soviet Union with respect to the United States, Europe, and Asia during the period of the Grand Alliance were barely perceived. After World War II both government and private funds began to flow into the universities, and institutes were formed in recognition of the fact that the country was sorely in need of information and specialists with critical knowledge about the world outside Europe. The cold war brought support for the training of Russian specialists. The Korean War brought support for the training of China specialists. But when the Vietnam War began, there were few Americans who even knew where the country was located, let alone its language. In the mid-1960s some support was found for the training of Vietnamese specialists. That ended with the conclusion of the war. In the 1970s the private foundations withdrew from foreign policy and area research; funds were diverted to studies of population control, ecology, urban planning, and the like. Programs in Russian and Chinese studies, as well as in other less strategic areas, have virtually ceased at many universities. And now, in the 1980s, we are witnessing the withdrawal of government funding from foreign policy and area studies and indeed from virtually all social sciences and humanities, which are viewed as nonessential not only to the power equation of the United States but to the American state and society.[10]

The Soviet challenge is all the more significant because power and diplomacy have never been separated in Soviet theory or in Soviet practice. During World War II the Soviet Union behaved in a way that manifested its peculiar understanding of Clausewitz's maxim that war is not only an act of policy but a true political instrument, a continuation of political activity by other means.[11] For this reason, even more that its goal of overcoming the relative superiority of American military power, the Soviet Union's challenge to the United States has been more political than military. Now that at least military parity and in some aspects even superiority has been achieved by the Soviet Union, there is every reason to expect that this capability will be employed to even greater political advantage.

More to the point, Soviet military capability is now the match of its foreign relations establishment, the extent and the sophistication of which beggar comparison.[12] Ideological controls were loosened after the twentieth party congress in 1956, when the Communist party recognized that an effective foreign policy requires expertise and initiated the construction of a research establishment built around the Soviet Academy of Sciences. While not ignoring cultural components, this enterprise is specifically charged with immediate and concrete economic, political, and military tasks. The Institute for World Economy and International Relations, with over eight hundred specialists, is the nucleus of a network of similar global institutes, such as the Institute of the World Labor Movement, the Institute for Scientific Information and the Social Sciences, the Institute of the Economics of the World Socialist System, and the Institute of World History. All have large staffs and excellent research capabilities, and all share access to a substantial Western currency budget, opportunities to send specialists abroad, and funds for publishing not only a wide range of monographs and special studies but also a number of journals and bulletins.

Interlocking with these substantive institutes within the Academy of Sciences are numerous area institutes, which employ over three thousand scholars and research analysts. The Institute of Oriental Studies, with over five hundred staff members, is responsible for key developmental issues in the Middle East and the Far East. After the 1956 party congress, this institute provided cadres and resources for the establishment of the Institute of Chinese Studies (1957), a Southeast Asian Department (1958), an Institute of Africa (1959), an Institute of Latin America (1961), and an Institute for the USA and Canada (1967). Because of political considerations, greater human and other resources have been given to the China and USA institutes. More to the point, there are direct lines of communication between all these institutes and the Central Committee of the Communist party.

The rationale for establishing these global institutes was to attain a scientific assessment of what the Soviet Union terms the "world correlation of forces" and the ultimate predictability of international patterns. The Institute for Scientific Information and the Social Sciences, with a staff of over three thousand specialists, is specifically charged with the task of providing the essential data base for the "scientific" management of policy-relevant knowledge. This attests to the overall Soviet intent to utilize comprehensive multidisciplinary methodologies in the aggregation of systemic forecasts of political, economic, social, military, ideological, and scientific-technological phenomena in order to ensure the "predictability" of foreign relations. It is this complex set of variables that constitutes the global aggregate known as the "objective correlation of forces." The scientific assessment of this correlation is presumed to give Soviet policymakers an edge over their Western counterparts. A recent study by the Stanford Research Institute acknowledges the intent of the Soviet approach and the possible advantages accruing therefrom:

With the advent of nuclear parity, the influence of economic, political, scientific, technological, and ideological factors is enhanced. At the same time, the strategy employing these nonmilitary factors can be devised and implemented by the Soviets in the competition between the two world systems of capitalism and socialism. Under such conditions the "scientifically" designed Soviet system of information collection, processing, and forecasting, which gives rise to their perceptions, is as important in systems competition as missiles would be in a contest of arms.[13]

Whatever the shortcomings of Soviet political control, the magnitude, scope, intensity, and quality of their unique foreign-relations enterprise contrast sharply with the wholesale deprivation of foreign policy and area studies and the whole range of social science and humanistic studies in the United States as part of the present administration's attempt to restore the balance of power with the Soviet Union solely by military means. Moreover, it has even reduced support for and is threatening to phase out the academic and cultural exchange programs with the Soviet Union and other communist countries that have contributed to our knowledge of precisely these Soviet developments. Along with the collapse of university and institute programs for foreign policy and area research, which at their peak were never the match of the present Soviet enterprise, this withdrawal of support menaces the power position of the United States no less than would a similar reduction of armaments or the phasing out of military technology.

In compounding past errors by concentrating exclusively on the military, the United States is retreating to a conception of power that is neither relevant nor realistic in terms of the "objective correlation of forces." Only a global conception of United States foreign policy is capable of responding to the transformation of power (and its relation to politics) that has brought the national interest to this critical juncture. Only an appreciation of the transformation of power and its relation to politics can inspire the global conception of United States foreign policy capable of reasserting the national interest.

NOTES

1. Hans J. Morgenthau, *The Purpose of American Politics* (New York, 1960).

2. The question of American security was brought to the fore in Norman Podhoretz's book, *The Present Danger* (New York, 1980), subtitled "Do We Have the Will to Reverse the Decline in American Power?" Podhoretz argues that the events in Iran and Afghanistan shattered the notions that the cold war had ever given way to genuine detente and that the political struggle between "East" and "West" had yielded in importance to the new economic conflict between "north" and "south."

3. Schwab's thesis is in part supported by the recent publication of a report on Western security prepared by the directors of the Research Institute of the German Society of Foreign Affairs in Bonn, the Council on Foreign Relations in New York, the French Institute of International Relations in Paris, and the Royal Institute of International Relations in London—Karl Kaiser, Winston Lord, Thierry de Montbrial, and David Watt, *Western Security: What Has Changed? What Should Be Done?* (New York, 1981). The report calls for a "political alliance of like-minded states" (p. 43) and speaks in terms of "principal nations" and "core countries." Whereas the report includes the United States, Britain, France, Germany, and Japan among the "core countries" (p. 45), Schwab includes a much wider constituency—the United States and Canada in the Western Hemisphere; England, the Netherlands, Belgium, France, Italy, the Federal Republic of Germany, Denmark, and Norway in Europe; Israel in the Middle East; Japan, Australia, and New Zealand in the Far East. But the report does not suggest, as does Schwab, any ideological foundation for such an alliance.

4. Carl Schmitt rightly observed that "rationally speaking, it cannot be denied that nations continue to group themselves according to the friend-enemy antithesis, that the distinction still remains actual today, and that this is an ever-present possibility for every people existing in the political sphere." See Carl Schmitt, *The Concept of the Political,* Translation, Introduction, and Notes by George Schwab, with Comments on Schmitt's Essay by Leo Strauss (New Brunswick, N.J., 1976), pp. 28 f. In his April 1980 address on "The Future of American Foreign Policy," Henry Kissinger stated the proposition in no uncertain terms: "Somewhere, somehow, the United States must show that it is capable of rewarding a friend or penalizing an opponent." See Henry Kissinger, *For the Record: Selected Statements, 1977-1980* (Boston-Toronto, 1981), p. 286.

5. Robert W. Tucker, "The Purposes of American Power," *Foreign Affairs,* vol. 59, no. 2, Winter 1980/81, pp. 243-274.

6. This line of reasoning is seemingly supported by the Mansfield Resolution. But the possibility of returning to a "fortress America" position is manifestly unrealistic in terms of the necessities of power and peace today. Moreover, recent suggestions that alternative sources might be Nigeria and elsewhere are at present too uncertain to inspire European confidence.

7. *North-South: A Program for Survival* (Cambridge, Mass., 1980). See also *Das Ueberleben sichern: Gemeinsame Interessen der Industrie-und Entwicklungslaender, Bericht der Nord-Sued Kommission,* Mit einer Einleitung des Vorsitzenden Willy Brandt (Cologne, 1980). See Barbara Ward, "Another Chance for the North," *Foreign Affairs* vol. 59, no. 2, Winter 1980/81, pp. 386-397.

8. U.S. Council on Environmental Qualities, *The Global 2000 Report to the President: Entering the Twenty-first Century. A Report Prepared by the Council on Environmental Quality and the Department of State* (Washington, D.C., 1980).

9. Jeane Kirkpatrick, "Dictatorships and Double Standards," *Commentary,* November 1979, pp. 34-45.

10. The United States is also falling behind the Soviet Union in its educational programs in the natural sciences, and in the years to come the weakness or strength of the United States will also be determined by the number and the quality of trained scientific and technical personnel who must design the next generation of weapons. Because without education there is no defense, education should also be a national responsibility. But explicit in the present administration's so-called New Federalism is the notion that education is not a federal but a state and local responsibility. In line with this reasoning, support for the National Science Foundation is being cut, federal help is being curtailed as the cost of college education rises, and huge cuts in aid to elementary and secondary education have been imposed. Albert Shanker, president of the United Federation of Teachers, has rightly argued that "by cutting taxes for the rich, wiping out programs for the middle class and the poor, and vastly increasing military spending, President Reagan is building a large antidefense constituency." The Soviet Union trains three times as many engineers annually as the United States; six times as many Soviet engineers are designing weapon systems. The average Soviet college-bound high-school graduate has had up to two years more of algebra and calculus than his American counterpart, eight years more of geometry, four years more of physics, three years more of chemistry, three and one-half years more of biology, and a year more of astronomy. All Soviet students take two thousand hours of mathematics over a period of ten years and must

take five years of physics and four years of chemistry. In the United States only one-sixth of high-school graduates have taken a junior- and a senior-level mathematics and science course.

11. The political dimension of the military has been stressed by Raymond Aron, *Penser la guerre, Clausewitz: I. L'age europeen; II. L'age planetaire* (Paris, 1976).

12. The information is taken from "Soviet International Relations Research," a study prepared in September 1981 for the International Relations Department of the Rockefeller Foundation by Daniel C. Matuszewski, associate director of the International Research and Exchanges Board in New York.

13. Quoted in Matuszewski, "Soviet International Relations Research."

Selected
Bibliography

Abshire, David N., et al., eds. *U.S. Global Leadership: The President and the Congress.* Washington, D.C., 1980.

Acheson, Dean. *Present at the Creation: My Years in the State Department.* New York, 1969.

Ajami, Fouad. *The Global Populists: Third-World Nations and World-Order Crises.* Princeton, 1974.

Bauer, P. T., and B. Yamey. "Against the New International Economic Order," *Commentary* 63 (April 1977): 25-31.

————. "East-West/North-South," *Commentary* 70 (September 1980): 57-63.

Bertram, Christoph. *Prospects of Soviet Power in the 1980s.* Camden, Conn., 1980.

Bosson, Rex, and Bension Varon. *The Mining Industry in Developing Countries.* London, 1977.

Brown, Lester R. *Building a Sustainable Society.* New York, 1981.

Claude, Inis L. *Power and International Relations.* New York, 1962.

————. *Swords into Plowshares: The Problems and Progress of International Organization,* 4th ed. New York, 1971.

Cockcroft, James D., et al. *Dependence and Underdevelopment.* New York, 1972.

Commission on International Development. *Partners in Development.* The Pearson Commission Report. New York, 1969.

Connelly, Philip, and Robert Perlman. *The Politics of Scarcity: Resource Conflicts in International Politics.* London, 1975.

Connor, Walter D., Robert Legvold, and Daniel C. Matuszewski. *Foreign Area Research in the National Interest: American and Soviet Perspectives.* IREX Occasional Papers, vol. 1, no. 8. New York, 1982.

The Council on Environmental Quality and the U.S. Department of State. *The Global 2000 Report to the President,* 3 vols. A Report Prepared by the Council on Environmental Quality and the Department of State. New York, 1981.

DGFK-Jahrbuch. *Zur Entspannungspolitik in Europa.* Baden-Baden, 1980.

Deibel, Terry L. *Commitment in American Foreign Policy: A Theoretical Examination for the Post-Vietnam Era.* National Security Affairs Monograph Series, 80-87. Washington, D.C., 1980.

de Vey Mestdagh, K. "The Right to Development," *Netherlands International Law Review,* 1981.

Divine, Robert A. *Eisenhower and the Cold War.* New York, 1981.

Douglass, R. Bruce. "International Economic Justice and the Guaranteed Minimum," *Review of Politics* 44 (January 1982): 3-26.

Edmonds, Robin. *Soviet Foreign Policy, 1962-1973: The Paradox of Super Power.* New York, 1975.

Falk, Richard A. *This Endangered Planet, Prospects and Proposals for Human Survival.* New York, 1971.

———— and Saul H. Mendlowitz. *The Strategy of World Order,* 4 vols. New York, 1966.

Finger, Seymour Maxwell. *Your Man at the UN: People, Politics, and Bureaucracy in the Making of Foreign Policy.* New York, 1980.

———— and Joseph R. Harbert. *U.S. Policy in International Institutions,* rev. ed. Boulder, 1982.

Finkelstein, Lawrence S., ed. *The United States and International Organization.* Cambridge, Mass., 1969.

Fukuyama, Francis. *New Directions for Soviet Middle East*

Policy in the 1980s: Implications for the Atlantic Alliance. Santa Monica, 1980.

Goldwin, Robert. "The Right of Foreign Aid," in *Political Philosophy and the Issues of Politics,* edited by Joseph Cropsey. Chicago, 1963.

Goodrich, Leland M. *The United Nations in a Changing World.* New York, 1974.

Gordon, Lincoln. *International Stability and North-South Relations.* Occasional Paper no. 17. Muscatine, Iowa, June 1978.

Hansen, Roger D., et al. *The U.S. and World Development, Agenda for Action, 1976.* New York, 1976.

Henderson, Conway. "Underdevelopment and Political Rights: A Revisionist Challenge," *Government and Opposition* 12 (Summer 1977): 276-292.

Herring, George C., Jr. *America's Longest War: The United States and Vietnam, 1950-1975.* New York, 1979.

Herz, John H. *International Politics in the Atomic Age.* New York, 1959.

Hoffmann, Stanley. *Primacy or World Order, American Foreign Policy Since the Cold War.* New York, 1978.

Independent Commission on International Development Issues. *North-South: A Programme for Survival.* Report of the Independent Commission on International Development Issues under the Chairmanship of Willy Brandt. Cambridge, Mass., 1980.

Johansen, Robert C. *The National Interest and the Human Interest, An Analysis of U.S. Foreign Policy.* Princeton, 1980.

The Joint Working Group of the Atlantic Council of the United States (Washington, D.C.) and the Research Institute for Peace and Security (Tokyo). *The Common Security Interests of Japan, the United States and NATO.* Washington, D.C., 1980.

Kaiser, Karl, et al. *Western Security: What Has Changed? What Should Be Done?* New York/London/Bonn/Paris, 1981.

Kaplan, Steven S. *Diplomacy of Power: Soviet Armed Forces as a Political Instrument.* Washington, D.C., 1981.

Keohane, Robert O., and Joseph S. Nye. *Power and Interdependence: World Politics in Transition.* Boston, 1977.

Kirkpatrick, Jeane. "Dictatorships and Double Standards," *Commentary* 68 (November 1979): 34-45.

Kissinger, Henry A. *For the Record: Selected Statements, 1977-1980.* Boston and Toronto, 1981.

————, *White House Years.* Boston and Toronto, 1979.

————, *Years of Upheaval.* Boston and Toronto, 1982.

Krippendorff, Ekkehart. *Die Amerikanische Strategie.* Frankfurt, 1979.

LaFeber, Walter. *America, Russia, and the Cold War, 1945-1980,* 4th ed. New York and Toronto, 1980.

Lenczowski, John. *Soviet Perceptions of U.S. Foreign Policy: A Study of Ideology, Power and Consensus.* Ithaca, 1982.

Marks, Stephen P. "The Peace-Human Rights-Development Dialectic," *Bulletin of Peace Proposals* II (1980): 339-347.

Mastny, Vojtech. *Russia's Road to the Cold War: Diplomacy, Warfare and the Politics of Communism, 1941-1945.* New York, 1979.

McNamara, Robert S. *The Essence of Security.* New York, 1968.

Myrdal, Gunnar. *The Challenge of World Poverty: A World Anti-Poverty Program in Outline.* New York, 1970.

Neff, Donald. *Warriors at Suez.* New York, 1981.

Nussbaum, Bruce, et al. *The Decline of U.S. Power (and What We Can Do About It).* Boston, 1980.

Park, Han S. "Human Rights and Modernization: A Dialectical Relationship?" *Universal Human Rights* (January-March 1980).

Pfaltzgraff, Robert L., Jr. *Energy Issues and Alliance Relationships: The United States, Western Europe and Japan.* Cambridge, England, 1980.

Pipes, Richard, ed. *Soviet Strategy in Europe.* New York, 1976.

Plischki, Elmer. *U.S. Foreign Relations: A Guide to Information Sources.* Detroit, 1980.

Podhoretz, Norman. *The Present Danger.* New York, 1980.

Riggs, Robert E. *US/UN: Foreign Policy and International Organization.* New York, 1971.

Rosencrance, Richard, ed. *America as an Ordinary Country: U.S. Foreign Policy and the Future.* Ithaca, 1976.

Rostow, Walt Whitman. *The Diffusion of Power.* New York, 1972.

Rothstein, Robert W. *The Third World and U.S. Foreign Policy: Cooperation and Conflict in the 1980s.* Boulder, 1981.

Rubinstein, Alvin Z. *Soviet Foreign Policy Since World War II: Imperial and Global.* Cambridge, Mass., 1981.

Rustow, Dankwart A. *Oil and Turmoil: America Faces OPEC and the Middle East.* New York, 1982.

Schmitt, Carl. *The Concept of the Political.* Translation, Introduction, and Notes by George Schwab. With Comments on Schmitt's Essay by Leo Strauss. New Brunswick, N.J., 1976.

Schwab, George. "Enemy oder Foe: Der Konflikt der modernen Politik" in *Epirrhosis: Festgabe für Carl Schmitt,* Hans Barion et al., eds. Berlin, 1968; English: "Enemy or Foe: A Conflict of Modern Politics" in *Carl Schmitt: A Modern Hobbes,* edited by Frank D. Grande. New York, 1983.

————, ed. *Ideology and Foreign Policy.* New York, 1978, 1981.

—————— and Henry Friedlander, eds. *Detente in Historical Perspective.* New York, 1975, 1981.

Spero, Joan E. *The Politics of International Economic Relations,* 2nd ed. New York, 1981.

Sprout, Harold and Margaret. *Toward a Politics of the Planet Earth.* New York, 1971.

Sterling, Richard W. *Macropolitics, International Relations in a Global Society.* New York, 1974.

Thurow, Lester C. *The Zero-Sum Society.* New York, 1980.

Tilton, John E. *The Future of Nonfuel Minerals.* Washington, D.C., 1977.

Tucker, Robert W. *The Inequality of Nations.* New York, 1977.

——————. "The Purposes of American Power," *Foreign Affairs* 59: 241-274.

Turner, Louis B. *Oil Companies in the International System.* London, 1978.

Ulam, Adam B. *The Rivals: America and Russia Since World War II.* New York, 1971.

United Nations Center for Economic and Social Information. *The Case for Development: Six Studies.* New York, 1973.

U.S. Congress, House of Representatives, Committee on Foreign Affairs. *East-West Relations in the Aftermath of the Soviet Invasion of Afghanistan. Hearings, Subcommittee on*

Europe and the Middle East, January 24-30, 1980. Washington, D.C., 1980.

U.S. Defense Policy in the 1980s. Daedalus (Cambridge), vol. 1 (Fall 1980); vol. 2 (Winter 1981).

Wells, Samuel F., Jr. "Sounding the Tocsin: NSC 68 and the Soviet Threat," *International Security* 4 (Fall 1979): 116-138.

Wolfe, Thomas W. *Soviet Power and Europe, 1945-1970.* Baltimore, 1970.

Yeselson, Abraham, and Anthony Gaglione. *A Dangerous Place: The United Nations as a Weapon in World Politics.* New York, 1974.

Index

imperialism, 30-32
Hoffmann, Stanley, 103
Hoover, Herbert, 93
Human rights, 49, 50; and the
Carter administration, 51-52, 149;
and dissent in Eastern Europe and
the Soviet Union, 50; historic U.S.
concern for, 149-150, 184; as an
internal determinant of Soviet
security, 51; precedent for voicing
international concerns about,
150-151; and the Reagan administration, 130; repression of, 50; and
the United Nations, 150-151. *See
also* Helsinki agreement on European
security

Inter-American Development Bank, 12
International Atomic Energy Agency
(IAEA), 29, 158
International Bank for Reconstruction
and Development (IBRD). *See* World
Bank
International Civil Aviation Organi-
zation (ICAO), 157, 158
International Convention on the
Elimination of Racial Discrimination,
150-151
International Development Association
(IDA), 111, 134, 153
International Fund for Agricultural
Development (IFAD), 105
International Labor Organization
(ILO), 157, 158
International Monetary Fund (IMF),
11, 67, 97, 105, 132, 153, 154,
155, 157, 158; figures of, on the
direction of U.S. trade, 124; and

monetary reform, 99, 105; and the
transfer of decision-making power in,
to the third world, 105, 106, 107,
117-118
International Planned Parenthood
Association, 202
International Rice Research Institute,
205
International Telecommunications
Union (ITU), 129
Iran, 12, 22, 82, 110, 177; effect of
the revolution in, on oil prices,
80-81; U.S. hostage crisis in, 55
Iraq-Iran War, 81, 84, 123, 141, 143
Israel: dependency of, on American
arms, 71; effect on, of Nixon's evenhanded policy, 69; and the
Palestinian Arabs, 143, 144-145,
183, 185; possibility of American
presence in, 182; and the third
world, 153-154; and U.N. Security
Council Resolution, 242, 144, 153;
U.S. commitment to the existence
of, 182

Japan: dependence of, on imported
oil, 71; and detente, 72; effects of
oil embargo on, 69; emergency oil
reserve of, 76; as one of the world's
leading oil importers, 72; productive
system of, 13, 96, 155; reaction of,
to Nixon's opening to China, 10;
reliance of, on American nuclear
protection, 72; trade of, with
mainland China, 9; turnaround of,
97-98; and the world economy, 101
Johnson, Lyndon B., 8, 9, 17, 19, 24
Jonas, Hans, 167, 186, 188

29, 48, 52; and the Federal Republic
of Germany, 41, 44, 45; the foreign
relations establishment of, 197,
233-235; and the Helsinki agreement
on European security, 47-48, 49, 50,
51, 181; image of, as the force of
the future, 49, 50, 51; imperialism
as a safeguard of the security of, 29,
30, 31, 32, 33, 42, 48, 50, 51-52,
181, 220; internal security of, 28-29,
30, 37, 39, 40, 41, 44, 47-48, 50,
51, 52, 53, 57; internal strains of,
45, 50, 51; and international terrorism, 48; and the invasion of Afghanistan, 10, 22, 27, 48, 55, 57, 84,
113, 140, 141, 147, 181; and the
invasion of Hungary, 7, 41, 42,
141, 147; leadership struggle in,
40-41, 43-44; and liberation movements, 113, 140; and the logic of
power, 57; massive military buildup
in, 44, 47, 48, 51, 52, 55, 57; and
Nixon-Brezhnev declaration, 47; and
the neutralization of Austria, 41, 42;
as one of the world's largest producers of oil, 72; and the open-
society bloc, 60-62, 220-222;
operations of, within the Marxist
Leninist framework, 57-58; 221;
policies of, of assertion and
accommodation, 28, 36, 37, 39, 40,
41, 44, 45, 51, 52, 53; and Polish
crises, 41, 46, 50, 51; and Portugal,
51; the primacy of the military in,
176; raison d'être of, 62; rapid
reconstruction of, 37; rapprochement
of, with the United States, 45; and
SALT I, 48; and Sino-American rap-

prochement, 47; and strategic parity
with the United States, 22, 47, 52;
and the third world, 41, 44, 48, 55,
113, 139, 140, 181; threat posed by
Hitler to, 30, 221; and trade with
the West, 45, 49, 50, 61; use of
Cuban surrogate troops in Africa by,
48, 55, 113, 140; and the use of
terror, 39, 40; 48; and the Vladivostok agreements, 48; and the
wartime aliance, 12, 32-35; and the
Western alliance, 44, 49; and the
"world correlation of forces,"
234-235; and Yugoslavia, 37-38, 41
Stalin, J. V., 11-29-30; aims of, 31;
the Allies' unwillingness to engage in
conflict with, 34; and the atomic
bomb, 38; attitude of, toward the
Marshall Plan, 36, 37; attitude of,
toward the Truman Doctrine, 36;
and confrontation with the United
States, 36, 37, 38, 39; creation of
the Cominform by, 37; consolidation of the empire in Eastern Europe
by, 38, 39; and Czechoslovakia, 37;
death of, 39; deployment of military
power by, 35; and the Great Purge,
30; imposition of the Berlin
blockade by, 37-38; insistence of, on
eastern European "glacis," 33-34; as
the leader of international communism, 37, 38; the linking of
imperialism to Soviet security by,
30, 33-35, 52, 181; permission given
by, for aggression in Korea, 38;
preparations of, for Soviet attack in
Europe, 38; refusal of, to join the
Bretton Woods agreements, 11-12;

the subjugation of neighboring states
by, 31, 33-34, 37; support of, for
the Spanish republic, 30; territories
incorporated by, as a result of war,
33; and Tito, 37-38; and Turkey
and Iran, 35; underestimation by, of
American willingness to sanction
Soviet control in Eastern Europe, 34;
underestimation by, of Hitler's
aggressive intent, 32; use of terror
by, 39; and Yalta, 35
Stalinism, 30
State Department, 19, 22
Strategic Arms Limitations Talks
(SALT): I, 48; II, 23, 53
Sun Yat-sen, 96

Technological revolution, 166
Thatcher, Margaret, 66
Third world: American strategic stakes
in, 139, 140-147, 226-227; concerns
of leaders of, 108, 226; and detente,
181-183; and the development
agenda of the 1980s, 133-134;
diversity of, 116, 126-128, 132,
141-142, 152, 224; essence of the
agenda of, 104, 132; the equitable
allocation of resources within,
166-167, 170-171; and the financing
of development and exports, 105,
121-122; and foreign aid, 111, 112,
156; and the Group of 77, 77, 113,
114, 115, 117-118, 125, 155; and
human rights, 177-178; and interdependence, 108, 109, 112, 128,
226; and the International Monetary
Fund, 105, 106, 117-118, 133; and
Israel, 153-154, 182-183; issues that

evoke solidarity in, 109; and the
management of resources and the
ecology, 140, 166-167, 170-171,
182; and nonalignment, 113, 183;
regional conflicts and structural
political instability in, 121-123,
146-147; and the Soviet Union, 41,
44, 48, 55, 110, 113, 181; threat
to, posed by explosions in world
population, 140, 166-170, 173, 196;
and the United Nations, 140, 142,
144, 145, 146-147, 148, 150-151,
152, 153; and UNIDO III, 107,
114-115; and the United States, 99,
103, 104, 110, 111, 112, 123-124,
126-128, 139, 162, 183; U.S.
exports to, 123-124, 133-134; and
the West, 143, 145-146; Western
assumptions about the priorities of,
in the north-south relationship,
105-106, 108, 110, 112, 132, 169,
225; and the World Bank, 105,
111, 114, 117, 133
Tito, Josip Broz, 37-38, 41
Toqueville, Alexis de, 3, 19, 218
Trade: and change in the world
economy, 101, 107; composition of,
77-78; the dollar's role as an international currency in, 98, 99;
between the East and the West, 45,
49, 50, 61; and economic interdependence, 66, 100, 101; and
economic nationalism, 99, 100, 101;
effects of crises on, 66-67; Europe as
the pivot of, 96; and the international division of labor, 101; and the
national interest, 88, 98, 99, 100; in
nonfuel minerals, 75, 140; in oil, 66,

cold war, 36, 37, 39, 40, 41, 45, 52, 99; conception of, of the aims of the Soviet Union, 56, confrontation of, with the Soviet Union, 36, 37, 38, 39, 42-43; creation of the North Atlantic Treaty Organization by, 38; the most critical areas of concern to, 143; and the Cuban missile crisis, 9, 22, 39, 43; decontrol of domestic oil prices in, 81, 83; dependence of, on oil imports, 71, 83, 84, 91, 182; and detente, 9, 39, 42, 46, 47, 48-50, 56-58, 61, 103, 110, 218-219; deterioration of relations between the Soviet Union and 25, 26, 27, 38, 39, 41, 42, 43, 48-50; and economic nationalism, 99, 100, 155; and economic world order, 94-98, 106, 108, 109, 110, 154, 155; effects of global oil price increases on, 71, 81, 83; effects on, of oil embargo, 69, 91; the election campaign of 1980 in, 73, 76, 84; and the European Economic Community, 13, 23, 65, 75, 99; as a food surplus country, 174, 210; and foreign aid, 156, 174, 175, 198, 200-201; and global issues, 128-131; and the Helsinki agreement, 47-48, 49, 50, 51, 181; and human rights, 49, 50, 51-52, 149-151; implications for, of the Havana conference of 1979, 113-114; and interdependence, 107, 108, 109, 112, 113; and internal strains, 45, 47, 48, 100; and international arms control agreements, 148; and the invasion of Afghanistan, 10, 22, 27, 48, 55, 57, 84, 110; and Latin America and the

Caribbean, 145-146, 198-200; and Mexico, 107, 114, 198-200; misperceptions of, of the goals of the Soviet Union, 25, 56-57; and monetary reform, 99, 105; motives of, in 1973 Arab-Israeli war, 69-70; the neglect of the security equation by, 56; and Nixon-Brezhnev declaration, 47; and north-south issues, 131, 132; as one of the world's major oil producers, 72, 73; and open-society countries, 58-62; perception of, of Soviet threat to Greece and Turkey, 36; *policies*: after detente, 55-62; of bridge building, 44; of containment, 36, 37, 40, 41, 143-144, 218; of evenhandedness, 69-70; of protectionism, 93; of rollback and liberation, 40, 41; raison d'être of national and international objectives, 94-96, 98, 99, 219; and the Rapid Deployment Force, 84, 182, 222; rapprochement of, with the Soviet Union, 45; and the restoration of the military balance, 51, 52; and revolutionary regimes, 145, 146; and stagflation, 10, 13, 100; and SALT I, 48; strategic petroleum reserve in the, 73, 76, 84; subsidies to farmers in, 75, 174; and threats to global survival, 166-167, 186-188, 195-196; and the third world, 99, 103, 104, 105-106, 107, 109, 111, 112, 113, 114, 123-124, 126-128, 131, 132, 134, 154-155, 183, 198; underestimation by, of Stalin's desire for endorsement of imperialism in the East, 34-35; and

Notes on Contributors

William Diebold, Jr. is Senior Research Fellow at the Council on Foreign Relations in New York City. Mr. Diebold's work has covered a wide range of international economic issues but most recently has focused on the problems of structural change in the world economy and American economic policy toward the communist countries. His publications include *Industrial Policy as an International Issue.*

Seymour Maxwell Finger is professor of political science at the City University of New York (Graduate Center and College of Staten Island) and director of CUNY's Ralph Bunche Institute on the United Nations. From 1946 to 1971 he was a career diplomat, serving the last fifteen years at the United States Mission to the United Nations, including four years as ambassador. His most recent book is entitled *Your Man at the UN: People, Politics, and Bureaucracy in the Making of American Foreign Policy.*

John H. Herz is professor emeritus of political science at the City University of New York (Graduate Center and City College). He has also taught at Columbia University, the Graduate Faculty of the New School for Social Research, and at German universities, among other institutions. In 1981 he held the Carl von Ossietzky professorship at the Free University of Berlin. His publications include *International Politics in the Atomic Age.*

Walter LaFeber is the Marie Underhill professor at Cornell University and was commonwealth lecturer at the University of London. He is the author of *America, Russia, and the Cold War* (4th ed., 1980); *The New Empire* (1963), which won the Beveridge Prize of the American Historical Association; and *The Panama Canal, The Crisis in Historical Perspective* (1978, 1979), among other works.

Vojtech Mastny is professor of history at the School of Advanced International Studies of the Johns Hopkins University in Washington, D.C. He has also taught at Columbia University where he directed the Institute on East Central Europe. He has published extensively on the history of East-West relations. His latest book is entitled *Russia's Road to the Cold War: Diplomacy, Warfare, and the Politics of Communism, 1941-1945.*

Nathan A. Pelcovits is professor of political science at the School of Advanced International Studies of the Johns Hopkins University in Washington, D.C. Formerly director of UN policy planning in the Department of State, Dr. Pelcovits is the author of *Security Guarantees for a Middle East Settlement* (1976), among other works. During World War II Dr. Pelcovits served as a combat intelligence officer with the U.S. Air Force in North Africa, Sicily, and Italy.

Dankwart A. Rustow is distinguished professor of political science and sociology at the Graduate School of the City University of New York. He has also taught at Princeton and Columbia. His publications include *OPEC: Success and Prospects* (with J. F. Mugno, 1976), *Middle Eastern Political Systems* (1971), and *A World of Nations* (1967). His analyses of Middle Eastern politics and the world oil market have appeared in *Foreign Affairs, The Wall Street Journal, The New York Times,* and other leading publications.

Arthur Schlesinger jr., writer and historian, holds the Albert Schweitzer chair in the humanities at the City University of New York. He has won Pulitzer prizes in history and biography for *The Age of Jackson* (1945) and *A Thousand Days: John F. Kennedy in the White House* (1965). His most recent book is *Robert Kennedy and His Times* (1978). He is working on the fourth volume of *The Age of Roosevelt.*

George Schwab is professor of history at the City University of New York (Graduate Center and City College). A vice president of the National Committee on American Foreign Policy, of which he was a cofounder with the late Hans J. Morgenthau, Dr. Schwab is the author of a number of works on great power rivalry, legal and political theory, and German history. His book *The Challenge of the Exception,* which appeared recently in Japanese, is now being translated into Italian. He is now preparing a critical translation of Carl Schmitt's *Political Theology: Four Chapters on the Concept of Sovereignty.*

Beverly C. Thompson is the director of studies for the North Central Education Conference Accreditation, professor of English at the University of Wisconsin at La Crosse, and professor at Phoenix Community College. Dr. Thompson has conducted a study of Mexican higher education focusing on

Monterrey Technological Institute. She is also the chairman of the Jefferson Area Transportation System, the chairman of the Charlottesville Faculty Book Club, and the chairman of International Relations for the League of Women Voters.

Kenneth W. Thompson is a vice president of the Rockefeller Foundation, director of the Twelve Donor Agency Review of Higher Education in Africa, Asia, Latin America, a director of the Institute for the Study of World Politics, formerly commonwealth professor of government and foreign affairs, and now director of the Miller Center of Public Affairs at the University of Virginia. Dr. Thompson is the author of many books, including *Morality* and *Foreign Policy and Foreign Assistance: A View from the Private Sector.*

G. L. Ulmen has long been associated with the Chinese History Project in New York, specializing in the social and political history of non-Western societies. His books include *The Science of Society* and *Society and History.* He has also published articles and monographs in such journals as *Slavic Review, Telos, Praxis, New America, State of the Nation,* and *Koelner Zeit fuer Soziologie und Sozialpsychologie.* A member of the Columbia University seminar on international change, he is also a member of the board of directors of the National Committee on American Foreign Policy. He is working on a book entitled *Five Modern Thinkers in Search of the State.*